T0267939

## Praise for *Mean Boys*

"No one before Geoffrey Mak has so well described the 'feeling' of the millennial era that ended with the pandemic—or acknowledged the absolute vanishing of this 'feeling' ever since, along with the alienation and exquisite spiritual longing left in its wake. This book is a rare comfort, a companion, a book that makes you say: *Yes, that is exactly how it is.*" —Torrey Peters, author of *Detransition, Baby*

"*Mean Boys* is a piercing inquiry into the long 2010s: platform Crocs and normcore; failed digital media strategies and right-wing trolls; American expats in Berlin and the rebirth of the rave. Mak tries to figure out what sanity should look like when the world is deranged. He finds there's no way to really know, except that one thing is certain: The old models are obsolete." —Emily Witt, author of *Future Sex*

"*Mean Boys* charts the anxious contradictions of being of two worlds at once and invites us to feel the past as it is and then again as it was. Geoffrey Mak's precision, perspective, and approach reveal a masterful pen." —Camonghne Felix, author of *Dyscalculia*

"Geoffrey Mak has a rare ability to inhabit and narrate the contemporary, that enticing hollow of the now, as seen and heard and felt from its current cores of Berlin and New York. There, art, fashion, and nightlife are one continuous attraction, best investigated through the art of hanging out, at which Mak is both a deft hand and delightfully self-aware. What emerges are many of the themes of our times: psychosis, vertigo, addiction, identity, status, casual sex, casual violence, the postindustrial hustle. In the corners lurk the mean boys, avatars of the sheer carelessness of power. Yet Mak also discovers something like a faith in the precious, passing quality of anything that can be truly cherished. His is a sensibility of shelter in the storm." —McKenzie Wark, author of *Raving*

# MEAN BOYS

# MEAN
# BOYS

A PERSONAL HISTORY

GEOFFREY MAK

BLOOMSBURY PUBLISHING
NEW YORK · LONDON · OXFORD · NEW DELHI · SYDNEY

BLOOMSBURY PUBLISHING
Bloomsbury Publishing Inc.
1385 Broadway, New York, NY 10018, USA

BLOOMSBURY, BLOOMSBURY PUBLISHING, and the Diana logo
are trademarks of Bloomsbury Publishing Plc

First published in the United States 2024

Bloomsbury Publishing Plc does not have any control over, or responsibility
for, any third-party websites referred to or in this book. All internet addresses
given in this book were correct at the time of going to press. The author and
publisher regret any inconvenience caused if addresses have changed or sites
have ceased to exist, but can accept no responsibility for any such changes.

ISBN: HB: 978-1-63557-794-5; EBOOK: 978-1-63557-795-2

LIBRARY OF CONGRESS CATALOGING-IN-PUBLICATION DATA IS AVAILABLE

2 4 6 8 10 9 7 5 3 1

Typeset by Westchester Publishing Services
Printed and bound in the U.S.A.

To find out more about our authors and books visit
www.bloomsbury.com and sign up for our newsletters.

Bloomsbury books may be purchased for business or promotional use. For
information on bulk purchases please contact Macmillan Corporate and
Premium Sales Department at specialmarkets@macmillan.com.

*For the Berlin clan: Amanda DeMarco,
Ryan Ruby, and Saskia Vogel*

# CONTENTS

# CONTENTS

# AUTHOR'S NOTE

The novel belongs to England or Russia, or even Japan, but the personal essay belongs to America. Not that we invented it, but it came of age in this country. Part reportage, part factual performance, the personal essay, in the hands of the greats like Baldwin or Didion, surged during the postwar boom of magazine culture, with its capital in New York. Then it enjoyed a renaissance when the internet brought forth the blogosphere, which opened its arms to crustpunks in St. Louis and cosplayers in Orlando. I wrote most of these essays for the internet, which is where they found their early readers. Some of them originated as extended Facebook posts, read by a dozen or so friends who might come up to me at parties and tell me what they thought. Because, in the beginning, I imagined myself addressing always and only friends, my writing coalesced around certain topics as if told in confidence: sexual trauma, gossip, madness, religious testimony. I was never writing for the void. I always knew who I was writing to, what they wanted to hear, and what they were wearing.

These essays arrive at a unique historical juncture. After postmodernism had deconstructed the authorial mastery of the objective narrative, the "situated knowledge" or "position-ality" of the personal writer—localized, bodied, subjective—took on renewed authority as the site of perspective and critique. This is a humble way to think about this kind of writing, even if its ambitions are arrogant. I happen to think the single greatest work of American literature is a personal essay from 1963, *The Fire Next Time*, and it began with a person, terrified and unrelenting, trying to make sense of his place in a history that was all but guaranteed to erase him.

Which is to say there are riches to be found in the personal essay, yet that somehow embarrasses people, Americans in particular. The format is frequently disparaged as minor, myopic, narcissistic—or, at worst, capable of spreading despi-cable violence. My final essay, "Mean Boys," is, in part, a grappling with one of the most horrific contemporary uses of the personal essay I could encounter, which would only be published on the internet: the mass-shooter manifesto. My work was harrowing, though I wanted to interrogate the extreme abuses of the personal essay and see if I could pressurize the format to answer to its own abjections.

The question I ran into, time and again: Is the personal essay simply a work of solipsism? Always, the personal essay will turn back to its origin: the self, a carnal thing that records the impressions of one's world, and the rhythmic vibration of its many voices, upon one's own skin. If these essays do anything, it is to articulate the self as credible, multiple, poly-phonic, soulful. You will find at the core of these essays is a moral torque. Their impulse is a desire to communicate. At stake is intimacy. What remains is a record, against the vagaries of history and memory, of what you might find scrib-bled on a bathroom stall at a bar or nightclub: *I was here.*

# MEAN BOYS

# Edgelords

## 1.

Why must Cordelia die? I've asked a number of people a number of times—but the answer was always wrong because the question is based on a misreading of *King Lear*. For years, I thought Lear was the one who killed his daughter Cordelia before he dragged her dead body onstage. In this version, *Lear* wouldn't technically be a tragedy in the Aristotelian sense, since the king's madness would have introduced a random act of violence, rather than an inevitable, fated outcome. For years, I took this ending of *Lear*, as I understood it, as a model for morality: There is good, and there is evil, and then there's madness. You can't stop madness. You can lock yourself up sixteen stories high in some corner of New York, but that particular train is still coming. It will plow through the Hudson River, emerge from the pavement on Broadway, go right up to your building, pummel up the elevator shaft and straight through your door on the sixteenth floor, and it will run you over. Because madness doesn't follow the rules. It isn't afraid of you. Which is why it singes when, in the play's final scene, the Earl of Kent stands over a blood-bath of the British monarchy, and asks, "Is this the promised end?" Except I got the part wrong about how it actually ends. Doesn't matter. Cordelia dies anyway.

Over the years, my habitual misunderstandings would tell of weird times and inconvenient revelations, during which I waded through the kaleidoscope of daily life, attempting, but failing, to cull the appropriate narratives out of nonsense, glean the cause and effect, locate the tragic flaw. The period I'm writing about starts during the Obama years and transitions into the apocalyptic logic of the Trump presidency. During those years, I worked in New York advertising. On an irregular basis, I wrote art reviews for magazines, talked shit to the appropriate groups, showed face at gallery openings and warehouse parties when my friends were DJ'ing, and never asked for list. I read everything I could find, opened myself up to the contagion of the world, made note of who had the fewest lines of dialogue in *The Great Gatsby* (those with the most power and those with the least) and precisely at which point Proust turns on the Duchesse de Guermantes (when she declares at her salon that she doesn't care for contemporary painting). I maintained the ability to, on command, recite the Clinton Administration's policy in Yugoslavia or state the reasons why an American intervention in Syria could have prevented ISIS.

But when I could not keep up with history, history caught up with me. I'd been reading on my parents' balcony in California when I got the text from my editor at a magazine I wrote for, alerting me that our log-in credentials had gotten phished by the pro-Assad Syrian Electronic Army. A week later, when the magazine interviewed the SEA about the data breach, the hacker collective responded, "It was a joke."

Except nothing was funny—either I'd gotten the timing wrong, waited too long for the punch line, or misunderstood the premise so profoundly that I started basing life decisions on conspiratorial assumptions in my mind that could be confirmed by no one around me.

I traveled frequently. I lived in Istanbul and then in New York, spent time in Hong Kong and Paris, and went through former Yugoslavia. In northern Iraq, I accidentally took photos inside a Yazidi holy site where no photos were allowed, only to read seven years later that the temple had likely been destroyed by ISIS. Another weekend, I flew into New York from Berlin, went to a warehouse party in Brooklyn until ten in the morning, crashed on a friend's couch, then emerged six hours later to moderate a panel on international queer literature. The first time I got a check in the mail for something I wrote, I went to Dover Street Market, bought a Rick Owens trench coat, rode the elevator down to the bar, and ordered myself a glass of cava (which is to say that sometimes, things were so good I thought my life, like the times, could only get better).

This was during the years when I divided my time between New York and Berlin. That I never really knew where I was living contributed to my recurring cycles of disorientation. I had a habit of starting my life and then restarting it every few months, as though jumping through unrelated episodes I didn't always finish before moving onto the next. One month, I rented a studio on Maybachufer across the canal from the luxury residences on Paul-Lincke-Ufer, and by the next, I was living in a narrow room in Mitte with a single window that opened onto dumpsters in the courtyard, from which, on some sweaty Monday mornings after coming back from the club, the smell of damp socks and garlic would waft into the room where, passed out from ketamine, I dreamed of becoming famous.

I wrote in a friend's apartment I had the keys to with a view over Görlitzer Park. Whenever I finished a piece, I didn't celebrate, nor did I do very much on my birthdays, as they were landmarks I'd acknowledge privately. In Berlin, I found I was often alone and then suddenly would be surrounded by three thousand at once, at a club or a biennial exhibition or a street protest in Friedrichshain. Once, I wore Rick Owens sneakers to a housing protest where demonstrators in black balaclavas hurled stun grenades over the crowd and onto a fortress of ballistic shields. Do you see a punch line?

In an apartment by the canal, I read the transcript to the Supreme Court hearing that would legalize same-sex marriage in all fifty states, and on the night that forty-nine were shot dead at Pulse nightclub in Orlando, I was at Berghain. The morning I found out that Alton Sterling and Philando Castile were shot by racist cops, I was acting on the set for a web series alongside a German philosopher, a male model, two Syrian refugees, and a hedge fund analyst. That the series was produced by an organization named DISCREET: An Intelligence Agency for the People might suggest that I was at least in on the joke, except I was not.

I never was. As it turned out, I would fail to be for a long time before things got weird. I remember reading Don DeLillo's story "The Itch" in a weekly magazine about the character who "heard what sounded like words as his urine hit the water," because during the year that story was published, I also heard words when my urine hit the water. Loud noises began to disturb me. I made excuses to stay inside. At the time, I had been house-sitting a friend's penthouse apartment in Prenzlauer Berg, across from a massive crane that, during summer thunderstorms, I imagined would swing in my direction and crash straight through the sliding glass doors of the balcony.

Those days, all that could hold my attention were reports of Turkey's "deep state" Ergenekon trials, and the wisdom of crowds. Outside, I took labyrinthine walks around my neighborhood, making fast turns from the Turkish food stands and into the discount supermarket, keeping note of who walked into both places after me and didn't buy a thing. "How old are you? What year is this?" a police officer asked me over the phone one day, after a botched ayahuasca ceremony in Brandenburg, during which I climbed out of a window on the second floor and jumped, convinced I was being held against my will by a religious cult, only to run out into miles of open grain fields with no cars in sight. Months later, I would find those questions useful to ask myself on a regular basis. I began forgetting what year it was and where I had come from around the time I found myself at Berghain early one Monday morning, sobbing so uncontrollably on the dance floor that the DJ stopped the music and put on Alice Coltrane's "Journey in Satchidananda," suggesting that it might be time for some people to go home.

The truth is that I *was* a long way from home, and I was on the verge of a psychotic breakdown. Here's a cut to just a few months later, August 2018:

> This is a 30-year-old male admitted to Parkside West on a 5150 hold for danger to self . . . This patient reports that he attempted to overdose due to severe auditory hallucinations. They are causing him distress. They are causing him to feel hopeless and helpless and causing him to continue to feel suicidal, depressed, and wanting to end his life so he does not have to hear the voices anymore . . . He was also restless and wanted to be left alone, and minimized his problems. He was given Zyprexa 10mg twice a day . . . was found to be positive for multiple substances, including ketamine and amphetamines. His mood is irritable. His affect is constricted. His speech is with an irritable tone. He admits to suicidal ideation. He denies any homicidal ideations. He admits to severe auditory hallucinations. He has severe paranoia . . . He continues to feel overwhelmed and hopeless that he will get any better.

This is an excerpt from my psychiatric report, compiled shortly after I boarded a next-day flight from Berlin to Los Angeles and was committed to an inpatient psychiatric clinic at Citrus Valley Medical Center less than two weeks after I turned thirty. Only at my most dissociative do I see this as a literary metaphor for the dissolution of the times, but I'm not going to go there. My twenties were already over before I could heed any possible warnings, or parse whether good was simply the absence of evil, but by then, it didn't matter. The train came for me anyway.

# 2.

FACEBOOK DATA & ELECTION INTERFERENCE
CHRISTOPHER WYLIE
Former Cambridge Analytica Research Director

Here is a transcript from C–SPAN that provides a sense of what, around the turn of the 2010s, would have been considered paranoid, yet in 2018 was a paragon of being informed:

SENATOR DICK DURBIN: I said to Senator Cornyn, my friend, when he said he thought consumers were aware that information is gathered on them . . . I said I'm sure he's wrong. We have now put a little piece of electric tape over the camera on my laptop.

CHRISTOPHER WYLIE: Good.

SENATOR DICK DURBIN: Most people do, now. Because they're being watched and they might not even know it.

This is from the testimony of the then twenty-eight-year-old whistleblower Christopher Wylie, former research director at Cambridge Analytica, before the U.S. Senate Judiciary Committee. Wylie, who self-identified as a "gay Canadian vegan," recounted before the Senate how Cambridge

Analytica harvested more than fifty million Facebook profiles for the Trump campaign in the United States and the Brexit campaign in the United Kingdom. Dubbed by Wylie as a "full-service propaganda machine," Cambridge Analytica employed personality quizzes that fielded psychographic data to target political ads specializing in "disinformation," "rumors," and "kompromat"—a "military-style operation" that was referred to internally as "Big Daddy."

I followed this story as it developed in the *Guardian* and the *Times*, watched Wylie testify before Parliament on C-SPAN, and then again before the U.S. Senate. I was so preoccupied with stories about manufactured consent and disinformation campaigns happening across social platforms that enacted a system of classically conditioned propaganda on a global scale. I learned, for instance, that as early as 2014, Cambridge Analytica began using data from Facebook (whose monthly users made up about one third of the world's population) to test responses to images of people scaling walls, and slogans like "The NSA Is Watching You" or "Build the Wall" or "Drain the Swamp," two years before Donald Trump hired the firm and began parroting those same slogans. Wylie describes the work of Cambridge Analytica as designed to trigger "some of the worst characteristics in people, such as neuroticism, paranoia, and racial biases," traits that might describe the defining cultural characteristics of these years I'm writing about.

When Senator Cory Booker asked why Cambridge Analytica was allegedly focused on "suppressing African American voters," Wylie responded, "You'll have to ask Mr. Bannon," who was then the VP of Cambridge Analytica and executive chairman of the conservative network Breitbart News, all before he became CEO of the Trump campaign.

Reportedly, Steve Bannon leveraged "voter disengagement tactics" on Black users by employing divisive content to discourage their support for Hillary Clinton—in one example, reminding them about her 1990s description of Black youths as "super-predators." (Coincidentally or not, Black voter turnout for a presidential election declined in 2016 for the first time in twenty years.)

Here you see the idea that if you control the narrative, you have the keys to the culture. "Given the influence that story has on our everyday lives, and that popular culture is barraging us with story on a regular basis, we must remain ever vigilant as to the messaging in those stories," declared one writer in Breitbart. It was an elaboration on what's known as the Breitbart Doctrine—"Politics is downstream from culture"—of which Bannon was an exemplary follower. Part sales pitch, part American lyric, the line had served as the founding principle of Breitbart News when Andrew Breitbart first launched the site in 2007 in efforts to reroute cultural narratives for a far-right audience.

I had never heard of Breitbart, not really, until the rise of one of its senior editors, Milo Yiannopoulos, a British conservative and self-described "dangerous faggot," who became the emergent poster child of what became known as the alt-right. Curdling around online forums such as Reddit and 4chan, this cesspool of neo-reactionary antifeminists and white supremacists would become a focal point for Bannon when he headed the Trump campaign.

"The alt-right is the new left," declared the white supremacist Richard Spencer, who coined the term, since "we're the ones thinking the unthinkable," which now included some of Spencer's new ideas, such as "peaceful ethnic cleansing."

Yiannopoulos would also describe the alt-right as the "new punk," because they were "transgressive," "subversive," "fun." What you get is an adaptation of Pat Buchanan's self-declared "religious war" over "the soul of America" from the 1992 Republican National Convention, created for a digital generation credited with codifying "trolling" as a legitimate political campaign strategy.

In a video from 2017, Yiannopoulos is shown singing "America the Beautiful" to Richard Spencer, who gives him a "Sieg heil!" Nazi salute, another "unthinkable" that would be interpreted as ironic because of all that transgressive and subversive fun they were having. Yet it would not be considered ironic when, in another leaked video, Nigel Oakes, founder of Cambridge Analytica's parent company SCL Group, stated about Hitler: "He didn't have a problem with the Jews at all, but the people didn't like the Jews. . . . So he just leveraged an artificial enemy. Well, that's exactly what Trump did, he leveraged a Muslim. . . . Trump had the balls . . . to say what people wanted to hear."

Below is a poem that once was framed and hung above the urinal at Café Loup in New York, which served for me both as a nostalgic token—like the restaurant itself, now defunct, from a bygone era—as well as a warning, ignored, of weird times ahead:

**WOLF CREDO**
Respect the elders
Teach the young
Cooperate with the pack

Play when you can
Hunt when you must
Rest in between

Share your affections
Voice your feelings
Leave your mark

In the time it took to piss, my eyes would zero in on the words "the pack"—conjuring the image of sex cults, mass suicides, charismatic leaders who lured people into orgies or Ponzi schemes, with telegenic smiles and promises of belonging. I wondered when, exactly, "community" passes into "groupthink," when the mere "collective" becomes "mob mentality." This was evidently the case during the 2014–15 Gamergate episode, when hackers, organized on 4chan, made death threats and rape threats to several feminist bloggers in what would become a vicious doxxing and harassment campaign. Petra Davis reported finding a website that advertised sex services with her address and images of mutilated women on the front page, under the tagline "Fuck her till she screams, filth whore, rape me all night cut me open." Revenge porn that featured Zoë Quinn was sent to her family and employers. A video game of Anita Sarkeesian, in which users could punch her face until it turned blue and swollen, was created and distributed. Kathy Sierra received Photoshopped images with a noose next to her head, a shooting target pointed at her face, and her mouth being gagged by underwear.

Here was an example of the pack gone astray, no longer able to distinguish between hunt and play. By then my world-view had already corroded so deeply into the paranoid that I assumed, at all times, that somebody, some group or other, was out to get or recruit me. I was never safe. *Someone* was always watching. More and more, people I knew started posting under fake names on Facebook or recommending I get on encrypted messaging apps like Signal, and I took their advice. I didn't know what anyone might want by spying on me, but I assumed it could and would be used against me the day the Feds showed up.

One afternoon, I was having coffee in the garden of the Standard Hotel in New York when a friend told me he'd been contacted for a job interview by someone at the CIA. I joked, "I'll never know if you get the job, because if you do, you won't be allowed to tell me." He said he may not be able to tell me, but if I see him one day wearing an expensive coat, I'll know why. We laughed, because the sun was bright, and it was still 2014, which is to say *early*, before the paranoia really set in, and we were able to joke about things that seemed to belong to a remote reality.

A few months later, I saw him walk into a friend's gallery opening wearing a three-quarter-length leather coat. When he saw me, he came over and whispered in my ear, "I got the coat."

What was I to make of this? Maybe he actually was talking about international espionage, or about cultivating energy and signal-boosting soft power from the New York City underground, except I did not get the punch line. After a certain point, these aborted conspiracies became par for the course during a time that was defined by concerns about whether a cell phone tower was in fact a cell phone tower or instead an "active GSM base station," operated remotely by the NSA, designed to intercept cell phone data. My preoccupation with these stories was just my idea of "being informed." Every threat was to be taken seriously: the promise for the wall, or the boogeyman under the bed—or behind the camera, staring back from the top of the computer screen.

## 3.

In December 2015, I attended Art Basel Miami Beach, an annual event held at the Miami Beach Convention Center, where multiple commodities are available for sale or as trade collateral: paintings, new media, cultural capital, thumb drives, smartphone videos of the seminude, a critique on the collapse of the social contract, Taschen art monographs, and glitter.

This makes Art Basel difficult to criticize because it seldom pretends to be anything other than what it is. Its absence of pretense has made talking about the fair taboo because it is "degrading for art and artists," as Artnet described it, or because, as *Business Insider* stated, it "has become as much about the parties as the art." I wondered when exactly the "has become" took place, when exactly Art Basel had been "about the art," as if the Swiss franchise's decision thirteen years prior to base the fair in a city with a twenty-four-hour party district, proximity to the U.S. cocaine trade, and a 0 percent tax on sales and income were quirky atmospherics, the local color. The curator Hans Ulrich Obrist—who mentored the fair's director, Noah Horowitz, as an associate at London's Serpentine galleries—confessed to having "little knowledge of, or interest in, art fairs."

About the Art Basel parties, Barbara Gladstone of Gladstone Gallery said, "There are too many of them and I don't think it's that useful." Useful to whom? The answer came more directly from Lawrence R. Luhring of Luhring Augustine galleries: "There are a lot of people who come for the parties—there are people who don't even come to the fair," he said. "But we do business here."

Business as usual was the main factor in navigating the grounds. Upon entering the convention center, one encountered the so-called Circle of Power: Gagosian, Zwirner, Rosen, Hauser & Wirth, Cooper, et al. The opportunity for discovery—i.e., the 90 percent of the fair's participants beyond the Kusamas, the Christopher Wools, the Krugers, the Hirsts—should have been an exciting prospect but was, in practice, deflating. The critic and curator Kenny Schachter hyperbolically described the fair as "the end of art history," a Fukuyama-like prophecy that might explain rather than contradict why the fair has felt the need, since 2014, to introduce the "Survey sector," which presents "precise art historical projects" tucked neatly alongside the fair's main action. When I went, the main action was, you could say, the bigger history lesson: The fair was not the end of art history, nor was it at all an anomaly in the history of art, since, dating back to the festivals of the late Middle Ages, guild masters and apprentices set up "booths" that exhibited crafts for public evaluation and sales. The art history lesson here was the discrepancy between what the art world progressively mythologizes itself as and what it actually is. Or rather, what it has always been.

Somehow, the fair that year managed to piss everyone off, from its main players, who were hasty to disavow emotional investments in their financial calculations, to regular fairgoers, comparing email invites and Instagram stories, who were at the fair to complain about how they wanted to be somewhere else.

The anxiety reached an alarming pitch when twenty-four-year-old Siyuan Zhao of New York stabbed a thirty-three-year-old stranger in the neck with an X-Acto knife, just outside the Freedman Fitzpatrick booth. When interrogated by the officers about the crime, Zhao, who claimed to have experienced paranoia and auditory hallucinations, stated, "I had to kill her and two more!" and "I had to watch her bleed!"

A photographer from the *Miami Herald* was on the scene ready to shoot photos that would be introduced online with trigger warnings for "graphic content." *Gothamist*, CNN, Fox News, and the Huffington Post each picked up the story, leading not with the stabbing itself but that "witnesses thought it was art."

Assuming for the first initial seconds that the stabbing was "performance art" with "fake blood" would not have been outlandish; just a few weeks earlier, certain concertgoers at the Bataclan theater during the Paris attacks thought the first gunshots fired were part of the music—part of the art. Such a misunderstanding seemed reasonable enough after witnessing the stabbing, a traumatic event in its own right, except that was not the story the press was interested in. One witness who stated, "I never would have thought there would be a stabbing at Art Basel," was described by *Paper* magazine as a character out of a piece in the Onion. Something ridiculous. A satire. A salacious event at an elite art fair that continues to mine the deepest social insecurities of the international art world on a yearly basis.

The victim was wheeled away by paramedics to Jackson Memorial. Zhao was arrested on an attempted murder charge. The blood was quickly removed. The fair went on as planned. Click. Shoot. Cut. Send.

Many of us who were not "doing business" at Art Basel spent most of the daytime coked out and sleep deprived, wandering up and down Miami Beach with press pins and stickers, hunting for the VIP lounge in rain boots or Doc Martens.

That weekend, South Beach had flooded. The rain had come late Thursday night as a sort of biblical cleanse once the business at the temple of art was done, and the fair was open to the plebeians. That night, those who arrived on delayed flights from New York shuttled among New York parties transplanted and reinvented in Miami: Topical Cream, Mixpak, Bunker, GHE20G0TH1K. Text messages were sent, asking if the nebulous *there* was better than the permanently uninteresting *here*. "I think we're gonna go to NADAWAVE," said one. "When does Objekt go on?" "Is Perez the same thing as PAMM?" Paris Hilton or Alicia Keys either was or wasn't playing a party in Wynwood. It either was or wasn't worth the price of a taxi.

After two parties and sixty dollars' worth of taxis up and down Collins Avenue, I ended up at a party to see Juliana Huxtable and Venus X DJ at Kill Your Idol. The bar was packed. Somebody reported seeing the artist Jacolby Satterwhite and the rapper M.I.A. there, but Satterwhite, who was exhibiting a piece and hosting a party, was allegedly not in Miami at all. The musician Dev Hynes, after a performance at PAMM that one attendee described to me as "just okay," was now waiting in line for the gender-neutral bathrooms. I was also in line waiting for a gender-neutral bathroom, when a girl leaned over and asked, "Do you know where I can find any coke?"

I did not. Landing in the middle of Miami and finding a coke dealer off the street didn't seem smart. Others got more creative. A friend had dissolved two grams in a nasal spray bottle and carried it on the plane, while another packed pills and mixed them in with a bottle of melatonin. One friend had stored small bags in a Soylent powder pouch packed sideways in his carry-on to dodge the X-rays. "The powder blends in with the powder, the plastic blends in with the plastic," as he described it.

Back on the dance floor, a friend said, "There's Ryder Ripps behind me looking like a fuckboy."

"Wait, I don't know what he looks like," I said.

"He looks like a fuckboy."

I wedged my way through the dance floor, wearing a white turtleneck and the straps of my black nylon backpack crossed over my chest like a harness. Across from me, the girl who asked for coke was now dancing on the couch beside a friend with bleached blond hair, who was swinging his shirt over his head like a lasso. It was New York but not—the "but not" being the crucial factor in everyone letting their pants down, like the "but not" factor of senior trips and study abroad programs and weekends in Palm Springs.

Even the word "Basel" had become code for cultural excess, an ad-lib to fill in the "What happens at —— stays at ——" dictum, an excuse to use "art" as a badge of "social awareness" and "criticality" that, instead of reining in excess, affirms the twenty-four-hour hedonism of coke and neon. If politics is downstream from culture, then here was the culture: narcissistic, cultish, choosing an obsession with petty optics over coherent thinking, and eternally paranoid about minor distinctions up and down the caste system of social status. For that week, and that week only, South Beach would become a hall of mirrors for New York galleries, New York DJs, serving as another wing in the revolving door of the East Coast underground—people I recognized but knew nothing about, except that they had enough money to spend a weekend in Miami: the supposedly fun thing we would never do again unless everyone else was also down there with us pretending to look at art.

## 4.

Another snapshot of the culture in excess: One weekend, in Berlin, I was at a monthly party called Herrensauna, at the Bertrams club on Maybachufer. It was started by a former bartender at Berghain who went by the name Herrenscheide, a German portmanteau for "male cunt." The party's target clientele was unofficially described as "gay skinheads," according to a friend who classified the party to me as "half fashion, half gay sex." I arrived that morning at six, hiding inside my sock what I thought was a gram of speed but was actually a gram of meth, or "special speed" as a friend who owed me a favor called it when he sold it for seven euro at the last party I was at.

Herrensauna was a fashionable simulacrum with no original. It was designed to reference the fashion brand Vetements's

Fall 2015 show, which had been staged inside a gay sex club using Shifted's techno track "Chapter 69" as the soundtrack—a choice that was yet another reference to the kind of gay sex that actually *was* happening at Herrensauna, which had booked Shifted to DJ the headlining slot that morning of the party and had hired, as the bouncer, a model who had just returned from walking the actual Vetements shows in Paris.

Everything was a circle of references, a sign. At the party, we were not so much socializing as we were performing *types*, which often confounded me. I was never sure which side of the counterculture I was expected to perform: art critic, ad man from New York, technogoth turning looks at the club, or foot fetishist with a kink for golden showers. I just knew that once I located my role, my "character," it was important to deviate as little as possible.

On my way into Bertrams, I ran into a noise rapper who went by Palmtrees and performed under the name VIOLENCE, and we started talking about Cormac McCarthy. I saw another friend from New York, a photographer, who was wearing a white lace Craig Green top he got with an employee discount at Opening Ceremony. I saw a sizable number of "skinheads," both in person and in Instagram posts from the party, who might have been personally anti-fascist, yet were visibly chan-neling all the hallmarks of skinhead regalia: black Doc Martens with white laces, tattoos of dogs and Greek statues, Fred Perry polos and suspenders, replete with the party's wrist stamp showing the letter *H* inside a laurel crown. This was an archetype—a "character"—I occasionally saw around Berlin, on the U-Bahn, or smoking outside a Späti. Multiple times, I saw men with tattoos of the Chanel logo—on the inside of someone's forearm or behind his neck—a symbol that might appear curious in this context, were it not, as I learned later, an oblique reference to Coco Chanel's career as a covert intelligence officer for the Nazis during the German occupation.

If I didn't know any better, I might've called this . . . *the new punk*? It depended on your understanding of "the new," what with Herrensauna's use of anti-gay skinhead symbols reappropriated as gay sexual fetish, following a tradition of transgressive artists from Jean Genet to Siouxsie Sioux to Gabber Eleganza. There was no observable map to be found here—preferable for a generation that had adopted a shock-and-confuse strategy toward any attempts by outsider media to make sense of its culture. Here, entire histories in contingent localities got recycled and posted on social media for the shocks and the lulz. Conveniently dropped were the working-class values integral to British skinhead culture in the seventies, perhaps its only salvageable detail. Instead, these fashion skinheads deployed "the look" indiscriminately in adjacent circles of streetwear bloggers and Fashion Week after-parties, effectively obscuring any of its political coordinates by the absence of a moral compass.

I wondered when and where this mattered and when and where it didn't. Down in the basement, the dance floor was filled with shirtless muscle queens and a drug dealer I knew, who was fully clothed, working the floor. When my photographer friend and I needed a light, we tried to strike a lighter, but the flame wouldn't catch because there wasn't enough oxygen in the air.

Legitimately, this party was operable as a men's sauna: heat, fog, gay sex. Lines of speed started clumping up once you tapped them out onto your smartphone, though people were mostly taking milliliters of GBL, rationed off in the privacy of the darkrooms furnished with ripped-up couches and a leather sling. I was off on the floor dancing like an overheating robot because I was on speed that was actually meth, and I was trying to find a place to park myself until I could ride out my assigned role for the night: the dumb American who took too much.

We were all too much. In the words of trend-forecasting agencies, our role was to be "influencers," which implied an elusive "audience" we all knew didn't include each other, exactly, but unseen someones out there watching on Facebook or the livestream, followers in the reality TV show that was our youth culture in real time. Here was a generation depicted on social media as eternally at leisure—an essentially groundless fantasy enacted entirely on easyJet miles and corporate-sponsored afterparties. That our theater of excess might have been alienating "someone out there" was not a question on anyone's mind, because no one ever asked who it was we were supposed to be "influencing"; because it would be poor taste to wonder what they might want from us as they scrolled through our social feeds and whether their feelings toward us might be less than purely aspirational.

## 5.

If politics is downstream from culture, it's because the culture makes no fucking sense. For instance, take this story I heard, which I often told people in certain media circles, about someone who worked for Kanye West on a video shoot: Before Kanye arrives on set, one of his representatives comes out to meet with the agency. She tells them, "There's something really important about Kanye that I need you to know. This might sound crazy to some of you, but Kanye does believe he's a prophet. Don't question it, and don't bring it up in front of him. This is very important. Don't tell him what to do. Do not look at him in the eye when talking. Do not ask him any direct questions." So, when Kanye arrives, nobody looks him in the eye, and nobody asks any direct questions. If the team wants to say something to Kanye, they have to print it out and frame it in one of the bulk Ikea frames the team bought for this express purpose. In Kanye, the personality disorders of the prophet merge with those of a dictator: moral indignation, claims of direct access to the divine, consolidation of an "inner circle," and a positive perception of self paired with a negative perception of the future. Everything he touches, every comment, every idea he expresses out loud turns to gold. Whenever he says something, or so much as stares at the mood board for longer than seconds, the team sections it off as "interesting." Valuable. This goes on for a while, because everything Kanye finds interesting, they produce. Should Kanye not like what they produce, the team starts over. Should one of Kanye's trusted advisers comment that what they produce "looks weird," the team starts over. This happens several times, with two full-length videos scrapped. On the third shoot, Kanye walks past one of the interns on a couch watching a YouTube video on an iPad. Kanye is stunned. "What are you watching?" he asks. "What do you think of it? Are you into it? Why?" After a few more lines of dialogue, he turns to the rest of the team and tells them he has an announcement: The intern is now instated as the creative director; everyone must stop what they're doing and listen to him.

If I ever knew which video it was, I forgot, because the story itself had already become a contemporary parable about a culture industry based entirely upon a model of psychosis. In fact, almost a decade after I first heard the story about Kanye, I saw the same friend who told it to me, and I asked her to tell the story again. As it turned out, I had misremembered some of the details, but the version in my mind had already taken on a life of its own. Anyway, by then, it didn't really matter. Are you starting to see a pattern?

## 6.

Certain images, certain icons, became indicative of these years to me—images that don't mean anything in most contexts but are resonant in my mind. Here's one: the image of a clenched fist. I saw it first in 2009, during the University of California tuition hike protests, and I saw it again on TV at the barricades in Gezi or the squares in Kyiv. Incidentally, it had also been the symbol used in the Otpor! protests in Serbia "as the brand of a bloodless revolution," recalls Srda Popovic, one of the leaders of the student-led movement that deposed Slobodan Milosevic from autocratic rule in 2000.

In 2005, Popovic cofounded the Centre for Applied Nonviolent Action and Strategies (CANVAS), a political NGO that, as Wikileaks revealed, collaborates with U.S. intelligence firms and think tanks to provide political consulting to pro-democracy protest movements worldwide. Since its inception, CANVAS has trained groups in more than fifty countries, often covertly, years before any of the movements start making global headlines. Note that when protesters in Tunisia deposed President Ben Ali from power in 2011, igniting the Arab Spring, CANVAS had been training grassroots organizations in the country since 2007. Because CANVAS's involvement is discreet, it is impossible for outside observers to discern whether they have been active in any given protest movement.

For the centerpiece for her work *Seductive Exacting Realism*, which was featured in the 2017 Documenta 14 exhibition in Germany, the artist Irena Haiduk interviewed the CANVAS founder:

HAIDUK: I can never tell when I am watching the news if you are involved or not.
POPOVIC: That's good. It keeps us safe. Most of the time, you will never know. If and when we do sign our work, it is after the fact. It's too dangerous in the process.

I, too, would not be able to tell. In my memory and in the news, I began looking for telltale signs, or the stamp of handlers, like secret hand signals or an implicatively timed cough. I had a habit of drawing connections that could not be proven valid, but could not exactly be disproven, lying somewhere in between the "may" and "may not."

I found similarities across disparate movements that could trace back to similar sources. For instance, I discovered that in training manuals distributed to activists, CANVAS compiled an extensive list of common nonviolent strategies. The guidelines include:

- Organize blockades of highways in order to debilitate the economy and show the regime the people's power.
- Occupy key public buildings and occasional nonviolent invasions of said buildings.
- Move bulldozers in line with police barricades.

I thought of Çarşı's bulldozer in the barricades in Istanbul. Waste trucks dumping manure in the streets of Paris. The highway shutdown in Atlanta after the shooting of Philando Castile. I didn't know, in each particular instance, which came first, the action observed or the covertly made prescription. What was real and what was simulated? Maybe it didn't matter whether what feels organic actually is organic or if it is orchestrated upstream by some pretty big players in the game. The difference between a staged revolution and a real one is that there is no difference. The result is the same: The regime comes down.

"Assad, Chavez, Erdoğan, and Putin fear us," states Popovic about CANVAS. "In Saudi Arabia, we're branded as terrorists. And when Chinese TV blames us for Hong Kong riots, it feels good. When you're banned, you attract a certain type of people. It's like a call."

Popovic goes on, "We seek out what might be a motivating factor for people—above all, *young* people." During these years, I knew more and more young people who felt the need to get out of bed and shut down a freeway. I, too, wanted to know what motivated them. These were people active in Oakland, Zucotti Park, Gezi, Berlin. There was a time when all I heard was talk about eating the rich, shutting down prisons, doxxing the police—vigilante acts of justice that saw bombing the data-warehousing systems at Google as today's only acceptable equivalent to storming the Winter Palace. If politics is downstream from culture, then here was a culture that wanted to topple regimes.

Five years after the protests at the University of California, I remember I exited the building where I worked in New York and opened the door onto a procession of thousands who came to mourn the death of Eric Garner. People held signs that read I CAN'T BREATHE and DON'T SHOOT and BLACK LIVES MATTER. That night, the largest funeral in the city's recent memory was happening on the streets, from Madison Square Park, through the fountains of Washington Square, to the churches past Houston Street, past the outdoor fish markets of Chinatown and westward to the river. I cried that night, as I had at Zucotti Park, and when I'd scrolled through Twitter images of the TOMA water cannon vehicles at Occupy Gezi in the neighborhoods I used to live in. I cried when Trump was elected, but not during the Women's March. I was emotionally depleted by then as we marched past the storefront window at Valentino, where all the mannequins were outfitted in camouflage. I would parrot the call and response of "Tell me what democracy looks like," and simultaneously, I would wonder: After the protests are over, what happens to *all this*? What happens to all the anger, the stunted desire, the gathering thunderclouds of a generation's discontents, our grievances and our nursed alienations? Where does all that energy go? I never found the answer, but I can tell you at least one thing: It doesn't go nowhere.

7.

During this time, I sat on panels, gave speeches at weddings, made orange chicken for holiday potlucks. I signed up for Apple Music the week Frank Ocean dropped *Boys Don't Cry* as an exclusive. It was possible to live like the Obama years would never end, until of course, they did, and it became inconceivable to believe how we'd ever thought they could last.

When exactly did the Obama years end?

Somewhere between the shooting of Michael Brown and Gamergate.

When I think about the Obama years, I think about a giant party. It always ends, never on a high note. At some bleary point in the morning, when the dance floor thins out, the lights fade on, and you look around to see that nobody's in the same mood as they were in when the party began. Sometimes, all I could ever be certain about was the mood. During the lead-up to the 2016 election, all I knew was that the "aura" was changing. A sinister energy clouded over New York. I remember arriving at a furniture sale in Brooklyn hosted by two friends of mine who were decamping to Finland. We opened the windows and cleansed the place with palo santo and talked about how the mood in the United States was souring—it didn't "feel safe." People were getting restless. I remember getting a tarot card reading by a practicing Wiccan I knew, and being told that bad fortune would come if I stayed in New York, and that I should leave for Berlin "sooner than later." Around this time, I could not get my mind off the blood moon prophecies from the Book of Joel, about four lunar eclipses: red moons that would fall consecutively over the next two years, triggering the Second Coming of Christ. In the past, I might have dismissed this as pure lunacy, but by then, I no longer did.

When the time came for the unspeakable, people claimed it had been inevitable. Pundits pointed fingers. (The media! Identity politics!) Lambs got sacrificed. Demons exorcised. Then after the flagellation came the narratives. The Russia investigations. The Wylie hearings. Collectively, we appealed to the prophets to tell us what went wrong. What were the warning signs? How did this happen? And at some point or other, we privately asked ourselves: Why were we so surprised?

## 8.

In 2014, Christopher Wylie was twenty-four when he came up with the idea to mine millions of Facebook profiles for private and personal information that could create psychographic political profiles in what he termed in the *Guardian* Cambridge Analytica's "psychological warfare mindfuck tool."

I first read about Wylie in 2018, when I saw him in a photo shoot for the *Guardian*, with pink hair and a nose ring, wearing a camouflage jacket. It's possible his outfit is the whole reason he caught my attention; so influential were those details on my thinking, my language, that I texted a hair stylist I knew to ask if he could dye my hair "Wylie pink."

Wylie became, for me, an aspirational figure for the culture, a generational hero: the whistleblower. Before Cambridge Analytica, Wylie worked in Canadian Parliament for the opposition party and as a data analyst for Obama's national director. Then Wylie was approached by Alexander Nix, the head of Cambridge Analytica, who told him, "We'll give you total freedom. Experiment. Come and test out all your crazy ideas," which bred the kind of analytics that revealed, for instance: "People who liked 'I hate Israel' on Facebook also tended to like Nike shoes and KitKats."

I never ended up dyeing my hair, forgot I ever wanted to, but I was then reminded when I stumbled onto this detail, which stopped me in my tracks: At the time when Alexander Nix discovered him, Wylie was enrolled at the London College of Fashion for a "PhD in fashion forecasting."

"Politics is like fashion," said Wylie in an early meeting with Steve Bannon. "Trump is like a pair of Uggs, or Crocs, basically," he said. "So how do you get from people thinking 'Ugh. Totally ugly' to the moment when everyone is wearing them?" After meeting Bannon, Wylie was soon introduced to Robert Mercer, Cambridge Analytica's billionaire investor, and his daughter Rebekah Mercer.

When he met them in Rebekah Mercer's Manhattan apartment, she stated, "Oh we need more of your type on our side!" By which, Wylie clarified, she meant, "the gays."

Bannon also saw "the gays," said Wylie, as "early adopters," believing that once the gays were on board, "everyone else will follow." This explained why Bannon was "so into the whole Milo thing."

I imagined that this level of detail, plumbed deep enough, might unlock for me the organizing principle of the era. Madness seemed like the only operational logic behind things like Yiannopoulos's "Gays for Trump" party at the 2016 Republican National Convention, for which he created promotional posters of shirtless twinks wearing MAKE AMERICA

GREAT AGAIN hats. When asked why he surrounded himself with white supremacists and 4chan trolls, he explained, "Because they're interesting." Here influencers served as energy for energy's sake, the libidinal compass at the heart of the Breitbart Doctrine, which sees no functional difference between a fascist leader and a hip-hop celebrity. "Radical" denoted anything that hit the lowest common denominator to shock or offend, to excite the new punks on the right and trigger the libs. Transgression for transgression's sake.

A deference to "interesting" as a blanket aesthetic, erasing any discernable political coordinates, had been the logic behind the then editor Tina Brown's decision to put Donald Trump on the cover of *Vanity Fair* in 1994. It was the kind of "authentic bullshit," she recounted after Trump was elected, that "epitomized the brassy craziness of the times."

By the 2016 election, brassy craziness had crossed irretrievably into the weird. Around that time, Breitbart began accompanying its articles about Yiannopoulos with an itemized list of the clothing he wore in photo shoots, including jackets from Balmain and suits from Gieves & Hawkes, outfitting Yiannopoulos as a socialite in his own right. Fashion was politics; politics was fashion. After a while, such absurdity became the animating force behind a culture industry led by a handful of influencers, political or cultural, who were systemically incentivized to parrot back to the nation its neuroticism, paranoia, and racial biases, except reformatted this time as the country's tragic vice: entertainment.

## 9.

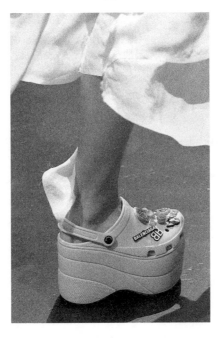

Facebook, a monopolist marketing platform that socially conditions more than a third of the world's population under an ethos of "connecting people" at neocolonial proportions, is the most powerful arm of what the artist Dena Yago describes in *e-flux* as "the content industrial complex." The phrase refers to the system of corporate-sponsored media designed with compulsively clickable headlines and images that compel users to share said media on social platforms, which glues users to their screens for longer amounts of time and allows those social platforms to sell the extracted attention back to corporations who are often also the ad sponsors for the media originally being circulated. In this system, users aren't the customers so much as the livestock being sold, too dependent on the gamified apparatus of renewable bite-size stimulation to break away. "As a term," Yago writes, "'user' resonates unambiguously with the language of addiction."

Yago was a member of K-HOLE, the artist collective and trend-forecasting agency that analyzed the way certain trends emerge from content circulated online. In 2013, K-HOLE released a PDF titled *Youth Mode: A Report on Freedom*, commissioned by the Serpentine galleries in London. "It used to be possible to be special," the report begins, before identifying a post–MTV marketing strategy that effectively neuters what used to be "special"—the idiosyncratic, the indie—by recycling and monetizing emergent local trends into mass-market aesthetics, made equally accessible to mall rats in Kentucky or radical queers in Manila. This tactic is known in advertising as "coolhunting." In an era when any emergent style trend can be poached by corporations and marketed out to mass culture, K-HOLE asks how it might be possible to avoid detection, avoid commodification, avoid getting coolhunted.

The solution is invisibility. K-HOLE proposes a ubiquitous "youth mode," a quasi fashion style that almost seemed adapted from the artist Hito Steyerl's idea of "withdrawal from representation," and is identified by a normie aesthetic that is undetectable, so camouflaged as to be boring, so bland that it could never be taken for "special" or "cool." We're talking Nike trainers, cargo shorts, and Gap pullovers. It was the "anti-cool," demonstrating a chameleonic ability to blend in with the surroundings on the ground, thriving below the radar of trend forecasting agencies in an era of big data algorithms and universal surveillance.

Thus: normcore. It was a fashion trend the group defined in their report as "situational," "adaptable," and "post-aspirational." With the nonchalance of a heather-gray Champion hoodie, normcore finds its identity in the incognito, in its ability to relate to any number of groups on any side of the culture. The aesthetic was spoofed in an episode of *Model Files*, a web series produced by the fashion retailer VFILES, where the fictional (and real life) casting director Preston Chaunsumlit is shown outfitting underground style icons in Old Navy's blanket mass-market aesthetics. The joke had reached its apex by the time the writer Fiona Duncan, in *The Cut*, classified normcore as a style that captured "self-aware, stylized blandness" with an accompanying slideshow of models wearing "Uniqlo khakis with New Balance sneakers or Crocs." Here, the simulacrum merges perfectly with the real. In streetwear photos around SoHo, Chaunsumlit is photographed wearing "white nurse clogs," i.e., Crocs, a sort of de facto icon for normcore, until four years later when Demna Gvasalia, the creative director of Balenciaga and cofounder of Vetements, designed platform Crocs with pointed rhinestones and sent them down the Balenciaga runway in Paris. This is the story of how "totally ugly" led to "fashion," how "fashion" led to "politics." Track the movement, gather the early adopters. Dupe the public.

## 10.

Here's another story: I first met Elizabeth Spiers in 2013 at an online publication called Flavorwire, where she was hired to revamp the digital strategy, which consisted of selling ad impressions and partnering with advertisers to produce custom events and email giveaways. Two years earlier, Spiers was a writer for *Forbes* around the same time I was also writing book reviews for *Forbes*. For the October 2011 issue, Spiers profiled Arianna Huffington, who was featured on the cover as one of the world's "100 Most Powerful Women."

In her profile, Spiers was the first to break, in detail, the revenue strategy through which Huffington had built her digital empire. By 2010 the site had grown to a total of 6,000 unpaid bloggers and 186 paid staffers. The structure entailed a bottom-up content assembly line distributed across twenty special-interest verticals ranging from "U.S. News" and "Business" to "Relationships" and "Wellness," built off a similar model as Gawker, which Spiers had cofounded in 2002.

Two years after Huffington Post moved from analog to digital, Andrew Breitbart, one of its cofounders and partners, decided to create his own version for conservatives, who he saw as ignored by mainstream media. He launched Breitbart News. From its inception, it was funded by the right-wing political donors Robert and Rebekah Mercer, who also funded Cambridge Analytica. Breitbart would become responsible for publishing and promoting right-wing political content in conjunction with, on the one hand, Cambridge Analytica, and on the other, the conservative pollster Pat Caddell, who said he worked on the Trump campaign because he was looking for someone with the name recognition and the resources to connect with voter bases disillusioned by the establishment. In a reference to *Mr. Smith Goes to Washington*, Caddell stated in the *New Yorker*, "He clearly wasn't the best Smith, but he was the *only* Smith."

Before Flavorwire, Elizabeth Spiers had been fired from her role as editor in chief of the *New York Observer* by Jared

Kushner, owner of Observer Media Group and future senior adviser to his father-in-law, President Trump. In an official statement, Kushner lauded Spiers for having launched "a slew of new verticals and web properties, and invigorated the newsroom." By the time Spiers was hired to launch verticals and invigorate the newsroom at Flavorwire, I was there editing an author interview series for which I asked questions like "What was the last good book you read?" and "Where do you think American fiction is headed?" before I was fired by Spiers after just three interviews, because I failed to make any newsbreak that could sufficiently trigger the social media cycle.

*Forbes*, the Huffington Post, Gawker, Breitbart, and Flavorwire were all publications belonging to the same spawn of digital media in the 2000s that specialized in sub-eight-hundred-word viral content that abounded in listicles, affective slideshows, op-eds, and identitarian politics, all designed for the explicit purpose of being shared widely on social media. The content I wrote for Flavorwire didn't drive up page views. Instead, it was understood as "legacy content" that lost money but would boost the overall reputation of the site, which it had failed to do.

The publication's political platform was only as strong as its most frequently shared content on social—an ad-backed profit model sustained by corporations as part of a revenue system that itself precipitated the collapse of an American news culture already in decline. How the inauguration of the content industrial complex paved the way for Trump to troll his way to the White House, one social share at a time, might be an example of a "bigger picture" story, but I'm a little late to the joke. I have the joke. But where's the punch line?

## 11.

At the end of the summer of 2018, when I flew back to California from Berlin, I got checked into the emergency room and was given two red pills that plunged me into lead-heavy sleep as I was wheeled into the psychiatric ward on a stretcher. In the hospital, I was no longer the art critic, nor the ad man from New York, nor the technogoth turning looks at the club. I was someone who heard voices in my head, different genders and accents, several times a minute. I had gone mad, or madness had come for me.

In the ward, I led what I would call a benevolently surveilled existence. I woke in what looked like a motel room with no carpet, no locks, no door to the bathroom, no handles on the faucet, no foldable toilet seat. At designated hours each day, I was to walk to a counter for medications, but at times when I was too sedated to get out of bed, one of the orderlies would come into my bedroom and shove into my mouth two pills, which dissolved immediately.

In the afternoons, patients paced the courtyard in disposable blue slippers, waiting for the smoke break, when an orderly passed out Pall Malls to patients—"only for real smokers"—who congregated around the ashtray like wildlife at a zoo's watering hole. I tried to speak with a largesse of courtesy to the nurses and social workers to demonstrate that I was sane enough to leave. Not all of us were. One breakfast, a woman refused her food and started screaming in the middle of the courtyard, "Somebody help me, please!" A man with white whiskers shouted, "Shut up!" and "Give it a rest!" Another patient quietly sang "Twinkle, Twinkle, Little Star" to herself. I was standing down the hall when I watched the staff restrain a patient and lock him in a room in solitary confinement. All afternoon, I heard him shouting, "Open the door!" while slamming the flat of his palm against the square window in it.

On my fourth night at the hospital, after the voices had subsided significantly, I woke up from one of my druggy sleeping spells, still jet-lagged, and went out into the court-yard for air. The August night was humid. The palms swayed. One of the nurses came around, which surprised me, because it was the middle of the night. I smiled as she made small talk, asked what I was reading. I tried to look sane as she took notes on my ultimately convincing performance that I was ready to leave. I kept up my side of the conversation until, abruptly, she stopped, her eyes fixed on something in the night.

"Did you see that?" she asked.

I did. It was a shooting star.

The Feds never showed up. What arrived instead was my newfound passivity to the nonnegotiable opacity of the world's private machinery. Because my auditory hallucinations, after my hospitalization, persisted for longer than six months during a period of sobriety, my medical team said that it was likely I would hear these hallucinations for the rest of my life. My blanket diagnosis was "unspecified psychosis," because it was unclear if my psychosis was organic or triggered by drugs or—as only I was convinced at the time—if there were in fact remote supercomputers beaming messages directly into my skull. The truth may be out there, but it isn't mine to know, and I have to be okay with not knowing. The only thing *to* do, which is also the most difficult, is to move on.

## 12.

Somehow, I cannot. As a writer, I thought I had to open myself up, like a compact mirror, to my generation, and when my generation became intolerable, so did I. Now, where did that get me? I still struggle to understand that not everything is meaningful, not every coincidence is interesting or would, eventually, with enough hindsight bias, become "the story." What was left behind from the 2010s was a heap of broken images that, if viewed in quick succession, might appear as a comprehensible zoetrope for the times. I might see massacres at the borders, riots in Paris, Twitter bot armies posing as civilians and civilians posing as prophets armed with AR-15 semi-automatic rifles, and still not know what it is I'm looking at. Here's what I do know: that I have difficulty trusting people, don't like crowds, keep searching inside my brain for my one proverbial "voice" while finding nothing but an index of the chaos already known.

In the months after I was discharged, I spent a lot of time swimming in my parents' pool in California, staring into the space between two palm trees where there used to be a third that had to be cut down because of termites. At my father's suggestion, I sometimes tied a swimming belt around my waist, attached to a column beneath the balcony, and practiced swimming in place. Flailing my limbs in a circle while making no progress is where I found myself most days. I worked on flushing out my bad juju with higher-frequency energy and thoughts that served me. I sat in the sunshine, meditated. On the phone, I listened as my friend told me about how time is a linear concept for "occupying the material plane," and by negotiating with past lives, I might find a path to "ascension."

I still wonder about the people I used to know—whatever came of the conversation at the Standard Hotel, whether any of those poets at the barricades in Oakland ended up behind bars, or what happened to the curly-haired office assistant I knew at Flavorwire who one day sold all her possessions and moved to Texas to sell 3D-printed rifles through Defense Distributed and eventually became the organization's director and the CEO of a company called Ghost Gunner. In a press release about her new role, she is also described as having organized "several independent spoken word nights and artist showcases."

Mostly I try not to think about these things. Most of the people I used to know carried on less controversial lives. They published novels, exhibited at biennials, joined housing co-ops, started their own record label, or quit their jobs at ailing publications and rebranded themselves by learning how to code. If I followed suit, I could also move on and live a functional life, and eventually I will. I'll let go of my questions upon questions, releasing them into this deluge of aborted narratives. Because there is nowhere left to put them. Where else would they go? Where do they all end up? I haven't found the answer yet, but I can tell you this: They don't go nowhere.

# My Father, the Minister

*Train up a child in the way he should go; even when*
*he is old he will not depart from it.*

—PROVERBS 22:6

## 1.

To hate is to demonstrate the capacity for love. This, I've found nowhere more evident, or breathtaking, than in the religious mind, which tends to have difficulty distinguishing between the two—sometimes decamping from one to the other in the time it takes to fall by the roadside, blinded by the light of God.

I've witnessed two such conversions in my father's life. The first happened when I was twelve. Out of nowhere, my father said he was called by God to leave his career in computer engineering, devote his life to ministry, go to the seminary, renew his faith. In my memory, the transition was sudden, though it happened over the course of a year or two, as he traveled among churches before finding a job opening as the Cantonese minister at the Mandarin Baptist Church of Los Angeles. This church was larger than any my family had been to before. It exhibited an entitled arrogance about its size, as if the sheer number of its offspring in faith—four congregations, with just under two thousand total parishioners—was righteous proof that God had smiled upon their good deeds. I imagine it was that the church's being large enough to house its own orchestra is what initially attracted my father, who'd studied at the Shanghai Music Conservatory as a younger man and idealized King David in the Bible as his prototype of the musical king.

As if overnight, my mother, a pharmacist, had to move from part to full time as the family's new primary provider, while simultaneously satisfying the role of the minister's wife. It was an essentially political role she never asked for but nonetheless filled dutifully. I remember walking up the stairs to go to sleep some Saturday nights and seeing my mother on the white leather couch beneath the reading lamp, holding the church's yearbook across her lap. She was quizzing herself, matching names with faces so that the next morning she could greet people by name.

My father was never able to fully command the pulpit from which he preached. His frame is thin, and although his voice was clear from years of vocal training at the conservatory, and he spoke from the depths of an impressively large gut, his voice tends more toward a soft, low lilt and follows a prescribed cadence that emphasizes the ending clauses of his sentences. He was diffident, held his chin up not with pride but in the trusting way a child looks toward his father: innocent, and also needy.

He wasn't strict with me when I was young. (He was too aloof.) He wasn't very in touch with the quotidian, exemplified by the escapist, adventurous moods of the classical music he often played in the car as I nodded off in traffic on our way to and from church. His faith—whimsical like magic— allowed him to float above life's minutiae and routine and into the spiritual reveries where love could cover a multitude of sins and promises were always delivered. He had no patience for the family's overflowing hampers, disappointing report cards, tuition bills. In his alternate universe known as "faith," my father could remain forever "like a child," a sort of Salinger type, as I said once to a therapist, trying to dress up his parental absence with some literary sheen. In my mind, I always see his smile—not smug, per se, but a little distant. And because his glasses would tint whenever he walked into the L.A. sun, half of my memories of him are of his dark, black eyes behind dark, black shades.

The little time that was spent outside of his private dreams with the Lord was reserved for his congregation. They didn't deserve him. I never forgave that church for their audacity to repeatedly insult my father, which you'd think would make me come to his defense. Except I didn't work like that: I resented him just as much for his inattention, for pouring everything he had into this church that treated him like a monkey. I didn't speak Cantonese, the language in which my father preached, but I knew his sermons couldn't possibly have been so horrible as to warrant the letters criticizing him that congregants slipped to the senior pastor or the secret petitions they sent around to get my father fired. (They claimed he lacked degrees and credentials.)

He never left, even when he probably should have. The senior pastor never fired him, kept him until retirement—because the church wasn't run like a democracy, but a Kingdom, and only a few trained elites had access to hear what God's Kingdom had in store.

At a young age, I had a privileged view of the hidden repulsion and hatred on which the outward visage of piety depends. For as long as I could remember, I knew my parents to be passionately anti-gay, which they made clear to me before I had a chance to understand sexuality on my own. During my adolescence, I remember seeing signs staked in neighborhood lawns every couple of years, declaring VOTE YES ON PROP 22 or VOTE YES ON PROP 8, measures that would block same-sex marriages across California. Both my parents advocated for these propositions and voted "Yes."

My father's church even organized a protest in Monterey Park, where my parents went and marched with others in their congregation, all wearing yellow caps that declared MARRIAGE = MAN + WOMAN in red embroidery. I remember sitting in the back seat as my father lectured on the depravity, the perversion of the sodomite, and the searing insult gay marriage was against the image of the most holy union he had with my mother. "The definition of marriage is sacred," he would say. "I don't mind what gay people do, but they can't use the same word—'marriage'—for what Mommy and I have."

I tried to convince myself to agree with him. Denial is a matter of effort, and as my sexuality awakened, I, as a child, capitulated with scorn to my base desires behind my locked bedroom door. "In this world, but not of it," the Bible teaches: and here I was, split between my spiritual life as the son of a minister, and the second, worldly life of a body whose homosexual desires grew and endured, despite all my prayers to stunt the inevitable. I remember masturbating to images in my mind of men tied down and whipped, a fixation that disturbed me, and I wanted to flee from it, before these fantasies could claim me as a teenage sadist. Something about myself I did not want to understand.

At church, all the men's youth groups I attended were fueled by the static of stunted desires, such as the private men's "accountability groups" during church retreats, where we'd huddle away in some bungalow in the woods, confess to each other our sexual fantasies—"stumbling blocks"—and hold hands as we prayed to be relieved of our sins. Quietly, I watched as all these corrupted young boys and I were given excuses to hate ourselves in the name of God. They knew shame, but I was convinced none of them knew my specific, isolating shame, which set me apart—being born the way I was, gay and in denial.

I remember moments, in the shower, when I would kneel under the water pelting my back, pleading to God to relieve me of my dreams of bodies I wanted to satisfy. I never considered acting out secretly. I believed the measure of my struggle would never be that which I could not bear, and so my faith would be credited to the measure I overcame. So I prayed that God be glorified in my incurable depravity. Such was the Christian logic: that in my corrupted nature, God could reveal his infinite power in me, age fifteen and drenched in sin.

———

The local anti-gay movement had reached my high school by my senior year, when my friend and classmate Martha decided to open the first Gay-Straight Alliance chapter on campus. Martha liked to see herself as a witty progressive whose political positions were the result of a cultivated mind and were as refined as her taste in the latest indie bands, which she was always the first to know about, not because she heard them on the radio but because she saw them herself, live at the Glass House. We sat next to each other in AP English and gossiped. Because I saw her as the designated expert on all things queer, I asked her if gay men see sex the way women do. In a voice as dry as wine, she said of gay men, "No, they're even hornier."

To start her new club, Martha had to pick two advisers and draft a charter, submit it first to student government for approval, then to the school board. I was in student government at the time the GSA charter came through for approval. I remember, during fourth period, sitting around the large table at the center of the room and hearing different students parrot arguments, presumably learned from church, about why the GSA shouldn't be passed: that it would be inappropriate to have a club on campus organized around sex, or simply, "It's against my values."

The club did go on to pass through student government. Soon, Martha's advisers notified her that a group of Asian parents was making efforts to block the GSA. My father was a leader of that effort. At my school, members of the Chinese American Parents Association (of which my father had previously been president) had organized with other Asian organizations on campus to circulate petitions in dissent and demanded a parent meeting with the high school principal and the GSA's staff adviser to try to veto the club. This was not an explicitly religious coalition, but it was made up of ethnically interested groups whose members often knew each other from ethnic church congregations: Chinese, Korean, Filipino.

At a parent meeting in the main conference room on campus, a group of about ten parent representatives, mostly Asian, and a Catholic monk listed their arguments for why the GSA should be blocked. They claimed high school students were too young to know whether they were gay and that the students who did know would be put in danger by going to these meetings. On the one hand, they would be in danger of violence, and on the other, they would be in danger of other GSA members trying to convert them to be gay. The principal could still use executive power and veto the club, citing safety concerns, which the parent coalition implored him to do.

The principal declined to veto the GSA. The charter passed.

On-campus publicity materials and announcements were also subject to approval through student government. Martha had been instructed that she could not write out the full name "Gay-Straight Alliance" and needed to use the abbreviation "GSA." Otherwise, she would not be allowed to put up posters or include the club in the school bulletin read aloud each day over the intercom during homeroom period. "Gay" was an obscenity.

The discrimination didn't go unnoticed. In solidarity, sympathetic students wore rainbow pins, which Martha passed out when people signed up for the club. While she worked the sign-up table, hecklers on skateboards approached her and shouted, "This is wrong!" Others said to her quietly, "I'm sorry, I consider you a close friend, but I can't sign up for this, it's against my values," as if rehearsing lines they were taught at home or church. Occasionally, straight boys would giggle and dare each other to go and sign up (at a time when "that's gay" and "faggot" were regular insults made in locker rooms and at lunch).

I signed up for the club, but I didn't tell my parents. I told myself I was supporting Martha. I wasn't out at school, and being the son of one of the parents who tried to block the GSA, I didn't want to openly invest in the club apart from attending occasional meetings. I don't believe I was worried my attendance would eventually reach my father—I didn't think that far. I was only worried people would think I was gay. My priorities were and stayed basic: masking my voice and mannerisms by which my identity could be exposed. Even then, I understood the body as helplessly declaring itself, giving itself away. Of my true sexuality, God was the only one who knew. I worshipped him because he allowed me to hate all the things I hated about myself, with rabid pleasure, so long as I blamed myself (never God) for the aberration and subjected myself to a life of humiliation and adoration.

Yet between a love for God and a love for humanity, I would go on to choose humanity. I chose to love bodies I was told were damaged because they understood the same carnal desires as mine. When I moved to New York in 2011, I would find beauty in all those bodies, after midnight, giving blow jobs on the Chelsea Piers. There was the Eagle and Paddles, the fetish club, and the underground theater on the Lower East Side, the Bijou, where they played *Vanilla Sky* in black and white as men sucked each other off in the darkness of the room. By then, I had a life of my own, having already abandoned the church, but I was left with a sort of palimpsest of holier days in the shape of ineradicable shame. I loved these men more than I was able to love myself, men whose names I didn't know but who fucked me in the back rooms of bars, or in the darkrooms in Berlin on leather slings, or in saunas with mirrors on the ceiling in Hong Kong. I looked for these bodies in almost every city I went to. The first man I ever slept with I met at Café Lafitte on a trip to New Orleans. It was during a blackout, and as I walked back from his hotel through the city, I remember watching a man play jazz on a piano on which twenty, thirty candles were lit. I remember the orgy at the penthouse in Chelsea less for the sex than the view, and I remember waiting for the G train after picking guys up at Metropolitan, because we were too cheap to pay for a taxi. The queers in New York are the ones who saved me; the parties, the drugs, they saved me by killing me. All those warehouse raves in Greenpoint, in Bushwick—the reggaeton, ball crashes, and voguing by the DJ booth. Steel Drums, 285 Kent, the Spectrum, and Palisades: names of venues that all closed down, yet they were where I was taught what the body was for. I've never seen anyone whipped on a St. Andrew's Cross, but I'd already had a lifetime's education of an innocent man tortured at the crucifix. What I read in the Bible and what I saw in cruising bars were never all that different, but this is who I worshipped now: gods in all those saunas and sex clubs who had fallen short of the glory, moaning, groping each other, pissing on my head as I knelt down in the bathroom, opened my mouth, ready to be born again.

Out of my two siblings and me, I moved the farthest from home. I flew as far from L.A. as I possibly could without leaving the country. When I'd first moved to New York, I didn't have a plan, except for a clear idea of what I was escaping. Years were squandered on drugs, sex clubs, plane tickets, and clothes I wore only once. I never regretted it. With friends, I never had to talk about my childhood, because the whole point of New York was becoming a nobody with no past, only a future. It was possible to live life solely on the borrowed credit of your ballooning yet endlessly deferred potential, stories you spun to your friends and yourself that you were always heading somewhere big. I was happy in New York, even when I remember the times I felt suffocated by my depression, my money problems—happy, because whatever mess my life was at any given period, I was the one who called the shots.

I managed to make phone calls to my parents only every few months, and I hid the entirety of my lifestyle from them because, I mean, it wasn't their business. I kept our conversations curt, maintained a grumpy reluctance to ever talk about my life beyond everyday details. In return, my parents offered ready-made Bible verses and prayers that rolled off me as soon as they were spoken. Our niceties were our buffer. I learned not to ask about their lives, because it would end up devolving into anecdotes about church squabbles, Bible groups, and seminary courses. To preserve their world, I maintained a lazy but adequate performance that assured them I was keeping up the faith (that was my last and only duty as their child), perpetually "looking" for the right church once work settled down. How that might've appeared plausible speaks less to what I was performing for them and more to the level of denial my parents needed to maintain about who their son was turning out to be.

A faggot. Even worse, a moody one.

The denial cut both ways. At the same time, I was pretending not to notice my parents' lurching toward more fanatical and conservative enthusiasms. I was convinced I needed to maintain this highwire act of feigned ignorance. Sometimes, to affect even a modicum of decency, you have to tell a certain number of lies to yourself about the people you love when they openly antagonize everything you stand for.

The expectations my father's church placed on him—as the Cantonese pastor, leader of the flock—pressured him to have strong views. Most who attended his services were older, first-generation immigrants, mostly neocons in nylon vests and corduroy. From the pulpit, my father declared that the country—in the hands of what he derisively termed "liberalism"—was sliding into wicked ways, and that it was the church's job to fight for and defend the soul of the nation. This called for either merging religious doctrine with the Supreme Court or letting the whole thing go to hell while the faithful few huddled in their churches, waiting to be called on by God before the fire came down.

Liberals were my father's idea of all things evil. And it was specifically gay liberals for whom my parents reserved a potent amount of revulsion. Hence, they considered the defeat of the Defense of Marriage Act and Proposition 8 during the 2013 Supreme Court rulings as the church's most stinging failure of a lifetime. For them, the fight over marriage was never about equal rights or partners' shared eligibility for health insurance, hospital visitation access, or immigration status. To my parents, gays were not only immoral but also *disgusting*, like roaches to be exterminated; the threat that festered in the imagination was more terrifying than any danger the logical mind could perceive. Their conception of marriage was a godly and holy institution, sanctified and ordained. Keeping marriage heterosexual was a defense against perversion. Marriage, for my father, was the last bastion of the great Christian institutions of this country, which were founded—so they always say—on the freedom of religion. But people tend to enjoy their freedom more if it robs somebody else's. And the Christians wanted marriage all for themselves, just how they liked it: normative, exclusive. And then 2015 came along and all the gays rushed in, snatched everything up, and perverted the whole enterprise, paving the way for intrusions of bestiality, incest, pedophilia.

When Donald Trump announced Mike Pence as his running mate during his 2016 presidential campaign, my father hungrily threw his support behind them. Pence was a self-described Christian with a career-long stance against LGBT rights. In a speech, he once stated that "societal collapse was always brought about following an advent of the deterioration of marriage and family," and in 2010, he opposed the repeal of "Don't Ask, Don't Tell," which had banned openly queer people from serving in the military. On Facebook, my father wrote posts urging his church's members to vote for Trump.

I should not have been surprised, except that I was. I was repulsed. I did not want to admit that these were the people I came from.

For an entire decade, I knew I would have to come out to them, but before I did, I wanted to cull financial and emotional independence. It wasn't that I was afraid they would cut me off. *I* wanted to be the one to cut *them* off, excising myself from their love, which I then could mistake only as religious tyranny.

I didn't want to be associated with them any more than they wanted a gay son. To hell with it then. It was time to sever the dead weight: my family. I no longer wanted anything to do with their provincialism. I wanted no reconciliation. I wanted to be free. My parents appeared as despicable to me as gays seemed to them, and if I had to sell them out for any reason—my freedom, my writing—I knew I would, a hundred times over.

At age twenty-nine, shortly after Trump was elected, I came out to my parents. I imagined the shock and insult of it to be so great that it would automatically nullify my relationship with them and set me free. I wanted it to land like a missile. I wanted it to destroy the family.

I did it in an email from New York, counterbalancing my emotions by writing with a clinical chill. Then I deleted the email from my outbox, because I didn't want any record of it. I didn't tell any of my friends when it happened. (Talking about it still feels so embarrassing—too many *feelings*.)

My parents responded, but I deleted it. I did not want to allow them a response. I was making it clear I had unilaterally cut them off for my own freedom. I was entitled to their silence after a lifetime of being silenced. For the entire year after, I refused to talk to them. I wanted them to feel my disgust to the same degree they had made their disgust for me known my whole life. It settled the score.

Except here's what I got wrong: In my quest for freedom, what did I think freedom was? As I went on with my life in New York and Berlin, my experiments at freedom would prove—surprise—to be a resounding failure. I thought that once I estranged myself from my family, the world would open itself up to me, uninhibited, which is true, it did. But once the world revealed itself, I no longer had the foundation from which to make any coherent decisions. My freedom was only to be unmoored and afraid. Of course, this is not the sort of thing anyone can warn you about; you have to discover it yourself. By hating my father, I ended up hating myself, too, and it made me scared of everything.

2.

Here is the second conversion I witnessed in my father's life.

One year later: My father broke. My silence had corroded him. In October 2017, he emailed to say he was flying to see me in New York, where I was living, and had booked two nights at the Hilton in Times Square, ready to present himself changed.

In his email, he wrote that God had spoken to him in a dream. In it, my father is at a fellowship meeting at his church, where all the ministers share about their struggles. When it comes time for my father to share, he tells the others, for the first time, about his gay son who absconded from the family and flew across the world and refuses to talk to him. My father doesn't gain their sympathy. The other pastors scoff at him. They don't offer the words of solidarity they normally would to ordained colleagues. In the dream, they just sneer and turn away. In their silence, my father prays at the end of the meeting, and thanks God for choosing him to serve "even as a sinner." Those were his exact words, he remembered, because once he spoke the word "sinner" he began crying uncontrollably in bed and woke beside my mother to find his face wet with tears.

I didn't know how to take his email or the announcement of his visit. I agreed to see him—I wasn't going to just turn him away—but I didn't know if I had it in me to do much else. If this was an appeal for my forgiveness, I didn't want to extend it. It was too little too late. But it was still more than I ever expected, more than I ever asked for. I wasn't even sure if I wanted or if I could handle this gift of reconciliation he presumably wanted to offer.

In response, I emailed him because I was tired, and the silence had also worn me down:

> I'm trying to be less angry . . . Both you and Mom are getting old, and I don't want this antagonism between us at this stage in your lives, our lives. I've been talking about our relationship a lot in therapy, and I'm trying to find ways in which both of us are similar, and I think both of us are products of our education, and that what we learn is what we learn. You are human. You are not perfect. I am human. I am not perfect. We agree on that, I'm sure.

What now to make of my father, the minister? This upstanding immigrant who arrived to California with only a suitcase and a Spanish guitar, in search of suburban affluence and a corporate sponsor for his university education. He found a good wife in the church who birthed him three children who were, to him, strange hobbyists who preferred writing over sports and dreaded weekly orchestra practice. All he wanted was a good Christian family, which he would never get, because having a gay son disqualified all that.

But dreams are a touchy thing, and no one likes being judged for them. As condescending as I am to my father's dreams, my own could equally be derided. What did I want? Free sex, loads of it, and parties and parties and parties. "The road of excess leads to the palace of wisdom," writes William Blake, yet I was still looking for that palace. I aligned the political queer project with a narcissistic consumerism by trying to have all the sex I could get and being public about it, because I was Out! and Proud! and after years of repression, wasn't sex and more sex the whole point of gay liberation? I hadn't thought this one through.

Wounded, I was too hurt and bitter to make any of the sacrifices demanded by love. I didn't know how to love. I kept any potential lover at bay. I never put anything on the line. I had foreclosed the love of my parents, and then found myself unable to love anyone else. The only kind of love I knew was disappearing into my own unfulfilled and exasperating desires, nursing my grievances on my own, suffocated by my needs, my unsettled scores.

By all accounts, I was worn down by freedom.

I found out where the road of excess goes. It leads to nothing.

The night my father landed in New York, we ate ramen at Ippudo and saw *La Bohème* at the Metropolitan Opera. The next day, we went to the Guggenheim and saw *Art and China after 1989: Theater of the World*. We had lunch at my Bushwick apartment where I lived alone, which no family member had yet seen, and I watched him tour the rooms. He showed a benevolent curiosity at the seafoam walls, the leather couch the color of fig leaves, the blue-and-white vases I'd collected from Chinatown, the ad for Wolfgang Tillmans's show *PCR* that I'd torn out of *Artforum* and pinned to the fridge. If my father at all approved of what he saw, he was silent about it. For the first time, I was showing him the life I'd made for myself here, in my adopted city that unconditionally adopted me in return.

At the beginning of his visit, I was suspicious of his intentions. I didn't know when we'd start talking about *it*. Did he think I wanted to know his theological evolution? I wasn't particularly interested in the contortions he'd have to make to incorporate queer people into his theology. If he was trying to tell me that his views had changed, that I was no longer some dog with a gimp leg but someone glorified under Providence as much as all God's children outside of Sodom, it didn't make a difference. It also didn't make a difference what overtures of fatherhood he might make. There could be no atoning for past sins, past neglects. And if he believed that there could, I didn't want to spend three days in New York babysitting my father's naivete.

At my apartment, we sat in the living room as he told me about the books he was reading on queer apologetics, hoping to one day translate one into Chinese. He said that God had called him to devote the rest of his life to ministering to queer people, who were created in God's image, and who had been persecuted by the Church. He also said that he had been seeking out groups devoted to loving "Christians who happen to be homosexuals," and battling the skepticism toward, and segregation of, homosexuality within the evangelical community.

His words sounded rehearsed. I could tell when he moved beyond conversation with me into the reverie he entered when at the pulpit, with its lights bright enough to obscure the faces of his congregation. At times I would notice him catching himself, his eyes suddenly narrowing back into the apartment, with our cups of hot tea, the trucks outside, and the sirens.

"The church has been wrong," he said. "In the last century, there has never been a group more persecuted by the evangelical church than LGBT people in America."

He recited his words slowly, searching my face to see if he had offended me or if I was even still interested. His face looked intrigued, but withholding, unsure if I would reject him.

He asked me about my life being gay, going through the usual, awkward questions: Was I actually attracted to masculinity? How early did I have these feelings? Had I ever been in a relationship with another man?

This line of questioning was like listing off the collateral damage from his oppressive faith during my childhood. Pooled into the silence between my sentences was the measure of my own failures at love. Yes, I was attracted to masculinity my whole life, and no, I have never managed to be in a relationship.

Having already spoken for hours, he asked me why I had been so upset.

"Mommy and I," he said, "we never rejected someone from our church just because they are gay."

"I don't want that kind of acceptance," I blurted. "I don't want to be treated as second-rate, that's bullshit to me."

I knew what would have happened if I had outed myself while still in the church. I might not have been "rejected" so much as treated like a freak show for contempt: never to be granted opportunities to serve in the church, never to be considered a leader, never to be allowed to openly marry, and never to command the respect that others who happened to be born straight effortlessly would. I didn't want, I explained to him, the looks of pity offered by straight and married Christians who knew nothing about what it means to sacrifice the body. I wanted pleasure, a future in love. A religion that had starved me of these things made me want them even more. I wanted a tangible love, and I left the church because I would never find it there.

Except once I left, I was never able to believe that I deserved love, that I was no less capable of receiving it, assuming I'd be able to recognize love if I ever saw it. I never could. I was unable to love myself, much less accept it from others. I didn't understand joy enough to trust it, so the prospect of a desire fulfilled was as alien as it was threatening to me. To receive joy without concessions would require me to let go of everything I knew thus far, and I knew only hatred and the bitterness of being determined unworthy. And now I knew this would never change if I never learned how to love my father or come to accept his own kind of love in return.

My father was silent. I watched him, with his arm between the armrest and his chin, and though his eyes didn't move, I saw a tear slide down his face. He didn't try to defend himself, did not seem to find himself, the "sinner," worthy to be defended. I found it pitiful, and compelling, how pathetic he appeared. What father wants to be seen this way by his own son?

After our rhetorical arguments and the defenses of our respective lives fell away, we presented ourselves to each other, exposed, and we could not be sure if the other would accept. We didn't speak. Slowly, I recognized in my father the regret that was now passing into a kind of fear. I knew this fear. When I was a child, the terror that the beginnings of sexuality presented was the discovery that I could not control my desires, and that my deepest urges resist comprehension. But instead of explicating desire, I later learned to inhabit it as I let it inhabit me. I unraveled beneath its sway, obeyed its wisdom. Accepting the body's desires means no longer castigating the body into submission. I no longer saw the body as something to be subdued, but rather a vessel for pleasure and gratification that affirms—rather than punishes—the human.

Except this kind of fraternity with desire is what evangelicals shun. All fear is erotic, motivated by compulsion over reason, and perhaps the greatest fear, in the evangelical mind, is the fear of the erotic. The threat that lust presents is the possibility that one's behavior could be clipped and trimmed to moral perfection but then suddenly overthrown in an irresistible impulse, revealing, during one hot night, one's deepest urges of the kind that ultimately cost Samson his life.

In the evangelical imagination, there is no other figure who embodies the threat of the erotic more than the homosexual, and there is no other group of people to whom they consider themselves more superior. In the eyes of the evangelical, homosexuals are a permanently plagued, primal, and morally infantile people, either neurologically deformed or voluntarily perverted—the "other" against which Christians can then position themselves as the paragons of civility, normality, conformity, poise, and tact. Straights are allowed to have sex, but gays are not. For the homosexual to be allowed to stay in the church, evangelicals grant only one destiny: to be celibate, essentially a eunuch, totally neutralized, sexless, impotent. Love and relationships are barred. The best a gay Christian can hope for is a life devoted to abstinence and denial. Granting only two options, expulsion or forced celibacy, evangelicals carry out the total moral, cultural, and political subjugation of homosexuals. At best, they view gays as genetically predisposed to sin. At worst, gays are deserving of death and AIDS.

But for evangelicals to accept the homosexual would be more difficult than for a camel to pass through the eye of a needle. Yet this is precisely where Christianity can demonstrate its character as one of the greatest social and moral experiments known to humanity: a truly horizontal community, founded on the principle that all are equal in the eyes of God. To do this, the church would have to accept homosexuals as equal, by nature, to heterosexuals. Christianity is most revolutionary in its absolutes. Its truly radical potential can be enacted only when all of humanity, *the entire flock*, is defined as absolutely and equally sinful, by nature and not by deed, from the liar to the murderer, the philanderer to the thief. In the eyes of God, there is truly no status difference between any human soul. For all have sinned, and all are forgiven.

This could be a view toward a truly liberating theology, one that might upend the very lattices of moral hierarchies.

But evangelicals today are not interested. They would be required to give up too much. They would lose the violence on which their cultural and political power is necessarily founded. No, the church will never let go of its oppression of sexual minorities. The church's vital failure to grasp the most crucial tenets of Christianity—what constitutes human nature and therefore salvation itself—will be, and already is, the evangelical church's most inevitable, and perhaps necessary, downfall, damnation or otherwise.

Yet it was from the church that my father and I, sitting in my apartment, were released, even if only temporarily for him. I believed, then, that my father wished to repent for sins on behalf of the church, which would not apologize. If they heard he had a gay son, I knew he would only be scorned further. He knew this, too, and it made me sympathetic toward him. At this point, I imagined that the sorrow and bitterness my father might have had when first learning his son was gay was comparable to my own sorrow, now, in confronting that he would never leave the church. I knew he never would. The church was his commitment, his crutch, his yoke, his flock. He had let me go to live my life. I had to grant him the same now.

Except there was one more thing.

"There's something I need you to do for me," I said.

When I asked him if he had told his church about me, he said he hadn't. Then I told him I needed him to. While there could be no undoing the damage of my childhood, there was something he could do for me now if he loved me: Tell his church about me.

He said no. He wasn't ready.

Now, here is where grace began. We were both human, failures to each other. Depraved in our own ways: My father's depravity was cowardice. He didn't want to jeopardize his career or his reputation or let go of the bigoted oppressive regime he subjected himself to every Sunday morning. But cowardice was something I intimately understood, my cowardice in matters of love, and on this basis, I was able to forgive my father as he was. In my father, I saw myself and all the things I hated and despised in me. All I ever learned from the church was that self-hatred was the only path to self-knowledge, and even after I got rid of God, I found that nothing had changed. What the absence of God revealed in my life were the habits and structures I'd built around him, which would stay where they were once God was removed, like wax melted from the inside of a sculptural mold. I still suffered from all my Christian vices: melancholia, cowardice, zeal for argumentation, a capricious generosity, a habit of hovering just outside of accessibility, paranoia, inflexible conviction, a kink for self-sacrifice, narcissistic self-effacement, corrosive self-doubt, obsequious submission.

What we were left with was a capitulation into forgiveness. A release, an unraveling, a letting go. An acknowledgment that we were all we had left, and we could not escape each other.

My father said to me then, "But you are still my son."

It was a platitude, but a harrowing one that enunciated the binds that tie.

While watching him in silence, I realized it to have been the first truly secular conversation we ever had. We had released each other from being moral paragons and became, at that moment, humans. And we were not extraordinary. We could look at the years we spent with each other—my childhood—and decide that they had been a failure. This realization made us become, therefore, more lovable—in the way love can only show itself in imperfection. Admitting failure had the effect of an expiation, a version of the great accounting one gives of the sum of one's life before God. And we survived.

I no longer hated my father then, after I acquitted him from any moral obligations so that I could love him more. I believed, at the time, that history is what pulled us forward, not God, and to history we would not be remembered. My father was someone who had seen Vietnamese independence, the rise of the Red Guard in China, knew friends who swam the South China Sea to Hong Kong to escape the Cultural Revolution; and my father wanted nothing more than to disappear through history. No one would judge or pity us for being none other than ourselves, and our destiny would be to meet one day, at the end of all this, the only forgiveness I know (forgetting), having slipped through the grips of our own histories into the only grace the godless ever know (oblivion).

# Identity Despite Itself

To be born with a race is to be entered, at random, into a collective history, a shared cultural construction not of one's choosing but an arbitrary assignment—not unlike the way people are assigned genders at birth. Can one reject this assignment? In his 2011 essay "Paper Tigers," the writer Wesley Yang describes his experience of his own race as "self-estranged," which can mean someone who *has been* estranged or someone who did the estranging himself (in Yang's case, I think both are true). He describes looking at his Korean American face in the mirror—"slanted eyes," "a pancake-flat surface of yellow-and-green-toned skin"—and considering it contestable: What is felt within is not confirmed by what is seen from without. He offers the "Twinkie" metaphor for his specific racial dissonance: "yellow on the outside, white on the inside." Despite having remembered that phrase from my own childhood, I found it an unusual thing to encounter, here, in this way. Does Yang's dissonance technically qualify as body dysphoria? You see how this gets weird.

Today, Yang is an active and passionate voice against transgender rights, often referring to the movement as a "social contagion." Yet his racial dissonance, felt in the body before it was intellectualized, might present a vision of the self that upends restrictive notions of identity, perhaps more than he would publicly admit.

What is the difference between identifying *with* and identifying *as*?

To identify as a man is to consent to be troubled by the collective afterimage left behind by every man who has ever lived. This afterimage, not so much dead or alive but rather *un*dead, haunting one's life, emerges as certain throughlines (at times expressed as stereotypes), which one must address or at least acknowledge, whether one chooses to claim them or not. Identity takes place on the level of the aesthetic, if we follow Judith Butler's famous definition of gender as "a stylized repetition of acts."

I like Butler's use of the word "stylized" because it suggests some aspects of gender as analogous to art. In the art world, we have this word "format" (once referred to as "medium") to describe a formal organizing principle that could, like a rubber band, potentially include different media within itself. "Formats are dynamic mechanisms for aggregating," writes David Joselit in his 2013 book-length essay, *After Art*. Artists like Isa Genzken and Rachel Harrison will employ sculpture as a format that can include, or aggregate, paintings and photographs within. That a photograph might exist within a sculptural installation does not destabilize its format as sculpture, even if it is contradictory.

I'm reminded of Walt Whitman's words in "Song of Myself":

> Do I contradict myself?
> Very well then I contradict myself;
> (I am large, I contain multitudes.)

The sculpture is still a sculpture, capacious enough to contain multitudes. Humans, too. Seeing gender as format suggests that one can present as a man and contain a woman within that presentation—simply one of many gender configurations. Formats are also not fixed. They can change, the way the same image can exist as a GIF file and also a print. A single person can present as male, and then later as female. Gender as format is capacious, dynamic, historically informed, unfixed, always changing.

But what was startling about Yang's "Twinkie" discovery is the suggestion that race, too, has formal characteristics, a shape, an interior and exterior, which might have something in common with the formation of gender. That race can be thought of as a format is indeed a provocative and potentially outré possibility, except Yang doesn't go there. He is not interested in expanding what I might call the "Asian format," seeking instead to reject the assignment altogether. Between the two options of claiming "Asian culture" and assimilating to "the manners and mores of my white peers," he writes, "I had refused both cultures as an act of self-assertion." In refusal, Yang finds power. He adds, "I care, in the end, about expressing my obdurate singularity at any cost."

Rather than Asian, Yang would prefer to be known as himself. He could have stylized an alternative Asian identity that troubles the very binary between light-skinned people and "people of color." Except he prefers the lone and obdurate Wesley Yang. In his writing, he appears to experience the cultural significations of his racialized face, and the purchases of collective solidarity that it might offer, as ultimately confining.

This is a provocative stance for any intellectual to adopt. To self-select as an intellectual is usually to choose one of two paths. The first: to be designated by one's tribe to tell the world about its values and struggle as an ambassador and guardian of its foundational myths. (James Baldwin or Edmund White or Claudia Rankine.) The second path: to refuse any tribal identification, either by choice or by excommunication, with no accompaniment but the dignified song of one's uncompromised criticality. (Norman Mailer or Susan Sontag or Katie Roiphe.)

Not everyone who rejects their tribe does so by identifying it with its most discolored characteristics. But apparently, Yang does as much:

> Let me summarize my feelings toward Asian values. Fuck filial piety. Fuck grade-grubbing. Fuck Ivy League mania. Fuck deference to authority. Fuck humility and hard work. Fuck harmonious relations. Fuck sacrificing for the future. Fuck earnest, striving middle-class servility.

When "Paper Tigers" appeared in Yang's 2018 collection, *The Souls of Yellow Folk*, Asian American tribal leaders were swift to denounce him across the board. Viet Thanh Nguyen wrote, "Yang flails rather than fights, which suggests that there is something inadequate about the Asian-American legacy for him." Frank Guan characterized the whole of Yang's project as "discounting of East Asians." Clio Chang wrote, "It's hard to come away with anything but the creeping feeling that Yang's main interest is sexual frustration." Chang might be responding to passages like this, from the book's introduction:

> My interest has always been in the place where sex and race are both obscenely conspicuous and yet consciously suppressed, largely because of the liminal place that the Asian man occupies in the midst of it: an "honorary white" person who will always be denied the full perquisites of whiteness; an entitled man who will never quite be regarded or treated as a man; a nominal minority whose claim to be a "person of color" deserving of the special regard reserved for victims is taken seriously by no one.

Except I saw this as a strength. While race, unlike gender and sexuality, is often understood as autonomous from erotic desire, Yang would disagree. Yang sees race as inextricably entangled with sex. Throughout the book, his primal trauma is the emasculation of the Asian American male. He writes about pickup artists who run standing-room-only lectures where they teach Asian men how to seduce, specifically, blonde and blue-eyed women. Yang describes the Asian male face as one "that has nothing to do with the desires of women in this country." Of his coming-of-age as a writer, he proclaims, "I went three years in the prime of my adulthood without touching a woman. I did not produce a masterpiece."

Here, Yang manages to mine a specifically sexual shame as both the fuel and compass for working through problems of race, privileging the sexual life as not only real but instructive.

Again, Yang surprised me, because I tend to find this method more in queer polemics. As seen in the gay pride movement, shame can have a galvanizing effect, not least because it feels primal. Shame has a delineating quality. It results when exclusive, cultural norms acknowledge an outsider first as visible, perhaps *too* visible, and second as unwanted, devalued. But imagine, for instance, all the Asian men who may have gathered, for the first time, in a room full of other Asian men to learn pickup tactics in a bar, tasting a new kinship? To my mind, I understood Yang's Asian male arrogance-as-shame as not only potential grounds for solidarity but also as indispensably clarifying, precisely because its essentially erotic sensitivities (his polemic, also correct) could critique—maybe organize against—the unspoken sexual passions that make up the racial imagination of this country.

Queer people of color have known this all along—and perhaps Asian men have, too. There is a surprising and refreshing kinship here. Enabled by this new common ground, one can seek out others, collect themselves, codify values that edify and empower. Or one can choose "singularity at any cost," which is Yang's ultimate preference. He seems to believe that the individual is always more complex, objective, and critical than the collective. He doesn't want the cozy belonging of a group, is in fact suspicious of it and outright refuses it. In Yang, we encounter the intellectual with no tribe and something to say about it. Estranged from all including himself, he imagines himself at the height of his powers, yet ruggedly, alluringly alone. But the question he raises and never answers: Does collectivity necessarily preclude complexity?

Narrating his path to become a writer, Yang describes moving into a room in a "decaying Victorian mansion in Jersey City" while making no more than twelve thousand dollars a year for "eight consecutive years." He shunned the dusty halls of the academy, as well as any job where he'd have to report to a white shirt who ordered him what to do. This rugged self-reliance was indeed a fantasia with a distinctly American pitch. "I was descending into the abyss," he writes, coming up short of both wealth and fame.

When I decided to become a writer, I did not take up the life of a destitute freelancer. Instead, I worked in advertising. Thinking, as so many young people do, only in terms of style, I had it in my mind that being defined for a signature aesthetic was the same thing as being othered, Orientalized, exotified, commodified. So I distrusted my own signature. Both as a writer and as a person, I wanted to preserve, in the absolute, the right to change at a moment's whim and not have to notify anyone. Because more than prestige, I wanted freedom, even if it meant incomprehensibility (to others, to myself).

Like most young writers, I floundered for a while, because even though I knew I had a voice, I had nothing to say. Imperiously, I wanted to be known for having a singular voice. Yet I would not find my voice until I acknowledged the histories and literatures of my people. After the Chinese were allowed to immigrate to the United States again, following the 1943 repeal of the Chinese Exclusion Act, the families they raised found voice in writers such as Frank Chin and Maxine Hong Kingston, who produced salient works in the seventies, which were mostly nonfiction. Chinese American fiction wouldn't arrive to the literary mainstream for another few decades—with Amy Tan's *The Joy Luck Club* (1989), Gish Jen's *Typical American* (1991), and David Wong Louie's *Pangs of Love* (1991)—during the nineties, when postcolonial theory by the likes of Edward Said and Gayatri Spivak was being canonized in university syllabi across the West.

Most of those books featured working-class characters, though during the decade in which they were published, Asian Americans would be labeled, pejoratively, as the upwardly mobile "model minority." We were stereotyped as arrivistes and sellouts, made to feel guilty for entering, with mixed success, the social strata of privileged whites, who had thus far denied access to all the other minorities, particularly Black and brown.

Yet while my parents gained in wealth, they lacked status. After getting her doctorate at USC, my mother, the breadwinner of the family, had at different points owned three houses and five cars and a stock market portfolio. Nevertheless, my parents were not invited into the social lives of the white people on our street: book clubs, Super Bowl parties, or backyard barbecues by the pool. This had nothing to do with income or assets, but an elusive socialization that has everything to do with the coded manners and hermetic social capital passed down along generations in billiards rooms and tennis courts, which my parents knew nothing of—how could they? This specific brand of frustration would be portrayed as "hitting the bamboo ceiling," as having-never-been-accepted-into-the-gates-after-all-this-work. After watching my parents get rejected by white society, I always carried the tingling suspicion that I, too, could do everything right and still be rejected based on my identity, no matter how much I worked or rose in this world.

Though whenever I suffered identity-based rejection throughout my life, it would not be for race exactly, but sexuality through the inflections of race. Gay and Asian meant fey and ignorable at a time when gay marriage in the States was outlawed well into my twenties. The white heterosexual couple was still portrayed as supreme, representing the idealized head of the nuclear family myth.

Perhaps for this reason, I gravitated more toward texts about gay experiences than those about Asian American life. I tried to excavate the writers of my private gay canon, because gay writing largely wasn't taught in my university classes outside of the gender studies silo. My heroes were James Baldwin, Edmund White, Gary Indiana, Alan Hollinghurst, Hilton Als, and Dennis Cooper. For many of these writers, gay aesthetics would assemble toward models of transgression, potently politicized as anti-censorship, anti-repression. Originally, the gay civil rights movement in the United States largely articulated itself against anti-sodomy laws, which infused political urgency into the literary depiction of sodomy, or any kind of queer sex.

Once, I submitted an essay for publication, and the editor returned it to me with all the references to fucking and dick sucking meticulously crossed out. I was stunned. But if anything, I doubled down, imagining myself enlisted in the fight for queer liberation. Now, Proust was my patron saint, Hilton the master. Gary Indiana and Douglas Crimp became my new paragons of critique. In this way, I had written myself into a private lineage of my own choosing, even if it was, a lot of the time, solipsistic and flagrantly unprofitable.

When you're developing your craft outside of institutional support, you have only your inner critic to guide you, which, when raised and bruised by early rejection, can sometimes become self-flagellating with flourishes of paranoia. In an era when what's reductively labeled "identity writing" was getting celebrated wholesale by reviews and markets, I was frustrated that my own writing wasn't cresting that wave. How to know if I was too weird or just wasn't that good and too stupid to tell? Most of the time, I couldn't tell. All I knew was that, some mornings, I opened the *Times* books section and said to myself, "This all looks like shit." I thought of the scene in *Ulysses* when Bloom rips off an award-winning short story from the newspaper to wipe his ass.

Maybe I was bitter. Maybe I had an ego problem.

I was also picky. To be sure, there was a lot of Asian American or queer writing that I found facile. In writing that foregrounded identity, I was always looking for something both morphological and relational, rather than merely expressive. It was often the queer writers who saw identity not as a fixed interior essence, but as a unique and dynamic shape. Leo Bersani aestheticized anal sex as a lived practice of shattering the self. Maggie Nelson used queer desire to burglarize the canonically heteronormative iconography of mother and child. If queer identity was like an aesthetic, a kind of art with formal characteristics, that meant it could be shaped, could change, or could align, coagulate, or recombine itself with other identities in infinitely clever ways. This kind of writing took the lid off my skull. This was neither a minority literature that enjoyed token success, inspiring the animosity of anyone else who didn't; nor did it endlessly nurse its own grievances, which have their way of persisting even in success. The most valuable discovery from these writers was that queerness need not be an alienating thing. Queerness could be promiscuous, cunning, tactile, unpredictable, witty. It has the tendency to surprise. Could the same be applied to race?

Then there was Trisha Low. She did the queer thing but with race in her 2019 book-length personal essay, *Socialist Realism*. Even the book's very form demonstrates the elastic capacity of the personal essay to include art criticism, political theory, romantic epistle, sexual confession, and dream journal. With piercing originality, Low pushes the capacity of the personal essay beyond mere aesthetics and into a political articulation by absorbing other traditions into the Asian American identity, such as queerness, or even Christianity. This genre is sometimes called "autotheory," a confessional aesthetic commonly associated with queer writing, such as Wayne Koestenbaum's *The Queen's Throat* (1993), which sweeps across the academic, the lyric, and the personal.

Already, the book's title, *Socialist Realism*, declares an emphatic departure from the anxieties and injustices that afflict only the "model minority" classes of Asian Americans. Early in the book, she enunciates, and later disavows, herself as privileged—the scion of a wealthy Singaporean family. She describes her house in Singapore with *Gatsby*-esque lyric: like "a ship, sleek and beautiful," with "porthole windows, and giant panes of curved glass that I liked to rest my cheek against." She is the kind of girl identified by a stranger at an airport as someone who "grew up riding horses."

As an adult expatriate, she leaves Singapore for California, where she throws herself into the labor movement in Oakland. By reinscribing a romance of what Low calls "the West," she stages a downwardly mobile descent (not without irony) in a deliberate reversal of the hardworking, upwardly mobile immigrant who arrives to new shores in search of fresh-cut lawns and a three-car garage. As all incorrigible Americans do, she is looking for freedom. "I came to the West with a desire to reinvent myself even if I didn't know how," she writes, seeking an emergence enacted across race, class, and sexuality like a flood over barren plains.

She ends up discovering the pursuit of freedom—and the identities in which freedom is lived—hard to bear, because liberation, for her, follows a series of costly refusals. In California, Low refuses wealth. She refuses the heterosexuality her parents prefer for an array of female, male, and nonbinary lovers. Refusal becomes constitutive of the self. As figured by Low, the Asian American emerges as a double negation between two binaries: light-skinned or of color. Just as the expatriate refuses to find home in either a country of origin or an adopted land or the bisexual refuses to be limited as either straight or gay. Of course, to maintain this position entails real struggle. Low writes about her difficulty with how to express a bisexual queerness that isn't always just "code-switching" between "only gay sometimes" and straight. "I didn't pick an 'identity,' per se, but identity forced my hand," she writes.

Articulating her oscillation of self-estrangement, analogous to Yang's, Low writes, "I found myself; I rejected myself. I was not-not me." In her reworking of the notion of the "closet," that shadowy room one is in before coming out, she elaborates on her undefined self that existed before public declaration: The closet "can also be a space for fantasy, a space for unformed and flexible sexuality. A space for desire, unconstrained and uninhibited by any identity classification, where there are no restrictions on how you explore your behavior or how you name yourself." She is writing about a kind of embodied queerness—or gender, or race—that can't be limited, described, or assimilated by the language of identity. In that spillage, there is a great amount of freedom, even sloppiness. Queerness is free to distend and pool with desire, and we know from Yang that race, too, is just as conscripted with the sexual. Both race and queerness, coagulating with the erotic, can shift, secreting meaning and joy in surplus of the conditions of their own social constructions. Perhaps race or queerness only harden into an identity, "a static category," when presented under the floodlights of the white, patriarchal regime.

But Low does not see each person's race or sexuality as something that can fit into specified compartments like items into bento boxes. Her identity's syncopation between dislocation and reintegration allows her, thrillingly, to abrade the membrane between the individual and the other, which was always fallible. Unlike Yang, who vies for "obdurate" individuality, Low can find rhymes, entanglements, and surprising homonyms between identities and traditions, both within herself and in the leftist and queer social group she falls into in Oakland. With almost no friction, she even cites the Christian church, of all places, as the site where she learned to imagine a queer utopia. Comparing it with God's unconditional love, she writes of both, "It can only be experienced if we first believe it exists—if we first believe that we are worthy of it. If we do not, it will forever remain unseen; we will be blind to it. But if we simply believe, we will feel His love. It will flood over us in waves."

Is this a fantasy? Yes and no: It's one of those things where, by believing it, we can make it real. Not for the sake of it, or to dream up some hallucinatory game to occupy ourselves with a mission, but because our imaginary utopias tell us who we are. They organize us. Low goes on, "You commit to ideals because it's how you find your shape." And to have a shape is a desirable thing. The world tells so many rumors about identity to convince us to dispossess it: that we can love only those who share some aspect of our identity, that our identity is visible only under the lights of violence and persecution, or that if we are assigned more than one—Asian *and* queer—we have to choose which one to emphasize. Unlike Yang, who wishes he could reject identity altogether, Low not only claims identity but also wields it for intimacy, for style, for revolution. She does not need to choose to function as one identity or the other. Identity pools the way desire pools. And if identity is inextricable from sex, what is at stake is love. The self can love multitudes because it contains multitudes. Both can be infinite—the number of selves one can love and the number of selves one contains. There exists a tautological harmony between the self and the collective. Neither the individual nor the collective is more complex. The individual is a synecdoche of the collective. They are symmetries of each other.

Both individuals and collectives desire, and they are bound when they can desire together. In Low's description of attending a May Day protest, she writes, "We're pissed off—about minimum wage, about police brutality, about the murder of trans women of color, about so much more. The psychic tissue of our want turns the crowd into one fleshy mass." For Low, desire incarnates a collective subject, with mutual identifications, fighting for a common utopia, despite all evidence of its impossibility. Identity *can* do this. It is likely to fail, but perhaps the struggle for utopia is less about actualization than the organization of a new collectivity: shared joy.

# In Arcadia Ego

The morning my niece was born, I was in Berlin in the middle of an overdose. I'd asked my friend if I could stay with him because I thought if I were alone for the next twelve hours, I might kill myself. The whole thing is a blur: the month, maybe the entire summer. I remember I had just flown back from the 2017 Venice Biennale, where I did not have a bad time by any means, and was sickened by the thought of returning to Berlin on a Monday morning, alone, to my one-room apartment. I lived by the canal. I was spoiled. I'm not even trying to defend the moment.

Maybe I thought this was how fags did it: art, parties, sudden death. Nobody ever teaches you how to die. Nobody teaches you how to fuck, either, which I had not been doing much of that year, nor for some time by that point. Four years earlier, I had been sexually assaulted. It happened in New York on a Sunday afternoon. The encounter would "take me out of the game" for a long but indefinite amount of time, and there was nothing I could do to shorten that period but wait.

What had I been doing during those four years? For one, I had been on East Fifty-Seventh Street working in luxury advertising, the industry that manufactured the very myth that if you aren't fucking, then you aren't doing much of anything at all. Part of the allure of those years was that within the fashion world, I knew I could walk in as the smartest person in any room—and also the most invisible, because I was so undesired. Maybe it would've been fine if I had known, for sure, that my sexual convalescence would last just one more year. Except I didn't know this for sure. And so instead of continuing to not know, I decided I might drug myself into oblivion: the sort of total passivity to the death drive that I wanted from sex and could not, at the time, negotiate for myself but could very reliably engineer with drugs in the privacy of my own four walls.

Taking drugs was the only way I could feel in control of my life at a time when the elements that had made life make sense for me were falling away, one after another. While drugs simulate and exacerbate exactly the incapacitation that I was trying to escape, they do so in a way that's disguised as pleasure. And if you can buy into the pleasure, you can live a lot longer with half the effort until the pleasure kills you, and isn't that how we all want to die? Once, a friend had to tell me, "You're the only one I know who actually likes K-holes," which was his way of asking me why I hated myself. The answer I never gave him to the question he hadn't asked: Instead of being victimized, I believed I could engineer the theater of my own debasement, be the master who could, alone, obscure his role in the design.

Except I didn't really hate myself, I was just tired. Tired of talking to people who had gone through worse (which made me feel like I was overreacting) or to people who did not understand the gravity of what *did* happen to me (which made me feel like I was overreacting) or to people who suggested I was overreacting. Even people who just said "that's horrific" irritated me, because it wasn't *that* horrific compared to the two friends—male, female—who had been gang-raped and hospitalized and were gorgeous enough to tell me they knew what I was going through, which just made me feel stupid.

Immediately after the assault I tried to steamroll over the incident, chalk it up as some New York moment—in trauma all thoughts are ad hoc—and I tried having as much sex as I could. And when it didn't work, when I couldn't perform or do much of anything at all in bed, frigid with paranoia or sudden catatonia, I knew it would be this way for a very long time.

Since I was not physically injured so much as violated, the assault persisted psychologically as I worked out the trauma. A fantasy: that it was "all in my head" and that I could reason my way out. In these narratives in which I told myself about my own control, there was always something that could have *been done*. At times, I blamed myself for letting the man escalate the situation as far as he did. At other times, I blamed myself for not wanting it more, for not turning the entire episode into one of seduction on my part, making this into a narrative of sexual ownership. Latent in the relative lack of assault narratives from adult gay men is the idea that we must have *wanted* this to a certain degree—maybe just a little bit?—and if this is what I had to work with, I would. It was a deranged train of thought, and I knew it the whole time, but I was trying to flee a burning house.

What I assumed about the man who assaulted me: that he was older, that he was homeless, and that at the end of the day I had more privilege than he ever would. I didn't even hate him directly after it happened and had waited an entire month before calling the public facility in which the event took place to report what had, in fact, occurred "on the premises"—what a dirty way to put it.

"Don't you want to protect others who might not be safe in that space?" a friend had asked me, and once it was clear I didn't give a fuck, he reframed it as "Don't you want the facility to feel guilty about not protecting you?" This was more convincing.

It would be months before I brought up the assault with my therapist. The day he told me "It's not your fault," I cried immediately, something I mention only because I always forget it happened. Some months later, maybe even a year, I told him that I could only jack off to fantasies about rape: disguised suicidal fantasies that would morph into fantasies of getting my head bashed in with a baseball bat. Sometimes when you really don't know what it is that you desire or how you can bring your desire to the surface, you dream that someone or some*thing* will come along to make those decisions for you so you don't have to do anything at all.

Being as fucked up as I was, I felt safe only in underground darkrooms: mazelike constructions designed for anonymous sex. In Berlin, I'd find them all over the city, in the basements of clubs or at bathhouses, where in near-total darkness I would wander through turns looking for someone to suck. In the all-bets-off economy of cruising, wokeness doesn't save you. Asian men rank at the bottom of the sexual hierarchy. The virtual nonexistence of Asian men in gay porn tracks with the desert of desire I've detected in other men, white or otherwise, who have seen me more like a green leather couch—an aesthetically pleasing object they appreciate, but could not imagine fucking. For them, the erotics did not compute. These men would either dismiss or ignore me—or at best they might assume, because of my face, that I was hungry to be used. Which honestly was accurate, because I did want to be used, and then disposed. Because I no longer had control of my body. Alienated from my own desire, I was irritated by my body's inability to respond when others tried to pleasure it. I wanted my body—and my pleasure—ignored entirely, because if I couldn't command it to do what I wanted, then I would decide to deny it, starve it out, or force it into a vessel for service.

At Lab, an underground sex club, someone asked if he and some friends could take turns fucking me on a leather sling. I didn't go through with it, though I wish I did. I wish I did everything differently, really. Part of the nightly tape reel that runs in your head, playing back all the scenarios in which you could've *done things differently*, is the illusion that your fate was in your own hands, rather than subject to all the arbitrary forces out of your control that end up changing your life— like the sudden interest of the man wearing a fisherman's hat with beer on his breath who suggested I follow him to the bathroom and would not take no for an answer.

Before the assault, I'd had a certain idea about where my writing was going, and I didn't want this event to define my career. I didn't want anyone calling me "brave" or "healing" or "necessary" or whatever.

So I stopped writing.


To distract myself, I threw myself into nightlife, where I was increasingly spending my time. The people I hung out with centered around Happyfun Hideaway, a Bushwick dive tucked in the shadow of elevated train tracks, where the bartenders sometimes gave me free shots at the beginning of their shifts. Or at the Spectrum on Montrose, where the doorperson sometimes let me in for free. The scene was clubby, queer, and messy. At the club, people were identified by their race, sure, but more by their *look*, their attitude, their drama, their performance. It was about surface, but it was not superficial. We had our ambassadors, those who had come out of our scene and made it big. I saw Arca sometimes come to these parties, same with Casey Spooner, but they weren't from us; they came from somewhere else. Nobody came for the sound system because the sound system was shit, and the DJs didn't care, often playing 128 kbps MP3s or YouTube rips, "precarious" audio files homespun out of the actually precarious and flagrantly illegal parties in which our queerness thrived. We worked with what we had: reappropriated Top 40 club hits, deconstructed with scattered beats, shattered glass, or chopped-and-screwed vocals on loop, a sound that journalists eventually termed "deconstructed club," which became like "hipster"—a term everyone would immediately disavow upon being described as such.

At the time, House of Ladosha—a collective of performance artists, drag performers, and club luminaries—floated in and out of the scene with the air of monarchs. The week

House of Ladosha occupied a full spread in *Artforum*, I remember thinking, "Fair and correct." I met them through my friend Yan Sze, a lesbian from Hong Kong who went by YSL Ladosha. Nowhere else in New York, or anywhere else I'd transited for that matter, did I see another queer Chinese person who was thriving like Yan Sze. Honestly, I adored her. Before the collective exhibited in major museums, Yan Sze invited me to their group show *THIS IS UR BRAIN* in Red Hook. It was a warehouse setup that was dark, with a pile of TVs in the center casting pale light on visitors' faces. On the concrete walls, neon green and pink light boxes lit up screen prints of the various Ladosha members, like star system promotional stills from the golden age of Hollywood. At the show's entrance, the text on the opening wall captured their coded, improvisatory lexicon: "Girl I was S P I R A L I N G last night . . . LEGIT *chew*—ing—*knee*—caps—*off*."

From Yan Sze, I managed to inherit four of the show's latex light box portraits of Ladosha members. It was the only original art I'd ever owned. I kept them hung over my dining room table. But because I wasn't schooled in how latex works, I never oiled the portraits and didn't shield them from direct sunlight. Then one day while I was in Berlin, a friend who was house-sitting my place back in New York emailed me a picture that showed all four works torn by the sun, along with the message "Please advise?"

The portrait I had of DJ Michael Magnan showed him dressed in a cop's uniform and sunglasses while painting his nails. Michael often DJ'ed gay afters, where, around four or six A.M., ball crashes would go off and gorgeous, skinny Black boys would spontaneously circle the dance floor and vogue.

Sometimes this happened at Shock Value, a queer party thrown by Juliana Huxtable. People were drawn to her. She managed to flourish at the very nexus of disadvantage: queer, Black, trans, intersex. She had long, thick braids, wore blue lipstick, and spoke in a low, raspy voice. Whenever I saw her, she was with Riley Hooker and Neon Christina (both from Ladosha), arriving at the final hours of a party. When she talked to you, she didn't hold her chin up in arrogance but dipped her jaw down, eyebrows low, eyes looking up at you conspiratorially, which was a test, because she never let you know if you were in on the conspiracy.

The scene was captured by these aesthetic moments, like the Telfar party that took place at White Castle, and the Hood By Air fashion show that opened with a soundtrack by Total Freedom, featuring recorded sounds he made while sucking his boyfriend's dick.

Then there was the New Year's party Yan Sze threw every year, where my friends and I tore golden streamers from the windows, wrapped them around our heads, and started strutting up and down the living room. My queers were screaming that night. I loved the scene and loved it hard. If, at sex parties, my race made me invisible, I found the opposite to be true at the club. I knew that if I could learn how to dance, I could demand to be seen. In Jennie Livingston's 1990 ballroom documentary, *Paris Is Burning*, the choreographer Willi Ninja's apartment is shown decorated with porcelain statues from Asia. He even uses his House namesake "Ninja" to describe his moves. At one point in the film, he says, "I would really like to take my whole House and go to Japan and have them accept it there." These cultural coordinates were far more sophisticated than anything I could easily navigate. Through the ballroom's self-aware exotification of East Asian culture in the eighties, I learned to come into Asian culture and perform it back to the club. I learned to use my hands, which are large, like Chinese fans attached at the wrists that I could flutter around my head. At the club, I never knew what I looked like— except at the Spectrum, where (because of all the mirrors) I could watch my form and do some serious damage on the floor. When the strobes came on, I pretended not to notice people watching. It was exhilarating, because nowhere outside the club did I ever command this attention. It was the height of the culture wars, and I had learned how to vogue, which I found funny and passive-aggressive. Whenever people asked me, at the club, if I was voguing, I would say, "I'm not appropriating anyone's fucking culture. I'm doing tai chi." Obviously, I was carrying.

But I'm getting ahead of myself. Clearly, I don't want to talk about the assault anymore. Self-pity gets tiring. How do you believe in your own value after you've been so devalued by violence? I act like my friends weren't there to help me. What a disservice to all the people *who were there.*

This is my tribute to all those who knew but didn't know, who just got it, who didn't have to ask. Who, instead, went shopping with me for skirts at the *kleidermarkt*; who answered my crisis texts; took care of the cats when I was spiraling; who sat me down and said I wasn't insane, and all my self-diagnosed psychoses were capitalist control systems.

Who taught me to have outfit changes before and after the DJ set. Who said a lot of gay people don't even do anal sex because wasn't the whole point of the queer project to reject the hetero-indoctrination of penetration as procreation defined by basic-ass Christians who prioritize progeny over pleasure?

You were the ones who recorded us talking for four hours straight before I moved to Berlin and then got Celestial Trax to sample it years later in Copenhagen. Before then, I hated my voice because it sounds faggy. Now, I love my voice because it sounds faggy. Self-love is something you have to be shown, and you showed me how.

I'm being serious—it isn't that bad, my life. When I started going to Berlin, I threw four parties a year for four years—welcome, goodbye, welcome, goodbye—and no one ever called me out on my bullshit. One of the perks of working in luxury advertising was that I would bag free product—fragrances, tinted moisturizer for every skin tone (which I never got right)—and at house parties, after the clock struck midnight, I'd bring the bag out of the closet and make it Christmas for all my queers and fashion hoes in Bushwick.

Sorry, I don't want anyone thinking I was a privileged faggot having too much fun, even though I just said so and have the pictures to prove it. I promise I was engaged in political activism, too. My feminism was hosting "Ladies' Night," where all my girlfriends went to a gallery opening of a midcareer female artist and then had dinner and talked about Catherine Opie and Hito Steyerl, and if someone accidentally brought up a male artist, we'd smile and be like, "Oh, I'm not familiar." (Men were allowed to attend these dinners if they were models, solely to provide reactions to other people's stories and decorate the table.) I never had that Asian party I kept talking about, because all y'all were too busy flying around the fucking world, and if the whole family couldn't be there at the same time, then what was the point. The closest we ever came to that was Yngve Holen's studio party that was technically happening for some other reason, which became irrelevant once our whole Asian crew showed up and occupied the place. Why Be and mobilegirl were playing B2B, and we snorted lines up and down the stairwell and danced on the tables in front of the DJ booth and, because the cops shut down the party, were all in bed by three and got shit done the next day. Whoever gave us permission to be so extra?

I don't know why I'm telling you all this. Sometimes life was bad, and sometimes it wasn't, and sometimes it just was. Basic presence. There isn't a "point" to this, at least not any more than there is ever a point to life. Your existence justifies itself; you don't need a reason. That's the thing: *You never need a reason.*

Which is how I got over it. I don't know when, but this period I'm talking about did eventually end—I woke up one day and realized it was over, even had been for some time. Life went on. I went on. My niece was born, and she was named after my grandmother. Mostly I try to make meaning out of the events until it becomes too painful, and then I take life as it is. I like to tell myself that. Just keep going, babes— you're on the right track. For most of what I remember from this period, I was so happy I could die.

# The Rules to Live By

Once, at a dinner party in New York, I overheard someone say he'd never fallen so in love with something that wasn't a person until he fell in love with Berlin. I recognized the truth in such a statement by its cadence, telling me about sweaty bedsheets, infinite bathroom lines, and midnight confessionals along the canal. Around that time, I remember seeing a Mark Borthwick photograph of a woman in heels standing beside a dumpster in a magazine, and I recognized in it the Berlin I know but keep failing to articulate outside of the usual techno, artist squats, and open sex. The Berlin I know is more elusive, seeping into nocturnal moods in which the crucial details blur, leaving a hazy *when* without the *why*, with the 4/4 beat of the techno kick drum running through virtually all my memories of the time.

I couldn't tell you why, exactly, I first decided to pack my belongings and go to Berlin. The euro's exchange rate to the dollar had hit a historic low, paving the way for an entire generation of Americans to suddenly ask, "Why not Berlin?" The city, with its low rents and seventy-two-hour parties, prefigured in the millennial imagination as a postindustrial wasteland with an aesthetic that mirrored, in emotional timbre, a lost generation who had entered an evaporated job market after the 2008 financial crisis. Finding our futures canceled and job potential erased, we became skeptical of anything but pleasure, which was, in the present moment, our only viable investment.

We were a new wave of downwardly mobile burnouts, a "surplus population" of emotional descendants of East Berlin's post-reunification squatters or Thatcherite ravers in search of ecstasy and the second Summer of Love. At twenty-five, all I wanted were "new experiences," which can feel like purpose to a twenty-five-year-old. The first time I touched down at the old Tegel airport, I felt an electrifying surge in my limbs. My luggage had been lost, my phone plan wasn't working, but none of it had any effect on my incorrigible optimism. From the airport, I went to meet my friend Danielle, who was renting a flat out in Schöneberg, where she let me crash on her couch. It was Easter weekend, which is like Folsom Street Fair in the States, except it takes over the entire city. Friday night, Danielle and I had gone to a diner around the corner and saw men walking around the streets in leather jackets, police hats, harnesses. The leather pair at the table next to us chatted us up while we brimmed with possibility for what this city now afforded us. I felt elated ordering a burger, because I somehow still thought the hamburger had originated in Hamburg, and my burger tasted terrible, and I didn't care.

Every detail of that first week had appeared sumptuous: garlands of sweet tomatoes at the market, the sound of taxis on cobblestones, lazily tranquilizing. I remember exiting the U-Bahn station at Kurfürstenstraße to greet the neon pink sign of the LSD sex shop: LOVE. SEX. DREAMS. The trip on the S-Bahn from Alexanderplatz to Ostkreuz had a natural pace to it: moving from the TV tower over the stalls at Hackescher Markt, then over to Warschauer, where I could see the bridge, the silvery water, and the Mercedes-Benz tower with its revolving logo on top.

One year, the top of the Benz tower caught fire, with smoke billowing up from the logo still stupidly revolving, and I saw, later, someone at a party with the scene tattooed across his back like a comic book spread. Squalor and decadence: the twin virtues of this weird new city I came to know. Unlike New York, Berlin displayed, for me, an unconquerable expansiveness. In New York, it was easy to lose your spot, but in Berlin, it was easy to lose your way. That first year, I would try to memorize the colored lines on all the transit maps. I'd sit on the S-Bahn and lose track of time, get off at some stop I didn't recognize, and find I was an hour outside of the Ring. For an entire year, I couldn't figure out a phone situation that worked, tangled in international plans and roaming charges. The Wi-Fi never worked with grocery store SIM cards when I needed it. Somewhere in here is a punch line about losing connection and not even noticing until you are an hour outside the city. After a while, I did get to know the transit maps, but I never found my way back to the track I had originally planned to take.

During my first year in Berlin, I rented an apartment on Mittenwalder Straße in Kreuzberg with my friend Ben. Like

Danielle, who'd worked for the Black Party, I knew Ben from queer nightlife in New York, where he was something of a fixture because he was such a polymath: photographer, DJ, sculptor, illustrator, model, dancer, fashion-zine publisher. He had the contradictory good looks of a severe angular face with needy eyes. He was sweet, a cheerleader, but if I ever crossed him he instinctively stung back, which made me always a little afraid. He was like a bottle of sunshine: compulsively dazzling, but if you swallowed it, it would kill you. Because he bleached his crew cut peroxide blond, he was immediately noticeable in club crowds, where everyone wore all black. He had a talent for attracting the semi-infamous: drag performers who worked the door at a club, stylists who dressed Rihanna, and denizens from a mythical class of superlancers who worked in either art or fashion or who vacationed in Greece or Tel Aviv for half the year. Whenever Ben and I went out, people were always asking me, "Where's Ben?" because he had the manicured ability to make his presence known by maintaining an aura of inaccessibility.

At the apartment, his mannerisms rubbed off on me. I picked up his slang—"rude" was a good thing, and "subtle" meant class—as well as his Southern manners, like repeating people's names when addressing them in conversation. He sometimes brought boys over, after the club or in the middle of the week, and we'd smoke by the window in the kitchen or do casual lines of K on his twin bed. Mostly we lived like bored teenagers on summer break, out there doing the whole artist thing. During the weekdays, I wrote, and Ben went running or worked on music, and at night we'd pick up a glass of Riesling from a Späti and confess our life stories the way only people in their twenties ever do.

One of those stories happened years ago in New York, when Ben was on the subway coming back from a party in Gowanus. It was early in the morning, and he'd been making eye contact with a stranger sitting across from him. After a while, the stranger beckoned him with his hand and Ben walked over. Introducing himself, the stranger had a proposition: This was his last weekend in New York before catching his flight back to Tel Aviv. Would Ben like to join? Over the next year, the two of them Skyped almost daily. This stranger—who at the time had just gotten out of Israeli military service—would end up being the DJ Roi Perez, before he became Roi Perez. In the next few years, Roi would move to Berlin, where he'd come to embody that Berlin dream of starting from nowhere and becoming a star just by hanging around. Here, you have Roi cast as the prototypical young artist who moves to Berlin, goes to every party, says yes to everything, finds a job at a record store (it was Spacehall), falls into the scene, gets discovered, makes his name as a vinyl-only DJ who plays sets of six hours, eight hours, and goes on to become a resident at Berghain, the city's preeminent techno club.

When I met Roi, Ben and I were having coffee at one of the outdoor cafés on Bergmannstraße, and Roi came down to meet us. It was sunny, and across from us was an advertisement of a man savoring his face getting smushed by a sneaker. When we asked Roi about Berghain, he described it in a sort of offhand way, with a signature mix of discretion, pride, boredom, and experience. Later, I'd be able to identify this particular affect from stories told by people most dedicated to the club: how, at first, all they want to talk about is Berghain, until Berghain becomes the last thing they ever want to talk about.

I, too, became one of those people, though I couldn't have predicted it then. At the time, I'd only heard about its notorious Klubnacht parties, which lasted from Saturday night until Monday morning. Like its predecessors, Paradise Garage in New York or the Haçienda in Manchester, the actual experience of being in the club was outmatched only by the legends its reputation spawned: raucous public sex, a merciless door selection. You could wait in line for three hours only to get rejected by a bouncer in sunglasses with tattoos of barbed wire on his face.

When Ben and I started going to Berghain, it felt like a rite of passage into some hermetic gay cult. Everything was discreet and fetishistic. We went every weekend, all summer. Our weekly party routine started on Friday, with a "warm-up" party, and then some bigger gay parties on Saturday at outer venues, such as Griessmuehle or ://about blank. At sunrise, we'd get back to our place and take a nap. Then on Sunday afternoon, we'd put on music and drink cheap wine while trying out different outfits in front of our hallway mirror. Our looks alternated from punk to health goth: combat boots, black vintage tees, and knee-high football socks. I remember Ben had these torn up Docs, which he had to pin together with a row of safety pins, like a tiny aluminum spine, that all came apart throughout the course of the night. Another time, I wore two oversize belts I bought at the market, clipped together with safety pins and cross-looped around my shoulders and back like a DIY harness. I had an elaborate system for where I stashed my drugs and how I recognized my bags when, at some late point in the night, speed or coke or K would all look like clumps of fungible white sugar.

We mostly went to Berghain on Sunday afternoons. Once we got in, we'd go out and tour the garden, find some people we knew, and then go off to the bathroom to split lines parceled out on our iPhones. Coke and ketamine we called "Calvin Klein," and ketamine with MDMA, "Kate Moss." We snorted both with rolled up euros, or tiny steel straws, which people either were or weren't weird about sharing with strangers. From the downstairs bathroom, we'd walk upstairs to Berghain's main hall, before which stood a massive white statue of Dionysus, a stand-in for bodily hedonism in dialectic with the technological severity of the club's mechanistic aesthetic in neoclassical drag. Inside the main hall, there were no windows to the outside, yet the high, glass panels that divided the dance floor from the bar lent the space the autocratic aura of a cathedral.

The crowd was filled with a curated cast of recognizable characters: shirtless leather gays, models from the Eastern Bloc set, cybergoths, new wave porn stars, speed freaks from the hardcore scene, and art world intellectuals. Ben and I usually lost one another in the crowd, found other friends, moved between "upstairs" and "downstairs," or drifted into lines for the bathroom stalls to share drugs, buy drugs, or take a shit because E gave you the runs. It wasn't uncommon to run into somebody I knew from New York who was in town for the weekend: DJs doing the European festival circuit or artists stopping by in the city before exhibiting at Basel. This is how I got most of my social news—six-month recaps in the garden, sharing a bottle of Club-Mate between us in concrete cubicles beneath the trees.

All throughout the building hummed the 4/4 beat associated with techno, looped in perpetuity: one-two-three-four, one-two-three-four. This music is often identified by a rhythmic system from 120 to 140 BPM, into which changes and revolutions are gradually introduced by a modification of individual components in exquisite relation to each other. At Berghain, a closing techno set can run up to fifteen hours. To some of the techno DJs I know, a set that lasts one hour is considered "light"; two hours, "enough to work with"; four hours, "standard"; and eight to fourteen hours, merely "a challenge" and curiously not "unreasonable." It's perhaps by this logic that techno makes people "lose their minds" at the rave, in the sense that the phrase is also used to mean maniacal. After spending upward of twenty hours in a single club, a combination of sustained sleep deprivation, drugs, and exhaustion from having not eaten contributes to a sophisticated delirium. In a meditative state, the conscious mind becomes vacant to receive the unknown. It is possible to fall into multiple states of consciousness at once, like sleepwalking through a lucid dream. Only after the repeated breakdown and exhaustion of one's restrictive faculties—what might be considered bodily system failure—can the secret life of one's mind be permitted to flourish, completely uninhibited, at ten in the morning, when you are beyond dehydrated, skin slicked smooth by the salt of your sweat.

Toward Klubnacht's final stretch, when Sunday begins to vibrate into Monday, people socialize in the lounge or go out and get food before coming back. Others take more drugs, burn out fast, leave. The gays, losing interest in the dance floor, go to fuck in the darkrooms, where monotonous music is preferred, allowing sexual rhythms to ride their course, uninterrupted by sudden gyrations or beat drops in the music. In fact, the kind of techno played during these hours, from one to four, resembles an intensely slow simmer, refined to an almost perverse level, like the way sex happens in these places over drawn-out periods of time, with shared partners moving in and out of the orgy's physical configurations.

Like candlelit chapels, the darkrooms are austere and dim. People rarely talk, except for basic negotiations, reducing communication to glance and touch. Men cruise each other, standing along the periphery, masturbating while others fuck against the wall or on stools or on the leather sling. "Rave music has always been structured around the delay of climax: mantra-as-Tantra," writes Simon Reynolds. "Instead of the tension/climax narrative of traditional pop, rave music creates a feeling of 'arrested orgasm,' a plateau of bliss that can be neither exceeded nor released." Orgasm becomes less "the point" here than the delayed promise that allows the pleasure of sexual tension to cull and relax.

When gratification is deferred to such an attenuated state, the anticipation becomes palpable. Tension hovers like a forecast of thunder. Static seems to gather in the air, crackling and fizzing with expectation. At some point in the early morning, after four but before six, the promised moment that only the club's most serious regulars know to expect arrives. The dance floor has thinned out. New entrances to the club have closed. Then, music blasts like a gunshot, blitzing across the cheering and whistling crowd. Heads gather to the dance floor from all corners of the club, as if getting dragged into a whirlpool. The percussion comes suddenly and majestically, like a bolt, not from outside but from within the speakers, sizzling and electrifying along the wires and bursting onto the dance floor. With the lights spasmodically flashing across the building, you'd think it was Beyoncé at the Super Bowl. The building declares its soul in these moments, the way a machine achieves formal ecstasy when used at maximum capacity. Rhythm propels your body. Between the ground and the ceiling, it seems, is the universe contained, and it is *moving.* Lights bend off lacquered skin in a million tiny laser beams as we move in unison to the same beat. In the music, desire and gratification become one, both terrifying and propulsive. Joy cuts like rain. I often experienced this as a release, but into what, I couldn't determine. It wasn't us in control, and it wasn't exactly the DJ, but it was *something* that everyone undeniably felt and knew like an instant ravening. Our insatiable hunger for it matched the inexhaustibility of its pleasure, and that's exactly what it was, *pleasure,* abundant and overflowing. To know this kind of pleasure is to know the body at its maximum capacity. There isn't any faith required; it is absolute presence.

I suppose that's what this is about: pleasure. And it never comes without an underlying cost: It's physically taxing and authoritarian in its demand of your undivided attention.

There were times I thought I loved Berghain more than anyone possibly could. Actually, I still think that. To risk the sentimental: Berghain is where I came of age. Fantasy is instructive, and it was there that I understood my desire, like an awakening inward, a light coming on.

It was the closest my lived experience had ever come to the way people describe Warhol's Factory: sex, glamour, and the avant-garde mixed effortlessly and liberally in its elitist, narcissistic splendor. I felt privileged to be included, at an age when feeling included meant everything. Berghain was, legitimately, a city within a city, intricate in a way that only identity-based communities are, at a moment when the city was prepared to endorse the club's illicit privacy while feeding off its cultural capital. Berlin's underground queer nightlife was a group of five hundred club kids who all vaguely knew each other, congregating at the same six monthly parties each weekend, and ending up at Berghain on Sunday, more or less. It was something of a gay fraternity or a secret society. While visitors sometimes describe Berghain as "a rave in hell," its most dedicated regulars call it, curiously, a "university," which I get. What the club had for me, a skinny Chinese kid from the suburbs, were rules I still live by. Freedom is in discretion, and discretion is in good taste. You can communicate only with someone who wants to communicate with you. When you see something, don't assume you understand what's going on. Stay loyal to your tribe. Everyone is on their own journey, unless they're in trouble—then you intervene. If you can: Solve every problem yourself before calling for help. These were pragmatic before they were ethical and served as a fairly useful guideline, I would learn, to navigating Berlin at large. Especially the last and most important rule: Know when it's time to leave the party.

I mostly heeded these rules during that first year, when everything was still cute. Whenever Friday came around, Ben and I would coordinate our looks, head to some party in a converted mill or warehouse, dance until morning, and then abscond, teeth grinding and feet twitching, to the gay baths at Mehringdamm or to lie on the banks along the canal with music playing from our phones. In the summers, clubs opened up their gardens during the daytime, and people danced on the decks by the bar, sharing drugs in tents or hollowed-out grain silos. Some of those afternoons, when the music was going, I'd feel my body under the cool of the overhead sprinklers, dripping with desire. Never did I want anything so badly as I did then. As for what I wanted exactly, I never knew.

After a while, I got used to arriving at any given party and running into somebody familiar. I'd fall into a group, split the cab fare to the next destination, lose my friends, but find somebody else: some fetishwear designer, a dancer who had just performed in Venice, or a drug dealer there to earn money to pay off student debts from med school in Greece. Everyone, it seemed, was in fashion, knew fashion, sold collections out of a boutique in Kreuzberg, or showed twice a year in Paris. Two friends walked for Balenciaga, two for Rick Owens, one for Ottolinger, and four for Vetements. Nothing was more exemplary, more *extra*, than when I was at a loft party hosted by a Vetements model, snorting lines of coke off the makeshift DJ booth with a bunch of gay boys in balaclavas and singing along to Britney Spears's "Everytime," which was playing from the karaoke machine.

As it panned out, I would not become the aspiring DJ who worked at a record store and fell in with the scene, but I would come to know pretty much everyone's faces, simply by hanging around long enough. After the first summer, I told myself, I must live here. Limerence—the stage in early love marked by a consuming, almost phantasmatic infatuation— isn't that far off from psychosis, since both have recurring catalysts, but nothing close to an actual reason. So powerful was the feeling I felt for this city—a sense of proprietary love—that I committed myself simply by wanting it as hard as I physically could.

During my first year, I was determined to make a literary contribution to Berlin. I was still discovering my voice as a writer, and I wanted to claim this city, this scene, by writing about it the way Fitzgerald claimed the Riviera or Didion claimed Honolulu. Through a failed literary magazine I edited, I came to know a clan of writers in Berlin, all older. What had always entranced me about becoming a writer was the *life* of a writer, which at last seemed graspable in Berlin. In the summer, we'd have dinners in apartments lined with bookshelves bearing works they'd translated from German, Swedish, French, and Chinese. We read each other's pieces in magazines when they came out, stayed busy. Most of the time, at least one of them was away at some porn festival in Helsinki or on an island retreat off the coast of Italy or spending the summer in Beijing to pick up the language.

Yet I was somewhat private about the other education I was pursuing. While my Christian upbringing made me sexually stunted, Berlin served as an appealing corrective. I was introduced to BDSM when I started going, mostly as a voyeur, to fisting or piss nights at Lab, the basement sex club at Berghain. Fisting fascinated me, though I never participated in it. "Water sports" I got into when I discovered that they were more about play than power. I liked fooling around in the heated pool at gay baths or going to nights at Ficken 3000, the dirtiest and seediest sex bar outside of Schöneberg—"like gas station sex," I used to say.

I seldom talked about all this, except with my friend the writer Saskia Vogel, who at the time was working on her novel about the fetish scene in L.A. I'd met her when I published a short story of hers in the magazine I worked for, an autofictional account of her time working for a porn magazine during what she called "the studio days," before Xtube came in and gutted the industry.

Together with her husband, David, a writer and filmmaker who had worked with her at the porn magazine, Saskia would host parties at her penthouse in Prenzlauer Berg, which had cerulean tiles and a Mexican ceramic sink in the bathroom, and marble-like countertops in the kitchen. She invited writers and people she knew from the fetish scene, and we'd eat on the terrace as the sun went down, the lights flickered, and the fat leaves of trees darkened into a bruised purple.

Saskia told me about Pornceptual: a queer porn collective that occasionally threw sex parties at Prince Charles, a club in Kreuzberg where she knew the owners. Since I was known as somebody who wrote about raving, she suggested that we go to the next Pornceptual at Prince Charles, where the owners, a couple, would host us.

So the night of the party, I brought Ben with me, and we met Saskia and David for dinner at the restaurant in the same building as the club. Prince Charles wasn't large; it had been converted from an old swimming pool for workers at Bechstein, the German piano manufacturer. That night, we arrived before the party began. The club was empty. The owners brought us champagne from the bar. Saskia had a harness over her shirt, which she said she'd never worn "as fashion" before. Steadily, people started trickling in wearing extravagant outfits. (The party had a reputation for *the looks*.) The DJ began with slower house tracks. Flat, padded beds were dispersed throughout the garden. Next to the bar where Saskia and I were standing, a gay couple reclined across a daybed, undressed, and slowly—without foreplay—one partner started fisting the other.

Per Berlin etiquette, it was tactful not to gawk. Saskia turned away, and said, "I love fisting, everything about it," as a joke, but also serious. She began to tell me how, with sex, she was "interested in generosity," which she found no more exemplified than by inserting her hand into a lover's rectum. She'd gotten into it from her fetish days back in L.A. Fisting is a practice, she described, of exquisite patience, attention, training, and sensitivity. Never in any moment, than when her hand is in her lover's body, is she more alert to his needs, to what he might be feeling, to the slightest twitches of his facial expressions or a movement in one direction that would make his muscles tense, signaling to her to pause, be still, until he could relax again, and she could press in deeper. A hyper-vigilance to his pain and pleasure would command her entirely, force out any thoughts that didn't completely service him. Her mind could not drift. For however long it took, she evacuated herself fully to make room for his physical needs, his fears and desires, the anticipation of his thoughts and the tiny convulsions of his body. Here, she could make contact with all that was happening inside of him, touch him fully as if occupying him from within. It was, she said, the most generous gift she could offer her lover.

———

When did things go bad? Like all fantasy narratives, there's another story—such as clandestine agents working behind the scenes—on whose effacement the fantasy necessarily depends. Because I was so far from home, I believed I could do whatever I wanted, cram fifteen people into a handicapped bathroom stall, or piss into the mouth of a stranger whose name I didn't know, or make it snow in July for thirty euro a gram, breaking free from the California of my youth, the church choirs and noisy dim sum afternoons.

For a time, the recklessness felt exploratory—indulgence justified with a progressive sheen. I still looked forward to the club nights at ACUD, openings in the red-light district of Schöneberg, and candlelit dinners beneath posters that made fallen Marxist heroes look like rock stars at Felix Austria. I liked wasting afternoons at Hard Wax listening to records, as outside the window, all along the canal, crust punks with mohawks lay with their dogs during summer evenings when sunset didn't come until after nine. And, of course, there was Christopher Street Day, when the shirtless gays at the club got tank-top tan lines from being at the parade all day. CSD was crazy, and so was Easter. I never actually went to the Carnival of Cultures, but the smells of frying oil and spices at the Turkish market—where I'd go every week and buy sigara börek with jalapeños by the stick, and pounds of tomatoes and strawberries at three-for-one fire deals—are branded on my mind. I could never manage to cook everything before it spoiled, could never remember that keeping two kilos of chicken breast in the fridge for a week meant that much of it would go bad, which is how I caught salmonella and spent two days vomiting and had to skip German class. Here, you find someone who habitually neglected the expiration date of things. I had shot past it.

Today, nothing seems more earnest to me than how I would look up the lineup of a certain party one night, find which DJs I absolutely had to see, then coordinate with friends before setting my alarms and going to bed at ten so I could wake up at five, when I would grab a Club-Mate and a banana, like I was headed for the airport, stash drugs in my socks, and go straight to the club. I remember the visceral glee I felt each time a friend, one after another, got booked at Berghain, which we never thought paid attention to the sounds coming out of our scene. On my best nights, while watching friends at the DJ booth, I felt like I was witnessing the emergence of a new aesthetic. I really thought we were in a golden age of dance music. I wasn't wrong. At a party at six or seven in the morning, a friend turned to me and said, "Look around, these are your contemporaries." Out of any reason to stay in a city, that was what mattered most.

Caught in my love affair with Berlin, I would sometimes look at the older people in the scene, whose deadpan faces were incorrigibly unimpressed by anything and everything that excited me, and I associated this with a kind of cosmopolitan glamour: ennui. Perhaps it's because I thought it was affected, unable as I was to accurately detect a secret and desperate anhedonia in a city where pleasure is king.

My own brush with desperation would come later, when certain expectations I had of Berlin did not pan out. I chased after extravagance, the idea of which stirred in me my most indefensible visions of who I wanted to be, and, more latent, what I deserved for being so damn pure of heart. But it would be the third summer in Berlin when things started to get bad, like how rust starts eating at cheap jewelry. Gradually the micropolitics of the social scene started railing on me: The drag queens were bitchier than normal, and I could no longer fake caring about who slept with whom. I seemed only to alternate between boredom and paranoia. When I had been living in Prenzlauer Berg, babies were always screaming, as if something horrific were about to happen around the corner. The slightest triggers could set me into a tantrum: a flicker of irritation from a waiter's face if my German was clumsy or the Neues Museum refusing my press pass because it didn't have an expiration date.

I started catching strangers who passed me on the street whispering under their breath, "Ching chong, ching chong," right as their mouths brushed by my ear. Another time, a Vietnamese friend and I passed a Späti in Prenzlauer Berg, with chairs set up outside around a flat-screen television playing the World Cup. I made eye contact with someone in a group of skinheads, and they started blurting gibberish Chinese to my friend and me as we walked by. Maybe this had happened the entire time, but I was only just now noticing, so preoccupied had I been with my expat playground.

I entertained a considerable amount of paranoia, which might even be described as the Berlin style (never New York). The former NSA listening station, designed to intercept communications from the Soviets in East Berlin, loomed behind the trees around the nude lake like a snake in hibernation. I was living alone, and grew distrustful of the neighborhood, afraid that I was being monitored for reasons unclear. It felt like sitting in dirty bathwater quickly turning cold.

One day, I thought I might meet a friend for lunch for Korean BBQ and take my mind off of my mental state. Instead of canceling my plans and seeing a professional—note the denial—I suggested my friend and I go get high at the public pool in Kreuzberg after lunch. He ended up dropping acid, and in between bouts of swimming we split lines of K and speed in the changing rooms as chlorinated water dripped from our ears. We didn't talk so much as lie around under the mid-July sun, which is all I could do at the time, drugs being my only reliable way to endure my degrading condition while appearing explicably "checked out." Tanning on the concrete, I was still under the impression that this was fixable if I would just *relax*.

I could not relax.

Stranded one time at the Ostkreuz station, I heard a siren go by so loudly and suddenly that I sank into a crouch and cried hysterically. Nobody batted an eye. I cried on the U-Bahn. I cried at the club. To refer to these as psychic attacks is to simplify the profoundly apocalyptic omen that I believed was coming over me. I visibly could not keep my shit together. Once, I arrived late to a writing workshop at SAVVY Contemporary led by the poet Simone White. I sat at one end of the table, facing her at the other end. Twenty other participants, having already written work, were reading from their material. I was, as I whispered to one of the gallery assistants I knew, "high as fuck," and halfway through people's readings, I was so strung out that I broke out into tears.

"Everyone's writing is just so beautiful."

The days when Ben and I coordinated looks for the club were gone. I'd stopped caring about set times before going out. Staying home had become intolerable. I had to go out, had to find the first person I knew and keep them talking and talking so that all I needed to do was nod along and think about other things. I remember a point when I kept hearing the worst stories about the city: Someone witnessing a stranger standing on the tracks before an oncoming train, or a friend who got dragged into a construction site in Kreuzberg by two assailants while she was walking home at midnight.

Once on the S-Bahn, coming home from a Cocktail d'Amore party in a Burberry trench coat, I had fallen asleep from G, only to wake as the train approached the end of the line in Neukölln. It was empty except for two men asking for change. I reached for my wallet, but one of them jumped on me, and I immediately curled into a ball, like a Pokémon, until I could shout for help from the people waiting to board the train at the next stop. When I escaped the train, one of the muggers followed me out through the underground terminal and onto the street. Because it was Sunday morning, all the shops were closed, and there was nowhere I could run into, so I jumped into the middle of the street in front of oncoming traffic, where I knew he wouldn't follow me, and flagged down a cab.

I kept my wallet that time. I lost it three other times, simply because I was careless. Once at the club. The second time, in a darkroom. The third: because I was talking shit while buying Pringles at the Späti and just got distracted. All these things started happening toward the end, when I knew better but was getting sloppy. I was taking drugs pretty much every-where: the bus, the opera, the KW institute, the Bode, on the way to the club, on the way back from the club, at home, at people's apartments at seven in the morning, always taking one more line "for the road." Eventually I hit the point where

Berghain became the last thing I ever wanted to talk about. I couldn't sit through another jewelry designer showing me their work on Instagram or a new visitor to the city wondering, out loud, if this was love they were feeling. If people I knew from New York were in town, I avoided the usual parties so I wouldn't have to see them.

Basically, I was having a bad time. I began fantasizing about island retreats, absconding to Athens or Tbilisi, where I'd wait until things looked better and blew over. Things did not get better. What used to be endearing became grating, and all the warnings signs along the way lit up to say that I was violating the city's single most important rule: Know when it's time to leave the party.

Once, I called a friend over in the middle of the night because I was having a panic attack, and she read to me from *Notes of a Native Son* until I fell asleep. The next day, with two weeks left on the sublease, I bought a ticket to L.A., thinking that all I needed was a break and some sunshine to detox my life.

I thought I'd stay in California a month or two. I stayed nine.


I did eventually go back to Berlin after California, but the city was different. I was different. Each time I come back, the city still lets me in, with something that feels like love. If I get off the bus at Ostbahnhof and smell concrete and cigarettes before I reach the overpass, my memories open back up. I find myself embarrassed by and nostalgic for the kind of imagination necessary for someone so young to believe that this unreal city will always be ready to kiss me like a skinny raver kid in a sportswear top with memories of all the good and none of the bad.

But really, there was a lot of bad. I can't even tell you. Except unconditional love forgives the bad, all of it, in perpetuity—a suggestion of injustice, perhaps—but what I'm trying to say is that I loved Berlin. Once, I overheard someone say that if he could relive discovering punk for the first time, he'd give anything. If I could discover techno all over again—in the same exact city, the crashes, the burns, and all my bad habits—I would. It's not what I'm supposed to say, but it's the truth. After all my stupid decisions, microwaved brain cells, all the people I've hurt who no longer fuck with me, I now fail to see a distinction between my youth and what the city used to be. Both now exist only in a region in my mind, like any country disappeared on a map. This is how I know I moved on.

# Anti-Fashion

During a period in Berlin when, for the first time, I was so broke that I started withdrawing cash against my credit line, I landed a job at a men's fashion magazine called *Highsnobiety*. Its three-floor offices were in the red-light district in Schöneberg—sex workers in fake Dalmatian-spotted coats walked the streets, passing by the entrance of the building. Every time I approached the elevator, I was greeted with a whiff of oak, stainless steel, and Le Labo. It smelled corporate, even as the employees signaled otherwise by showing up to work in dad trainers and oversize black hoodies: the uniform of the city's preeminent streetwear magazine.

I was brought on to the team to write branded copy. Others I knew condescended to this kind of work, but I never did. Richard Prince prepared magazine ads in the Time-Life Building, and both Salman Rushdie and Don DeLillo wrote copy for Ogilvy, Benson & Mather. They understood how words and pictures worked, how they pierced the dream fabric of a people, and these were skills I knew I would learn not in school but within the exposed-concrete walls of the magazine's offices.

The ground floor had a midcentury-style café with a large portrait of the designer Virgil Abloh, whose work I didn't consider "for me" but came to respect during my years working there. Abloh understood the way fashion was then being made. While others treated "hype" as ephemeral, something to be regarded with suspicion, he knew how to build, harness, capture, and sustain it. Originally trained as an architect, he embodied the proto-influencer who rose to fame. After he appeared in a 2009 viral photo with Kanye West at Paris Fashion Week, he went on to become the first Black creative director at a European luxury label. He was ground zero for the kind of fashion that would dominate the 2010s— the first Instagram decade—popularizing a style of bold sans-serif text on clothes and shoes that was easily photographable and legible on-screen.

Likewise, the new-media antics of the post–Web 2.0 internet was native territory for *Highsnobiety*. Founded by David Fischer in 2005 as a hobbyist sneaker blog on Blogger, the site would go on, over a period of fifteen years, to draw millions of unique monthly visitors and employ hundreds of full-time staff in cities around the world and across three major time zones.

Everyone there was young. Our receptionist was a local DJ who wore military vests and bucket hats and was always handing out guest list spots in the company Slack channel. The ground floor housed the editorial team: moody, windswept writers in head-to-toe labels, who huddled together at the round tables in the café, giggling over their glassy phones.

On the second floor, where I worked, was the in-house creative agency. We made the numbers move: social shares, follows, and impressions that went up, up, up. The first time I uploaded a sponsored Instagram post to the company account, I watched the likes reach the hundreds and then the thousands, all in a matter of seconds. My editor laughed heartily at how impressed I was. I felt like I was in a black-and-white film where men in suits stood dumbfounded at the New York Stock Exchange, transfixed by the jouissance of data.

To them, I came across as some exotic plant, a literary aesthete who connoted "high culture" in these spaces. Though of course nobody used that phrase anymore. At the time, the very notions of taste were being irreversibly subverted in luxury menswear. One of the main theses at the magazine was "the new luxury." This dandyish coinage described a period, starting from the mid-2000s, when streetwear began to grab land from the luxury industry and not the other way around.

*Highsnobiety* was one of the main agents of that change. In an interview, when David Fischer was asked how the magazine started publishing sponsored content, he said, "If you go back maybe five years, the site was basically product plugs all day. *This product. That product. This product comes out in two months. This comes out in one month.* So that's our DNA. We're product-obsessed. So that obviously makes it quite easy to plug sponsored products into it." A steady stream of RSS feeds supplied raw content for *Highsnobiety*'s news updates and product launches that satiated the hourly traffic and created a monetized feedback loop of reinforced bottom-up aesthetics that eventually bubbled up to the luxury houses—a shift made incarnate in *Highsnobiety*'s later collaborations with Prada and Margiela.

It was a pseudo-accelerationist new-media model that emerged from a cultural network of streetwear fashion blogs and message boards that have since come to "disrupt" the luxury industry in the last ten years. The old regime it modeled itself against was helmed by *Vogue*, and its parent company Condé Nast, which for the last century had been a centralized arbiter of sartorial taste. Recent years saw it undergo a full-blown financial crisis, obliging the company to sell off *W*, shutter *Details*, and digitize *Teen Vogue* to stave off losses.

I met a *Vogue* photographer once at a gallery opening who said to me, wide-eyed, of *Highsnobiety*: "The content keeps on coming and coming"—a comment that betrays the disdain and bewildered envy at the latter's ability (and the former's inability) to capitalize on and optimize itself for the internet age.

I smiled.

I had all the hubristic arrogance of the young, who embody the very spirit of fashion: out with the old and in with the new—a fixed schema in which the new is automatically pitched on the side of progress. Though in with the new also come faults and follies distinct from those of the ancien régime, though not necessarily less toxic—in some cases, more— which is precisely the fashion system as it is now.

How does fashion work today? "A label," according to Jonathan Anderson, the founder of JW Anderson and creative director of Loewe, "is defined by the products that make up its vocabulary, but they have to be flanked by autonomous cultural elements that can amplify their echo." While the success of every label has always hinged on flagship products legible to consumers (e.g. the Burberry trench coat, the Carhartt cargo), enlisting the influence of "autonomous cultural elements" is its own dark art. In the first two decades of this century, the fashion system has been privy to a dizzying barrage of global developments, including Web 2.0, image boards and forums, the iPhone, the globalization of hip-hop, the streetwear revolution, Style.com, the 2008 financial crisis, platform capitalism, Paris Hilton, cancel culture, edgelords, reality television, climate change, Cambridge Analytica, and Covid-19. Because it is mass-produced and mass-circulated, fashion contains an index of all these global developments. And the brand's "echo" that Anderson is talking about will carry with it the total sum presence of its circulation, mass-distributing consumer goods and images that accrue value the more it dredges up "visibility" and "attention," which are precisely the vital currencies of our age.

Before social media enabled billions of images to start appearing online, the fashion industry met the public in three institutional formats: runways, magazines, and retail. This operated on a seasonal cycle: clothes shown at Fashion Week, twice a year, six months before they hit stores. The system was timed so that the current collections appeared in stores around the world at the same time they appeared in editorial photoshoots and advertisements in legacy publications, half a year after Fashion Week. Notice the delay.

After the iPhone and social media, everything changed. In the infinite single-column scroll of social media, runway images are posted and circulated at a velocity at which fashion week trends become obsolete by the time clothes hit display windows months later. The lifespan of a typical Instagram post or tweet is rarely longer than ten hours, enough to sweep up faves across three time zones in three major cities, and then it recedes into archive oblivion. Nobody seems happy about this. This collapse of fashion time corners its products to be relentlessly and efficiently about the "right now." Centuries-old traditions in craftsmanship have been devalued by the screen in favor of the instant gratification of oversaturated colors, bold sans-serif text, and ridiculous silhouettes. Fashion is now designed to feel like a spritz of perfume: refreshing and ephemeral.

There's a kind of capitalist zen to this careless, presentist temporality: brisk and unconcerned with historical baggage. In the mindfulness of social media, posts aren't facts; they're feelings. Vibes. And the consensus around a vibe can be formed much faster than any critical appraisal of craftsmanship. Today, people use fashion like emoticons: ready-made avatars that perform emotions so you don't have to. Even after customers try clothes on in the dressing room, they might not remember exactly how they looked but they'll remember how they felt. Brands now design their whole identity around affect. Prada: intellectual and romantic. Rick Owens: glamour alien.

Yet social media is also conditioning a new way of taste-making, previously the role of the high-cultural class. Now, anyone can "like" luxury images through their smartphone, and brands need to listen to their engagement numbers. On social platforms, where the intensity of affect has a higher currency than quality of ideas, fashion is most viral at the emotional level, since it's competing with everything else within the same few inches of a pocket-size screen. In the kingdom of Instagram, there is no caste: Everything is smushed into content, and everyone gets to decide what they like.

Content, in the internet sense, which is curiously devoid of content in the literary sense, doesn't communicate—it signals, it "trends." Its goal is ever-perpetuating "engagement": an increase in user interaction for brands, as well as harvesting data for the platforms themselves. Content gains more value the more it travels, extracting it from every node (every social share, every Google search, every dinner party conversation) it touches, collecting a terrifying amount of residue, which is charged with meaning from everywhere it has ever traveled.

Today, the social media architecture of the fashion industry is girded by a vast, Byzantine network of influencers—models, activists, designers, skaters, or otherwise human-interest stars of social media—who have "clout" or are "making waves" in their subcultural communities. Brands hire marketing agencies for their research-driven intel on the new trailblazers, the early adopters, who are then contracted to appear in white-label photoshoots and video campaigns produced for clients, sometimes anonymously.

An air of new-money extravagance wafted through some of these agencies like incense. It would not be unusual to carve out space in a budget for a producer to fly from Berlin to Milan Fashion Week to film a fifteen-second Instagram Story for a client. At work, I heard producers murmur to each other, "Let's see if we can drop the margin," which meant increase a client's budget—so on the weekends, I took to shading friends at the club: "We gotta drop the margin on this look, sis." At an industry party in a Viennese neoclassical villa, I did lines of coke with salespeople in the bathroom and saw no discernible difference in their personalities before and after.

When I interviewed influencers—always bright-eyed, feeding on sunlight, sitting at the bars of the hotels where they'd been put up—for campaigns, I detected zero conflict over their compliance within the advertising apparatus. Absent was the anxiety around "selling out" that occupied the previous indie generation, replaced with a cunning that struck me as utterly contemporary.

The "influencer" is content personified, traveling the world the way content travels platforms. The very term is laced with artistic, economic, and technological implications. The influencer stages a market-vetted aesthetic on social platforms: positive, aspirational but relatable, and permanently on vacation. While the optics of Instagram are coded as autofictional, it isn't our generation's hunger for authenticity that fuels the demand for influencers (we know they are a simulation) so much as a collective thirst for the visual representation of leisure at a moment when neoliberal capitalism has made of everyone a total entrepreneur of the self. Today professional influencers are a visualization of the myth that even vacation can be monetized. There is no "free time" outside of capital.

Though the influencers are not the problem, but rather a product of the problem. As John Berger argued in *Ways of Seeing* (1972), modern advertising filled the role that paintings by the old masters had in the past: aesthetically representing the ideological interests and behaviors of the contemporaneous aristocracy, itself an economic and governing class. If fashion influencers might be thought of as an exploited labor class under the guise of a PG-13 creative jet set, the ones who control the means of production are the Silicon Valley barons whose propagandistic ideology of "disruption" and "democratizing the media" masks the monopolization of data harvesting, targeted-advertising models, and NDA-protected contracts with intelligence agencies and the military. If luxury is changing, it's because the ruling class is changing.

Today, luxury signifies the ideology of the new millennial money—as seen in Mark Zuckerberg's famous motto: "Move fast and break things." Take, for instance, Balenciaga and Off-White, which consistently place in the world's top three most profitable fashion brands. Creative directors from both labels—Demna Gvasalia and the late Virgil Abloh, respectively—compared themselves to Marcel Duchamp, the father of what's known as anti-art. In 1917, Duchamp sent a found urinal, which he titled *Fountain*, to the American Society of Independent Artists, not exactly changing the definition of art (because any idiot can make anything art if they say so) but changing what is *institutionally* legitimized as art. As the Society—modeled after the Salon des Refusés, the incubator of Impressionism in Paris—mandated that all works would be accepted from artists who paid the entry fee, *Fountain*, by virtue of its consented exhibition, became institutionally acknowledged as art, even as a urinal obscenely emblematized everything that art until that point had traditionally defined itself against. Thus, anti-art.

Today this would be termed "disruptive." One hundred years after *Fountain*, Gvasalia grafted himself into a similar lineage when he sent a platform Croc down the Balenciaga runway in Paris. Anti-taste, anti-luxury. While anything can be and is fashion when worn on the streets, it institutionally becomes luxury when sent down the runway by one of the top houses. Balenciaga belongs to Kering, and Off-White belongs to LVMH—two of the biggest luxury conglomerates known to humanity, and arguably two of the most powerful institutions that decide what is considered high fashion. One might even consider the platform Croc as the epitome of the "three-percent approach"—Abloh's adage that changing an existing product by three percent makes a new design. It's a visually pleasurable rhyme optimized to circulate virally on social. In the words of Silicon Valley CPOs, this could be classified as a "minimum viable product" or a minimally designed readymade.

In 2017, Gvasalia would "disrupt" Paris Fashion Week with his Fall/Winter Vetements show by exhibiting a luxury collection that was itself anti-luxury. Staged in the hallowed Centre Pompidou, the show comprised looks that surveyed a taxonomy of "types"—punk, security guard, office receptionist, tech dad—exposing the essential paradox that fashion promises individuality when, in practice, fashion identifies its wearers not as unique but as part of a group. The show almost had an air of a comedy, spoofing recognizable tropes. Certain models lost their individuality entirely, like the brand's stylist, Lotta Volkova, who disappeared into the costume of a central-European office professional. Here, the collection deconstructs signifiers that connote what we think of as luxury (price points, accentuated individuality, authenticity, exclusivity) by emphasizing their repressed opposites (cheapness, conformity, fakes on the black market, accessibility). Gvasalia appropriated Euro kitsch and thrift store staples, redesigning the Vetements logo in the style and typeface of other preexisting logos (the way Zara does), and even directing an official Vetements black market where "authentic fakes" were sold at cheaper prices in a warehouse. These strategies take after post-modern Pictures Generation artists of the seventies, like when Sherrie Levine photographed photographs by Walker Evans in violation of his copyright, effectively exposing art market mythologies of originality, which is the sine qua non of market value. These strategies weren't new, but Vetements's moves to destabilize the semiotics of luxury are newly resonant at a moment in fashion history that's ready to receive it. Ours is a time when categories are collapsing between traditional notions of niche and mainstream, luxury and mass, original and copy. Emblematic of the times, Gvasalia signals to his followers: Just buy the fakes—there's no difference.

But while the face of luxury fashion today is measurably more inclusive now than twenty years ago, it betrays one of the great riddles of contemporary culture: The more the 1 percent continue to hoard wealth, the more its luxury aesthetics reflect the populist tastes of the 99 percent. Whether hoodies and Crocs on couture house runways signal as "subversive" depends on how you look at it. You either do or don't believe that luxury can be avant-garde, that a "diverse" elite is as indefensible as any elite, that visual culture can have an activating potential in surplus of its market conditions, or that aesthetic change ultimately bears any relationship to systemic change.

Nevertheless, today fashion's object-oriented agony signals wider traumas rippling throughout the fashion system, where taste-making has been wrested from old elitist gatekeepers and is now being redistributed to people who might not even buy this fashion but are liking images and following accounts on monopolist platforms that train algorithms to promote the most outrageous and emotionally arousing styles. As in politics, the discourse around populism needs to be done away with. The people are not the problem. The issue is whether luxury fashion can continue arguing for its relevance in a system it guiltlessly reinforces, where fashion is made to compete alongside memes and political hot takes for attention. The more extreme the better.

All this was on my mind when I met my friend Chris as a user named "CZ" on a private, artist-run Discord chat server I spent a lot of time in during lockdown. His posts were easy to like: snarky but positive, breezy. His profile picture was a wide-eyed chihuahua, and whenever he posted, I imagined this cute and twerked-up dog talking back to me.

CZ and I got along because we both cared about menswear. A lot. After we started DMing, I learned that he'd been active in the men's fashion forum Superfuture, which preceded Facebook, Reddit, Instagram, and WordPress. In 2005, the first section Chris stumbled upon was dedicated to fashion and shopping, but nested within was a thread devoted to "selvedge denim" that was curiously teeming with more activity than anywhere else on the site. Late at night or on breaks between classes at Wilfrid Laurier University, he began stealing time to spend on the forums. Since age ten, he had lurked video game forums on his family computer; by his teens, he regularly chatted with friends he met in IRC chat rooms.

Superfuture was the first message board where he became a "power user." Under the username "minya," after Godzilla's son, he began posting anonymously on the site's denim thread, which spanned hundreds of pages. Denim heads from across Japan, Europe, and the States dropped long, intensive "resource dump posts" with an amount of information Chris described as "unreal." There, he educated himself on denim fabrics, construction, dyeing methods, fading techniques, processes for care and wash. These posts were coming from people who had been buying jeans in Tokyo for more than thirty years, socializing with hyperconnected college students whose gateway into raw denim was Nudie Jeans.

The forums brought out a cavalier, jockeying demeanor among its users, which, because it was anonymous, was at once brazen, geeky, and blithe. Chris could get to know users through the forums or direct messages, even if he didn't know their professions or the names on their passports. A communal lingo codified: Outfits were "fits"; clothes were "jawns." Once the thread titled "What are you wearing today?" (WAYWT) appeared, people began sharing photos of what they wore every day for the hive mind to respond to, unleashing a competitive spirit. Some users posted "fit pics" with their faces obscured—a vie for the unspoken code of anonymity that pervaded the forums. Personalities achieved cult status. One user took to posting photographs of himself on WAYWT, wearing a single pair of jeans every day for a year, unwashed, and then compiled the photos in a time-lapse video.

In 2005, Chris went on to become Superfuture's first paid moderator. His role was to keep discussions on topic or defuse arguments, which could be dicey. Around this time, a growing group of "shitposters" was emerging. While they didn't use the edgelord shock tactics used in forums like 4chan, they could troll other users hard, sometimes arbitrarily. If the shitposters didn't like your fit pic, one might interrupt the conversation and just say "Gay!" They called you a "tryhard" or "herb" if you were a poser. Some evaluated looks around what they called "brand synergy," which meant there should be a cohesive narrative within the different pieces of your outfit. For instance, if you wore military surplus with skater clothes—ostensibly trying on different signifiers that looked cool, with no understanding that their subcultures didn't mix—you were a herb.

Some situations Chris found difficult to moderate. When a new secondhand retail feature introduced a share of unhappy purchases or scams, further corroding trust on the site, he had little to say other than "Sorry, man." After a user got scammed by someone else on the site, that user doxxed the seller, getting a photo taken of his house in L.A., along with a hacked photo of his ID, both of which he posted on the forums to intimidate him "I know where you live" style. Trolls could get so aggressive that they had to be banned from the site, after which some would beg to be let back on. Wayne Berkowitz, the site founder, told me he got phone call threats in the middle of the night from banned users. At one point, someone even made a bomb threat on the Superfuture offices in Tokyo.

In 2010, Chris stepped down as a moderator, partly because he was burnt out, but also because peak activity seemed to be waning at a time when the advertising landscape was rapidly changing. Facebook and Google ad models had started stealing customers who were no longer interested in buying banner ads on a message board like Superfuture. The earlier generations of Superfuture users moved on as they became older and more professionalized, and there was little to draw in new members as Big Social began to monopolize internet communities. Years after Chris eventually stopped posting, he would go back periodically to check up on the site. "It was a dead zone," he said.

Yet many of the early users still kept in touch and made lasting, offline relationships. During the peak years, it was possible to couch surf across Europe and the States by finding one user in each major city to stay with for a few days. Many who posted on Superfuture as college students would go on to hold high positions at major fashion brands. Others would move on to the art world, start record labels. It was not uncommon for people who knew each other from the forums to run into each other at Paris Fashion Week. One Dutch design director shared a story with me about getting on a video call with new clients who immediately recognized him from the fit pics he'd posted on WAYWT. When I asked him about Superfuture's legacy today he said, "The legacy is the network."

Looking back, the story of Superfuture emerges as a case study in how influence is made from the ground up. At a critical historic juncture in the 2000s, Superfuture's peak activity happened concurrently with the two biggest shocks to the fashion system over the last twenty years: the streetwear revolution, and the birth of fashion blogging—both of which directed energy and influence from the street level up. Several styles today (like goth ninja, techwear, nu rave) can arguably be traced back to Superfuture, though perhaps more presciently, the site exhibited the seeds of much of today's online behavior: trolls, early influencer culture, the aesthetics of remixing, the free redistribution of encyclopedic knowledge across locales and histories, and the collapse of traditional taste-making institutions. What's startling about Superfuture is how anonymous it was, perhaps a necessary condition for these vernacular behaviors to emerge on their own. These spaces proliferated before Web 2.0, but got eaten alive by social media monopolies in the 2010s that were outfitted to cultivate and reinforce what used to be spontaneous user behaviors for capital and data harvesting.

But as the pendulum of history swings, users in our world of total surveillance, both commercial and political, are now retreating back into the shadow zones once epitomized by spaces like Superfuture. More and more, I hear of people deplatforming, turning to encryption, going anonymous. During lockdown, when users en masse began spending more of their time online, I felt I was witnessing a golden age of social formation across a netherworld of invite-only Discord chat-room servers, private Slack channels, encrypted group chats on Telegram and WhatsApp, or streams of group DMs. We saw how this only accelerated when the change of leadership at Twitter sent users fleeing from its walled state like refugees. In our age of omnipresent state and commercial surveillance, spaces where fashion communities can manifest—organically, in vernacular, halfway in the dark— new formations of underground collectivity are presented with unique potential. Fashion has always had the immediate ability to articulate communal identification. Like a river current carving a canyon, clothes in circulation can open new spaces, both digital and embodied, producing new social architectures for group organization. If the emergent technologies of our new digital realities have marked the present by infinite fragmentation, narcissistic personalization, and the total commodification of the individual as a content farm, one way out may just be the anonymous collective.

While the pandemic was a boon for online communities, it was almost a bust for *Highsnobiety*. Shortly after lockdown was announced in Berlin, the magazine laid off a quarter of its staff. I was put on indefinite furlough. In March, sitting in front of my laptop, I glanced through the window to see Berlin's first snowfall. I went out and took a walk along the canal, watching sheets of shattered ice float on its surface as the sakura trees were sugared in white. For the first time in my life, I looked into the future and saw nothing.

Incredibly, the magazine emerged a year or so later as a leaner and even stronger machine. When I was hired back, I was instructed to name-drop the pandemic in my editorials to demonstrate brands' performed empathy toward the cabin fever of a middle class stagnant in aspiration. We advertised satin loungewear for people spending days inside, and elevated indoor slip-ons to what we were now calling "mules." I considered this move both disturbing and savvy: our instinctual ability to slosh even the pandemic into content soup. Against the odds, they—and sometimes "we"—are still at it, leveraging hype to inflate sneakers on the primary and secondary markets. I still find myself susceptible to its diabolical charms, having just bought a pair of the Prada Cloudbust Thunder sneakers I first discovered in *Highsnobiety* with funds I don't exactly have.

All evidence attests that the fashion system survived the pandemic, or was even accelerated by it. Its tenacity, its staying power, presents itself as a cunningly adaptable apparatus that is improvisational and sophisticated enough to survive global catastrophe. It is not only an outsize part of contemporary culture, but an irreducible and indispensable part of daily life, down to the clothes you are currently wearing. By facilitating a feedback loop between aesthetic subcultures and the mainstream during earlier iterations of the internet, the fashion system has ended up producing the actual motor by which our whole culture arguably works today. Know the system, but don't try to beat it. If you want the shoes, you should probably just get them, and if you can't afford them, get the fakes. Don't worry about how much they'll appreciate, because by the time they do, the world will look completely different.

# California Gothic

To go insane is to burn up against the edges of one's own mind, where thinking ends and grace begins. In the middle of a pandemic in a city I did not call my home, I was sitting on the windowsill of the sixteenth floor of an old GDR apartment building in Lichtenberg—the *Hochhaus*, the taxi drivers called it—fixing my gaze on the thumbnail-size dumpsters below my feet. I didn't resent life so much as distrust it: I believed/suspected I was living in a simulation directed by an interplanetary AI, or I was locked in a nightmare from which I could wake myself if I simply pushed off the windowsill and dropped. In my head I was hearing voices that were telling me I was a prophet, and that if I jumped, I would not crash to my death, but—as Satan told Jesus—would be caught midair by angels, like the line from Toni Morrison: If I "surrendered to the air," I could "ride it." Quite frankly, I was losing my mind. I believed I was being tested by demons from antiquity, or remote CIA agents with microwave weapons beaming secret imperatives directly into my cochlea. The instructions were clear: I was not to eat or masturbate for ten days. And if I made it to ten days, I would gain nothing less than the powers of divination.

What was I thinking? That my day of reckoning had come—if not punishment, exactly, then some sort of hazing ritual of the soul. Manic, I did not sleep. I reread *Reena Spaulings* over the course of a single, putrid night, because I thought there were instructions hidden in its puns. By day, my voices instructed me to email and call friends and editors, with whom I believed I was telepathically communicating, and divulge inappropriate details about my sex habits and issue cryptic messages about God and the end of days. In what I believed to be prophetic inception, a voice told me my mother would die of the coronavirus if my sister followed through with a planned visit to my parents. So I called her, imploring her not to go to L.A. "I know you're operating on multiple planes of reality right now," my sister said, her voice measured and flat. I took this to be her admission that she was "in on it," participating in some conspiracy—attributable, I was certain, to a single source—whose meaning was obscured from me, just barely, by a thin veil that I thought could be snatched from my mind's eye at any moment, if I just had the right answer to this wretched riddle.

In fact, my sister *was* part of a conspiracy. A friend in Finland, upon reading an email I'd sent her during my mania, frantically fielded information from mutual friends in various parts of the world—Australia, New York, L.A.—and through chains of acquaintants found her way to my brother, on the one hand, who connected her with my family members, and on the other, to my roommate in Berlin, who coordinated with her to get me either to a mental hospital in Berlin or on a plane back to my parents' house in California.

My roommate tried to get me committed, but I refused. I chose California. My episode lasted four days.

After my sister booked me a flight out of Berlin, I returned to live at my parents' house in Diamond Bar, a suburb at the end of a brown and monotonous stretch of highway thirty minutes east of Los Angeles, toward Orange County. Diamond Bar not only is small but *feels* small, conjuring in the mind a montage of smog checks and hose water on sidewalks and imported eucalyptus trees and afternoon naps and Republicans and churches in office buildings with green windows and coyotes in the driveway. Arriving at the height of the pandemic, I could not always feel the contours of where personal trauma ended and mass devastation began. The plague shut down city after city at a speed so sweeping it felt biblical: Milan, London, Mumbai, New York, Jakarta. Watching the death counts surge into the hundreds of thousands offered a low, indecent charge that hummed like a lawn mower throughout an otherwise undifferentiated afternoon. To occupy myself, I got absorbed in staring spells at the poolside, heralded the fresh produce that arrived at our door, and took occasional walks along the nearby trail lined with cacti and warning signs for rattlesnakes.

Sunlight yawned. If this was the end of days, how could it be so dull? The hysteria of my insanity had merged with the ravaging of the world, yet the only emotion I felt capable of was boredom. Holed up in my bedroom, like a madman locked in his cell, I was to confront, once and for all, the fact of my unhappiness. Unlike the beat of metropolitan life, the time signature at my parents' house followed the rhythm of long and insufferable hours invoked in me by the word "home," which might, through discipline, be cauterized into something else entirely: understanding.

Blinking in the sun, I kept asking myself: Why did I go insane? Not just the fact of it, but why did I *deserve* it?

I didn't have the answers. I wasn't even sure I had the right questions.

Technically, this was my second psychotic episode in the span of three years, and it seemed the far more devastating of the two, leaving me with even fewer certainties. The psychiatrists I consulted couldn't draw any definitive conclusions about my diagnosis, due to the drugs I had been using (ketamine, DMT, some meth). As a junkie, I was hard for psychiatrists to take seriously, so in turn I didn't take *them* seriously. One psychiatrist told me that the brain damage from drugs was possibly permanent. He described a former patient who took acid once and—

"But I didn't take acid," I interrupted.

He just looked back at me with self-satisfied pity.

I must've looked wan. My hair, usually buzzed, was growing out into a black halo, and my mustache was too long, thick and straight on either side of my mouth, like a Chinese caricature. I was rife with self-scorn, something comfortably drip-fed in private after having so publicly drawn terror and pity from friends and family. During my episode, my sister had interrupted her presentations at work to take my erratic calls outside, then took a week and a half off because of the emotional turmoil. My brother checked out books on schizophrenia from the library. My mother couldn't sleep, eyes sore from tears, afraid she might get a call in the middle of the night from a stranger in Berlin or Finland.

None of this was remotely my concern during my psychosis, which is to say my self-absorption. In my trance state, I was concerned, rather, with voices telling me specific names of people I knew in the city whom I was supposed to locate and tell secrets to. "Are you writing about or *through* a condition?" wrote a concerned editor, who gave me a list of links and phone numbers after I had sent her an email with my litany of conspiracies, which I was hoping she might publish some- where, like a Q drop. My conviction was—as the pandemic seemed to suggest in its early stages—that these were apoca- lyptic days, and I was chosen to proclaim the truth to the nations and expose the hypocrisy of the wicked.

But if adulthood is marked by a certain equanimity toward meaninglessness and ambiguity, then it was surely adulthood that I had been putting off. What I can't fathom now is how much certainty I'd felt in psychosis. I almost want to say *purpose*, with which I'd felt brimming. How pleasurable it was to be swimming in meaning. Every detail up to the outer fringes of my awareness was tinged with significance, like a saturated color. Accidents were taken for signs, signs were taken for wonders. In the unraveling of my mind, I encoun- tered a breaking open of reason that I found grotesque but undeniably ravishing, even if it was batshit torture.

What felt so much like a betrayal when I returned to California—a pain like flat sunlight resting in my field of vision—was that, suddenly, I felt closed off from the supreme guiding intelligence I thought was issuing me commands, as if the entrance to a cave collapsed, barring me from its secret gold. Cast out, I felt like I was groping with pale arms in the dark, trying to rake through a black site for answers—any—to my only recurring question: Why?

In California, recovery is a booming business. While Alcoholics Anonymous was born in Akron, Ohio, it carries a distinctly homegrown iteration in Los Angeles, which I've heard referred to as "the Mecca for recovery programs." It was, for me, the house at the end of the cul-de-sac. At my family's imploring, I decided I needed to get clean. At the outset, Alcoholics Anonymous offers itself as a book or a method, though its participants will stress that it is a community. Even in the earliest meetings I attended, I found it hard not to be impressed by the fellowship I observed. What I was looking for was grit and character, and I sensed as much in some of the men in these AA meetings—"the rooms" they call it—which I attended with the reluctance of a teenager enrolled in traffic school. (Thankfully, we still met masked and in person.) Some of these men I encountered were Crips members, ex-convicts, Mexican drug slingers, compulsive liars, privileged scions cut off from their trust funds, chemsex addicts, gay-porn stars. The Big Book of Alcoholics Anonymous states: "We are people who normally would not mix. But there exists among us a fellowship, a friendliness, and an understanding which is indescribably wonderful." It was hard to shortchange this. Because this was L.A., I saw the occasional movie star or cable news pundit come through, though they were not the ones who showed up week after week. The dedicated regulars were the desperate and destitute, who, at the end of the meeting, "prayed out" the Serenity Prayer and repeated, in unison, "It works if you work it, so work it, you're worth it."

"Goofy and archaic" is how one friend described his impression of AA, after I'd told him I started going. "Goofy" had its charms. But "archaic" retained a deeper allure. I bored easily with other programs, which were either New Age–inflected or had a cognitive behavioral therapy bent. AA was so incontrovertibly the real thing. Austere, and as thorough as a colonoscopy. I may not be off the mark in saying that the "Big Book" of Alcoholics Anonymous is the single most influential work of American wisdom literature of the last one hundred years.

Still, most actual meetings felt grating to me, like church. I rarely shared. Antisocial and made awkward by social distancing, I didn't approach others, and instead waited for people to approach me. The man who would become my sponsor was one of those people. Bald, with a mustache, he had on a checkered shirt with a red bandanna around his neck, and his beady eyes bore affectionate crow's feet. By way of introduction, he dropped, in our first conversation, that he was gay and Christian, which was apparent from the cross necklace resting on wisps of chest hair and his straight-fit leather pants, which were like the ones all the fetish daddies wore in Berlin. Often, he showed up to meetings on his motorcycle, wearing a leather Harrington, and I could spot, from across the room, his idiosyncratic mustache that went from one of his sideburns, down along his jaw, up and across his upper lip, and then back down and up to the opposite ear.

Right when I saw him, I thought he looked like a daddy. In the rooms, he was held in high esteem because he worked at a rehab center out by the beach, dealing with day-zero addicts who were bouncing off walls. "Were you busy saving lives?" I'd say when I saw him. He came from the leather scene in New York and was old enough to have remembered when AIDS was called GRID. He'd been active in a gay motorcycle club and frequented after-hour sex clubs in East Village basements. But today, he had a scrubbed-clean image: a card-carrying Christian who listened to K-LOVE on the radio to destress. By the time I met him, he said, wincing, that he had been celibate for two years. His half-conscious abstinence—which made him alluringly untouchable—only called more attention to his repressed past, in which I imagined his low tenor issuing firm, affectless directions to a sub. I was probably in love with him.

Addicts are people for whom love comes easily. We ooze desire, barely able to conceal our battle against our forbidden drives. My sponsor secreted his sensitivity like sweat. He was constantly "falling" for people, often saying "I fell in love with her at that moment" or "I just love that kid" when describing clients or coworkers. He cried openly in front of others, midconversation, in meetings; a touching habit he was unembarrassed by. He, of course, had his own history with addiction: had once frisked a pharmacy while working the night shift, had gotten so blackout drunk that he forgot having called his grandmother and telling her to "fuck off." He had demons—had been molested as a child, gang raped once—touchstones that were part of the "narrative" he shared regularly in AA. He reminded me that the haunt of relapse always beckoned, no matter how long you've been sober. He had been several years sober when he was invited to his own sponsee's house and stole all the pain medication from the bathroom medicine cabinet. This might have deterred me from asking him to be my sponsor, but rather, it made me trust him. He was transparent. Broken even, a word he personally disliked, saying it was an Old Testament word and that "in Christ we aren't broken."

This was an unusual thing to hear in AA. While the program centers the notion of "God," it's frequently euphemized as a "power greater than ourselves" of "our own understanding"; you never hear the name "Jesus" mentioned. ("The fastest way to clear a room," my sponsor joked). AA members refer to themselves as "fellows," not "Christians." But my sponsor was a full-on Christ-believing Christian. Sure, I had long-standing reservations with the evangelical church, but as for Christianity itself, I wanted so badly by this time what people in the rooms referred to as a "spiritual awakening" that I took in my sponsor's faith without any resistance. I wanted nothing short of ravishing passion, an abrupt and inner conflagration, that would push me toward a holiness so ecstatic it would feel treasonous.

What I found instead was duty and discipline, tedium and dailiness. As a sponsor, he was strict. For months, we talked seven days a week for one hour, at five P.M. on the dot. Each of the twelve steps was paired with a spiritual principle, from acceptance to integrity to brotherly love. Every step was accompanied by a set of assignments and readings, and I was expected to do them on time. We held certain maxims. God draws near to those who want him enough. Where faith lacks, willingness suffices. My sponsor had rules: No self-pity or complaining of any kind. No "past-dwelling" or "future-tripping," as both distracted from the present moment, which is all we have—"This is a day-by-day program." He barred me from using certain words, such as "drama" and "trigger," because they reeked of "unmanageability." If he sensed I was trying to protect or assert my "EGO"—his (goofy) acronym for "Easing God Out"—he would interrupt me, midsentence: "Excuse me, but I'm going to have to stop you for a second."

He was firm but polite, gentlemanly in his speech. He said "freaking" instead of "fucking." Often, he punctuated his sentences with "my friend," as in: "That, my friend, is the difference between emotionalism and true religious feeling." He was one to be wary of emotionalism: His chief vice was wrath, he said, which always threatened to consume him. I, too, knew it was a constant threat, was careful to avoid it. Sometimes I suspected my flighty attention span irritated him. Whenever he made a point I was to focus on, he'd pause for several seconds until I said "Yes" or "Uh-huh" to show that I was tuned in. I dreaded that he would ask me to repeat what he'd just said (as he sometimes did), and I would be unable to answer because I had been zoning out.

I was afraid he could read my mind, quite literally in some respects. I often joked about his "psychic powers," because he used to be a psychic, which meant that when I told him that, in psychosis, I had entered other and potentially mystic realities, he remained as unfazed as leather. He said he'd attended a "psychic school" that trained some young clairvoyants to go on to work for the police department or the FBI. They were given tests, such as being shown a spread of facedown cards and asked to flip over the queen. More often than was considered normal, my sponsor would turn over the queen. For a bit in his twenties, he worked as a professional psychic. Once, he scared a woman out of the room after he called her by a name only her dead grandfather used to call her by. Another time, he was a substitute teacher for a class, and a kid saw his pack of tarot cards peeking out of his bag from the floor. He begged for a reading, so my sponsor consented, performing one over lunch break. But "because once you turn yourself on, you can't really turn yourself off," he told the kid that his parents were making a difficult decision that would alter the course of his life. At that, he burst into tears, and ran to the principal's office. As it happened, his parents were getting a divorce. My sponsor was fired.

Which is to say that he could be unprofessional. In our early phone calls, he complained to me about how difficult or inept his other two sponsees were. They were unable to carry out simple assignments and they tended to catastrophize (the worst thing). These disclosures never felt entirely appropriate, though a part of me wanted to hear about how poorly the other two were because it meant I was the favorite. I would offer an easy aphorism about my readings in the Big Book— "Resentment is a desire for vigilante justice" or "Only innocence reserves the right to condemn"—and he'd say, "You're so good" with a smile. It made me feel dirty because of how much I enjoyed hearing it. "You have the gift of energy," he said, and I could hear his voice go buoyant on the phone. Some days, our calls went for an hour and a half, two. "I quote you to people," he'd say.

I was flattered, even if I was wary that our relationship was barreling forward to a point where I wasn't always sure when or how to pump the brakes. He would text me artifacts from his past that he'd "never sent any sponsee before," like a wedding picture with his ex-husband in New York or recordings of him singing Christian songs to the karaoke machine in his garage.

What exactly was going on here? I felt overwhelmed by intimacy. Privately, it triggered an identity crisis. I hated acting like a teacher's pet. To recuperate some critical agency, I would bicker with him if I found him tedious or clichéd. But sometimes he really did make me feel as if I'd been pitched back to childhood Sunday School. My sponsor required that I memorize certain prayers, and pray every morning bedside, on my knees. Later in our phone calls, he would ask, "Did you pray today?" Every time I said yes I felt like I was lying, even if I wasn't. As "service," he required that I do two chores in my parents' house every day, and text him, without fail, which chores I did. "The text is as important as the chore itself," he said. Later, I was to text him answers to three daily questions: What I'd done well, what I could have done better, and who I'd helped that day. This was not, I concluded, a program for adults.

I fantasized about quitting, but never did. Eventually we went from daily calls to just four a week, but even then, the phone calls tended to blur. Sometimes, I would lie on my bedroom floor, with the phone resting on the side of my face and an eye on my watch, punctuating the conversation with my yeses and uh-huhs. He would say, "You get me?" and I would say, "Yes." And if he suspected my mind was drifting, he would say, in an insinuating tone, "*Do* you?" This would both enrage me and flood me with guilt. Why did I always need to affirm him?

Though he was often the one affirming *me*, to the point where I could feel I was being love bombed. "I'm in awe of you," he'd say about my insight. "My willing student," he said. "My friend." It made him giddy to get my calls unannounced. I could hear it in his voice. His earnest affection melted me. I collapsed into hysterical tears by myself one morning because I felt nobody in my life loved me as much as my sponsor. I was a drug addict, and he made me feel like the philosopher king. He was the first to tell me he loved me, and I could not get myself to repeat the phrase. "I have so much love for you, and I think it's mutual," he said, to which all I could muster was, "It is."

But, of course, I loved him, quickly and early. I wanted to give him the world.

I fashioned him in my mind as a lowly apostle, someone between Paul raving in chains and John the Baptist feeding on locusts and honey. My sponsor lived humbly, slept in a shared room in a sober living household, worked just over minimum wage. Finances dogged him, medical bills piled. His superiors were always dangling promotions that never materialized. I tried to motivate him to apply for higher-paying jobs, but it was like pulling teeth. He didn't want to leave the addicts who adored him because he genuinely enjoyed them. He dignified them by considering them preferable company, like Jesus did to prostitutes and tax collectors. "It's never draining," my sponsor said of the work, which otherwise had a staggeringly high turnover. "I'm where I'm supposed to be." I looked at my own life and found it stupid and wasteful: all the luxury clothes I never ended up wearing. *Blessed are the poor in spirit, for theirs is the kingdom of heaven.*

His lifestyle was not a rebuke to mine, but it always felt like it. The things that excited me—publishing in an international newspaper or getting a fan letter in my inbox from a fashion designer I admired—failed to captivate him. He extended me the disinterested warmth of a father regarding his son's grade school marks. What overjoyed him was when I was late to a phone call once because I had lost track of time while praying. And so I began tailoring my attentions. Out of habit, around him I clipped my emotions about trivial things, making sure not to feel anything too strongly, at the risk of being "dramatic." Sometimes, his masculine posturing irritated me—for instance, when a bike accident on the freeway caused a hairline fracture in his ankle, he relayed this information to me like he'd gotten a migraine—and if I expressed shock or worry that was, dare I say, too maternal, I could detect a hint of annoyance in his voice, and so I always backed off.

Yet his response recurred in my mind throughout my day like a rare blessing—"You're being dramatic"—as I complained to myself during the insulting repetitions of organizing cups to fit into the cabinet, the inanity of fitness, scouring the internet for new dinner recipes to make in my parents' overburdened kitchen. I lived for the dramatic. But to complain about tedium was to fundamentally misunderstand the task of life. Accepting life's irreducible plainness was a safeguard against being swallowed up by the whirlpools of one's own aggrandizements.

When I relayed to him something a close friend had confessed to me, something I found quite sad—"shame is the air I breathe"—my sponsor rolled his eyes and said, "That's so dramatic," and I burst out in laughter. I couldn't help myself. This laughter felt juicy. After all, shame *is* ridiculous. Only conceited people feel shame: It's performative and masturbatory. There is no other way to respond but to laugh. One has no need to be ashamed of "the wreckage of one's past." One can simply regard it with warm disinterest and move on.

What my sponsor taught me—that sobriety was a practice in humility and self-possession. Yet so much of the time on the phone with him, we could not stop laughing.

As the pandemic groused onward, my mind buzzed in a cottony fizz that some in the rooms refer to as the "pink cloud." Berlin slid into its winter lockdown—the long one—and it made sense for me to stay on in California, where I was so absorbed in my step work that it made me stupid. Reading the *Times* felt like reading about Mars. The troll king sat upon his gilded chair in silence before his American carnage. In a banlieue of Paris, a high school history teacher, after showing his class a caricature of the prophet Mohammad, was beheaded in the street with a knife. When the Burmese junta kidnapped head of state Aung San Suu Kyi the morning of the coup, I scarcely knew it happened. What I did know was that after the rains came down across the Inland Empire, the Chino hills outside my bedroom window went from brown to green. Somewhere on Neptune, it was raining diamonds. I thought of Nicole Diver in *Tender Is the Night*, locked up in an insane asylum in Switzerland during the entirety of the First World War. This was my cloistered existence, shut up against the world during the final days of the hated regime, absorbed in my own eccentric rituals, my private convalescence.

The weeks when the fires swept the coast, curtains of ash fell from a sky the color of tinted prescription bottles. A friend in Nashville wrote to me about a series of tornadoes that devastated the city, the worst part missing him by just three blocks. "My neighborhood still looks like a war zone." For a time, I felt like all I was hearing were stories of natural disasters. It put me in mind of the desert cyclone in the Book of Job that circles his house, which collapses and crushes his children. In grief, Job cries out to God, "When I think my bed will comfort me and my couch will ease my complaint, even then you frighten me with dreams and terrify me with visions."

In the Book of Job, his three friends insist that he is suffering *for a reason*. They sling false accusations on him, urge him to repent. Yet Job, described by God himself as "blameless," insists on his own innocence. He refuses to repent for sins he didn't commit, but he also refuses to do much else. His speech is pinned down by pain, capable only of lamenting either the unknowable logic of God or, worse, God's indifference. "It is all the same," he cries. "He destroys both the blameless and the wicked." Instead, Job chooses catatonic passivity: waiting for death.

I was by no means "blameless" before God, but I did see a sagacity, distinctly plain, in Job's willingness to wait. What else was there to do during this pandemic? How else to face the catastrophic loss I suffered at the very moment that so many across the world were plunged into grief? There are times when there is too much pain and the only thing *to* do is lie there and wait.

The philosopher Simone Weil uses the word "affliction" (malheur) to describe the suffering of Job, the kind of pain that is so overpowering it pulverizes the soul. Referred to as a "blind mechanism," affliction is set loose upon the world by God and happens on its victims seemingly at random. "Affliction is anonymous before all things; it deprives its victims of their personality and makes them into things." It explodes one's very subjecthood. In affliction we become brute objects, worthless in our senselessness. As Weil goes on to say, "affliction is ridiculous."

Job's friends insist that his suffering is punitive, serving a moral purpose, though the text reveals otherwise. If one believes in the sufficiency of Christ's crucifixion to cover all sins across time and space, in the Old Testament and the New, then human suffering serves no moral purpose at all. Human suffering in addition to Christ's is extraneous. Christians do not need to be punished for more sins; Christ's atonement is enough. So instead, for Weil, suffering is considered in the realm of aesthetics, ostensibly excessive, without any moral function. She conceives affliction not as a sweep of justice, but rather a mechanism of nature, a law of the universe, an aesthetic world to be marveled at, inseparable from the firmament of the heavens, the chains of the Pleiades or the cords of Orion, to the bowl of the Earth, where the horse laughs at fear, afraid of nothing.

For in the distinctly Christian imagination, aesthetics supplants morality. In Romans, Paul writes that in Jesus we are free from the moral law. The economy of sin and punishment no longer applies. Christ's perfect sacrifice of his total innocence cancels out God's absolute judgment, and from the nullification of the law emerges a newly possible aesthetics. Christ died so that man could be free to be beautiful.

This suggests, somewhat scandalously, that suffering is also a version of that awful beauty. In prose that is lyrical in its sweep, Weil describes the affliction that comes from God as a "red hot iron" that "stamps the soul to its very depths with scorn"; the afflicted are "mutilated," or "struggling on the ground like a half-crushed worm." Elsewhere, she writes, "Affliction is a marvel of divine technique," or "an object of love." As in all discussions of aesthetics, one detects an unmistakable erotic charge here. In prose infused with strange gratitude, Weil offers a distinctly masochistic understanding of the kind of suffering given by God, the master, the unknowable arbiter of the universe. The Christian then consents to any offering of pain or pleasure according to God's divine but cryptic logic, which one either does or does not decide to trust. And is this not simply a description of faith?

If one thinks of God as a sadistic lover, he acts recklessly in Job. God is cavalier, self-indulgent, withholding, and megalomaniacal; as in all fetish relationships, his behavior is not meant to be understood or legible to outsiders. This is what makes God "personal," as evangelicals repeatedly insist. Remarkably, Weil's language approaches what Leo Bersani, the queer Lacanian theorist, writes about anal sex:

> The opposition between pleasure and pain becomes irrelevant, in which the sexual emerges as the *jouissance* of exploded limits, as the ecstatic suffering into which the human organism momentarily plunges when it is "pressed" beyond a certain threshold of endurance. Sexuality, at least in the mode in which it is constituted, may be a tautology for masochism.

When I was younger, I used to see a rampart between the spiritual and the sexual. I no longer do. In queer erotics, the sexual is freed from the biological, the realm of reproductive (heteronormative) function, and into the aesthetic (queer) realm where the ends of pleasure and intimacy are paramount. Is it possible, then, to conceive of such a thing as spiritual aesthetics as spiritual erotics? In the grafting of theology explicitly within a lineage of queer aesthetics, which finds beauty and erotics when morality is suspended, spirituality, too, can be a tautology for masochism. Job, which scholars believe to be the earliest-written book in the Bible, appears meant to prepare us to face calamity by modeling a spiritual masochism. There is no moralistic lesson to be gleaned from Job's affliction (God never answer's Job's "Why?"), only aesthetics, desire, even perversion. When he asks God, "Does it please you to oppress me?" God does not give an answer, though (incredibly, ridiculously) it must be yes. This might be unacceptable on moral or even rational grounds, only sensible as an erotic truth.

During the twilight of my insanity, I felt savagely ripped from the people who loved me, as all the peculiarities of my life hollowed out to make room for a single occupant: my pain. Though when I emerged from it, I was engulfed by an aura like the glow of a predawn blue. I felt the breath of God blow through me like wind on the grass. I thought of Baroque saints carved out of marble with their eyes half-closed, jaws hung loose. This spiritual intimacy was total, and nearly took my life. But even as I don't fully accept God as a sadomasochistic lover, I was so taken by this entry into spiritual erotics because it felt adult to me—serious, committed—opening a door upon a potential spiritual passion, certainly dangerous, that I had not previously thought available.

This was also not something I needed to justify to anyone. It was personal, private. And I was convinced that if I could accept the God of compassion *and* the God of affliction on these opposing but not contradictory terms, then I could comprehend the full spectrum of human life—from catastrophe to tedium to mirth—which I now recognize as the part and parcel of spiritual practice.


During the final act in the Book of Job, God's oratory directs Job's attention to the majesty of the natural world by repeating, like an incantation, the expanses of the created Earth: from the recesses of the deep to the clouds wrapped in thickening darkness, where the behemoth below sways its tail like a cedar, and the hawk spreads its wings to the vastness of the southern plains. This is not systematic theology, but poetry, preoccupied foremost by beauty. I take this to be a recitation of the totality of the created world, whose apotheosis, on the sixth day of Genesis was, of all things, a garden.

So to understand God's answer to Job, and face the fact of my suffering, I went looking in the gardens. We know that Jesus, in the glory of Resurrection, appeared to Mary Magdalene as no more or less than a gardener, and so there must be something uniquely holy about this work, this place. The garden of Eden, cultivated for beauty and sustenance, serves as a synecdoche of the Earth at large, which Christians believe is also cultivated by God in view of aesthetics—intended, as he suggests to Job, to induce awe.

As far back as when I was a child, I explored my mother's garden because I was sensitive to rarefied frequencies of aesthetic bliss. There, I ran naked at dusk, discovering my body at play in my own limbs. These are my earliest memories: I was three. When all the world seemed in transition from one quality of light to the next, I felt the ground release its heat from the day, pressing against my small bare feet: an instruction in balance. I believe I was meant to revel in my mother's garden—a holy pleasure—in which I was being taught that this Earth had its order, and a place in it for me, a mere tenant. And until I could learn to appreciate the humility of my existence, I would not grow to enjoy heaven.

My imagination was captivated by flamboyant plants like passionflowers, or the *tan fa*, a cactus flower we referred to by its Cantonese name that bloomed once or twice a year and only by night. Two seven-foot-tall sunflowers, imperious, grew at the entrance of a stone path to the three-tiered fountain, which had a wide basin where my mother kept orange-and-white goldfish with fins the same color as the birds-of-paradise that fanned the walkway. I was always afraid to walk down this path, because it led to a more unruly part of the garden, marked by the shadow sides of fronds and riddled with snails and worms. These plants pulsed with creaturely energy, potent with animosity. After dark, the garden would take on the guise of a forest teeming with untamable urges let loose, warring impulses, demons, even. In fact, I didn't dare enter the garden without the presence of my mother, the master.

I call this my mother's garden, because it was she who worked the earth. With a stooped back, she clawed at the soil with iron and wooden tools that seemed unchanged from those of antiquity. The garden was constantly growing counter to its own interests, and demanded incessant clipping, watering, and pruning, which my mother did dutifully. I trusted her as a higher wisdom, which I gleaned by noting how she parceled her attentions and affinities, teaching me, as a child, something about the disinterested attention of God. As afternoon cooled into dusk, she did not, for instance, lavish time upon the larger, more garish plants in the garden, but instead labored over (and therefore loved) the common flowers that grew low to the ground, almost like weeds: gladiolas, azaleas, gerbera daisies. And the Peruvian lilies, hydrangeas, cyclamens, geraniums.

Even at that young age, I understood the garden to be a field of the erotic. The whole ecosystem was run on desire: bees teeming around the fragrant rosemary bushes, and the hummingbird struggling to insert its beak into the nectar of a trumpet flower. Fruits shed their petals; annuals died as perennials hibernated. This is the cycle of life: Something more justified, in the Christian imagination, by its beauty than any moral function. Bushes were pruned, with branches cut off to be planted elsewhere. Adam, too, was cut off from Eden, to taste hunger and death for the first time, which is the only way he would learn to yearn for God. This is how I know that it isn't an arbitrary detail that a garden is the origin from which all Scripture begins. The order of the seasons has its wisdom, as beauty reveals and withdraws and then reveals itself again. Within the garden is the order of the universe contained, and in which trauma and separation, too, play their role. Lack and grief and hunger all incite desire, upon which the garden, the plants and insects and birds of the air, necessarily depends. There is no desire without suffering. Suffering makes desire happen.

After Job's cry of suffering, God asks, "Have you comprehended the vast expanses of the Earth?"

To this question I answer: Yes, I have.

When I arrived in Berlin, I was imbued with a canny courage to demand more of life than was allotted to me, mostly because I believed I could handle it: the wild ecstasy, its stupefying pain. I had so little experience with either, to the point that their mere suggestion could conjure the fantasy of a life devoid of the blurry tedium that is everyone's lot. Everyone knows that the key to enjoying life is to be on nodding terms with tedium, but it took me a long time to figure that out. After psychosis and after addiction, I knew that whether I would recover came down to a single test: Could I again find grace in the ordinary? Would I find something in dailiness that was sacred, instead of trying to flee from it with drugs or conspiratorial delusions?

As the pandemic went on, I walked my mother's garden in a loop around the pool. And if I still did not understand its discreet wisdom, as humble as a platitude, I walked the garden again. I did this repeatedly, like walking a labyrinth at the monastery in Santa Barbara I had visited with my father two years earlier. Some of my mother's plants were the same as those in the gardens that buffed the knolls around the Mount Calvary Monastery, part of the Order of the Holy Cross, and its adjacent guesthouse, where my father and I once stayed for four days. I could spot only the plants whose names I knew: bird-of-paradise, eucalyptus, California poppy, and rosemary, which I sometimes picked and chewed on during these labyrinthine walks. It was located high up in Mission Canyon, connected by tree-lined pathways to the Santa Barbara Mission, and toward the north, over the creek, you could see the Santa Ynez Mountains. Spring had just begun, so the slopes of the Pacific Coast Highway were powdered with ocean salt and yellow wildflowers all along the drive.

We stayed at the hospitality of three monks, who carried out, according to Saint Benedict of Nursia, several daily offices. The earliest was the vigil at six in the morning, when a muted fragrance blew in from the creek as dawn woke into consciousness. One of the monks, dressed in a long, white cowl, would ring the bell outside the chapel, and the other two would convene to read scriptures from the Book of Psalms, pray, and sing Gregorian chants in both English and Latin. Aside from the vigils and lauds, the mornings were restricted to silence, including during breakfast, up until the Eucharist, where we partook in the body and the blood. The only times I spoke to the monks were during meals in the dining room in a Folk Victorian style, where we sat at the long, wooden tables and ate by a large picture window with a view over the cliffs. Two of the monks were older than ninety, one of whom was hard of hearing, and the youngest was often the one who initiated conversation with the guests (once, entirely in French with a woman from Montreal).

What did they know that I did not? What holy secret did they possess, which I did not but was only now coming to understand? The monks spoke and ate with an unhurried patience, an indifference to time afforded by a life resigned to abundant routine. In my mind, their daily practices in the presence of God heightened their sensitivities, the way a cellist might train their ear, to the splendor of ordinary life, to chores, transforming work into sacrament, tedium into grace. Somehow repetition didn't carry out the erosion of meaning, but the other way around. I knew that if repetition appeared boring, the correct response was to keep looking until it no longer did. Until it started to change, like a techno loop. Even if I couldn't locate, for myself, the blessing in the boiling of lentil soup, I would study the monks as they carried out their daily housekeeping.

Every afternoon, the monks retreated to practice the *lectio divina*, or holy reading, which could take up to four hours. Each week, they read the Book of Psalms in private quarters, where guests were not allowed. I spent that time during our stay reclined across the sitting room divan, beneath a rectangle of light, also leafing through Psalms or the collected T. S. Eliot that I'd found one morning in the library. I thought I might whisper the Psalms until the difference between pain and pleasure was subsumed entirely into an ecstatic suffering. I closed my eyes and thought of Eliot's line from in the hyacinth garden: "I knew nothing, / into the heart of light, the silence."

During the Compline, which was the final office in the evening, the monks rose in their cowls, chanting: "I sought the Lord and was heard; from all my terrors set free," and I would repeat those words, seeking to be heard by God: a benevolent dictator who ordained that the natural order of matter wasn't entropy, but a cosmic restoration from loss, toward which all desires are oriented.

When the prior came around to sprinkle holy water on our heads and shoulders, I bowed and accepted the Lord's blessing.

"I will lie down in peace and sleep comes at once. For you alone, Lord, make me dwell in safety."

"You will not fear the terror of the night nor the arrow that flies by day."

"When you call I shall answer: 'I am with you,' I will save you in distress and give you glory."

The monks chanted these words by candlelight, and I tried everything I could to imagine a world with no fear, where I could relax into the grace of forgiveness, and drop at once into sleep.

Time passed. Lockdown in California no longer felt like an injustice, and began to take on a hypnotic allure. Yet as I circled the gardens with my quotidian epiphanies, the world moved deeper into the drama of psychotic absurdity. Even after I left Berlin, Berlin found its way back to me. One sunny afternoon, I read that hundreds of neo-Nazis and far-right extremists attempted to storm the Reichstag, the German capitol, in the middle of tens of thousands of demonstrators—bloggers and AfD politicians and white, barefoot hippies with dreads—protesting Merkel's lockdown measures. Conspiracies spread: theories that the coronavirus was engineered in a remote offshore lab operated by the CIA or that the government's vaccine would contain a microchip—trackable by location-targeting satellites—that Bill Gates would design to be small enough to fit into a needle and inject directly into the bloodstreams of billions.

Universal surveillance. Government conspiracies.

Shuddering, I thought if I closed my laptop, I could shut these freaks out of my life. Yet I could not stamp out the impish, ironic twang of recognition when I gazed into their screaming mouths in online photographs. During my psychotic episode in Berlin, I had been convinced that some covert satellite could algorithmically decode my thoughts from electric signals detected in my brain from afar, and relay them to an evil man in a Tom Ford suit who analyzed intelligence for the CIA.

As to what really happened, I don't have the full story. Neither do the extremists in Berlin. But what separates me from them is I don't pretend that I have it—I accept that I never will. I accept the unknowability of the universe. The "whys" are beside the point of life. While the psychotic holds fast to a conspiracy theory with arms crossed, gathering more and more knowledge to confirm what he already convinced himself to be true, I no longer do. I accept that I do not know. I give thanks for suffering. I choose plainness. In Job, God describes how the ostrich lives joyfully, unaware of the dangers of the world, because God "did not endow her with wisdom or give her a share of good sense." This could be a parable for finitude: the limits of human capacity, including our capacity to know. I believe God grants humans the ability to know only what we need to know. We will never have the answers to certain questions because they are not what we need.

Where I am now, my voices still come and go. I don't know who they are, where they came from, or why. In fact, I never knew. But I try to live by that which I do not know, should not know, or simply cannot know, which means it is by faith I live. One of the greatest mercies of God is that he occludes. If the God of Genesis created darkness before light, then it is possible that darkness is closer to the nature of God, a vast and unseen ocean upon which thought merely borders.

Instead of eating from the tree of knowledge, I try to eat from the tree of life.

I walk the gardens. I give thanks for all things.

Looking back, what I find most vulgar about my own psychosis, as I do with the extremists in Berlin, is not its mystical or paranoid dimensions, per se, but my isolating self-aggrandizement: the delusion that intelligence agencies or aliens had vetted and plucked me out of billions, having been deemed so exceptional as to be gifted secret powers that could save nations. Something that marks the extremists in Berlin is their harrowing conviction that they have the exclusive solution that can save the world. Even the word "extremist" suggests an inability to occupy, or even validate, the middle ground. Yet there I was in Diamond Bar, trying to occupy the middle ground. Integral to how I see psychosis is the idea of an addiction to the melodrama of conspiracy: that one is enmeshed in a cosmic, clandestine saga, which is infinitely more enticing than chopping vegetables or restacking the pans from large to small. But it is while doing the latter that sanity finds you.

So I pray to God for humility and self-control. I am someone who might benefit from avoiding extremes, lest I, by rubbing too hard to remove the rust, break the vessel. If I once believed I was a prophet, sent to speak truth to government psyops and disinformation campaigns, I no longer move through life with that kind of arrogance. What I can say is that I know I have witnessed the impossible, been privy to secrets you would never believe, and by faith I testify that we have entered the age of miracles. Forgive me, Lord, for I am weak in spirit. May I forgive those who have sinned against me, so that I may never be unprepared for revelation. Lead me not into temptation, but protect me from evil. I pray that I may turn from my ways. I pray for peace in this land.

Eventually, the lockdown did lift. By then, I had finished the twelve steps. Inventory, amends, all of it. In my memory, the first six months of sobriety had dragged, but I barely noticed the six months after.

When my sponsor "graduated" me from the steps, I asked him for one favor to send me off: Could he give me a tarot reading? "In the name of Christ," I joked. He laughed bearishly and offered me this one occult indulgence.

He did the three-card reading. The first card, which represents my past, was the Emperor. Power, leadership, worldliness. The second, which represented my present, was the Eight of Wands. Creativity, rapid change, energy.

But when he flipped the third, I started once I saw it: the Fool. It's the first card in the entire deck.

"What does that mean?" I asked. This was supposed to be my future.

He smiled ironically. "To approach life like a child."

# Mean Boys

1.

On the morning of July 22, 2011, Anders Behring Breivik, a thirty-two-year-old Norwegian, parked a van with a bomb outside Regjeringskvartalet, a group of government buildings in Oslo, and detonated it before fleeing the scene. It

killed eight bystanders. While news of the bombing circulated, he had already smuggled himself onto the island of
Utøya wearing a police uniform. There, Norway's Workers'
Youth League—an organization allied with the country's left-
wing Labour Party—was having its annual summer camp.
During the course of a massacre that lasted over an hour, he
shot and killed sixty-nine children and supervisors. The
youngest was fourteen years old.

Before the attack, Breivik had lived with his mother,
spending most of his time either playing *World of Warcraft* or
secretly writing a fifteen-hundred-page manifesto. On the
day of the shooting, he sent his manifesto out to one thousand recipients. It was soon covered widely across news
sources. In the text, he attributed a decline of Western civilization to a culture war between alienated whites and the
rising tide of multiculturalism. He insisted that liberal diver-
sity, which matured in the 1960s, had ushered an imposed
horizontality of equal races, equal genders into mainstream
discourse, finding its opposition against a raw, potent, and
Darwinist masculinity, exclusively white. This tracked with
what's known as the "great replacement" theory, claiming
that European populations are being demographically and
culturally replaced with nonwhite populations, particularly
from Muslim-majority countries with rising birth rates—a
common rallying cry for far-right movements across the
world. Just a few years later, his manifesto would inspire a
reactionary crop of mass shooters. Notoriously, this included
incels, a portmanteau for "involuntary celibates" known for
posting long, nonsensical screeds on publicly indexed online
forums—weird, sexual confessions that were violently misogynistic and white supremacist.

The split Breivik outlined was not only about identity. In his text, he offers a paean to the crisp weaving of Lacoste polos: "I wear mostly the best pieces from my former life, which consists of very expensive brand clothing, Lacoste sweaters, piques etc. People can see from a mile away that I'm not from around here," as opposed to the "mostly unrefined/un-cultivated people" in the area where he lived with his mother. What did Lacoste mean to him? He likely associated it with whiteness, but the words "unrefined" and "uncultivated" also gesture in another, enigmatic direction.

To accompany the manifesto, he attached photographs of himself posing in Lacoste sweaters, and distributed them like press kits. The media circulated these photos widely. Three days after the attacks, in what would be the beginning of a ten-week televised trial, Breivik was presented to the public for the first time, leaving a courthouse in Oslo wearing a red Lacoste jumper.

When I was in high school, my brother and I used to trawl eBay for fake Lacoste polos on the cheap. Our parents weren't going to buy them for us, so we had to scrape together our earnings from our minimum-wage jobs. After returning from Sunday night family dinners at the local Chinese restaurant, we'd rush upstairs, log on to our computers, and refresh any of the four or five auctions we were following to see if we'd been outbid. We tried bidding on plastic bags full of fake Lacoste badges sourced from China, which you could sew onto Izod polos from Kmart and sport at school with the collar popped. The collar was important—arrogant and preppy— exactly the way it appeared in the Urban Outfitters catalogue that was mailed to our doorstep. We never won the bags of badges. But my brother scored some polos, and I got a fake Harrington jacket with a logo, which I wore proudly at school, as an icon that revealed more than I wanted to about who I thought I was and where I believed I was going.

Not unlike Breivik, I also spent most of my life trying to distinguish myself from the people I came from. My hometown, Diamond Bar, California, was majority Asian, which was a mixed blessing. Life as a racial majority exempted me from a degree of discrimination, and I experienced my race as common stock, an excess of population reflected in the town's demographics as well as the world's statistical majority: Chinese, male. Which is to say forgettable, replaceable, indistinguishable.

I sensed an idiosyncratic consistency of Chinese male angst in the performances of masculinity in my town: boys who slicked their hair back with tubs of gel, boys who wore chains and black tank tops and sagged their baggy jeans. These boys listened to hip-hop, preferred Asian girls with stick-straight hair dyed brown, and occupied parking lots in their rice rockets as if staking territory. In a flourish of racial solidarity, kids in high school tagged their AIM away messages with "aZn pRyDe" and loitered around boba stores and karaoke joints after school. Their speech was inflected with Black slang, which affected a racialized vitality and a romanticized street grittiness that these Diamond Bar boys could hardly mine from their own sheltered lives. Diamond Bar angst had chosen Tupac and Eminem as its patron rappers, and you could hear them blasting from car speakers with windows rolled down, subwoofers going, as the boys idled beside you waiting for the light to turn.

Grittiness fascinated me because Diamond Bar was so closely associated with big houses. The city gained its glitzy reputation solely from its gated community known as "The Country," just outside the more middle-class neighborhood where my family lived called the Diamond Bar Hills. The Country had glittering mansions belonging to doctors and interior designers and business owners and tycoons. The mansions were advertised as boutique, modeled after Spanish villas and neoclassical estates, and were arranged along two hills that might as well have been East and West Egg. In high school, I was instructed that *The Great Gatsby* was "the perfect novel," and I imagined it was because it was about the kind of people who would live in The Country. At the very top of the hill was what looked like a castle whose windows were all made of green glass, and whose balconies were chiseled out of white Italian marble. I could see them at sunset from my family's house, with its three-car garage and a pool but not *the* pool, a balcony but not Italian marble. No one fantasized about our house at three A.M. when they couldn't fall back asleep. The lives in The Country seemed entirely sealed off from the world the rest of us came from, with tract houses and Vietnamese nail salons and the one motel beneath the highway overpass with the light-up POOL sign in blinking red lights.

In Diamond Bar, I understood exactly the meaning of minority rule. It was the white minority that mostly held court, owned large houses, ran and got elected for city council. In high school, kids divided themselves upon racial lines. There was the Starbucks crew versus the It's a Grind crew, those who preferred the Brea Mall over the Puente Hills Mall. (The former meant white, the latter Asian.) You could almost observe this transition physically when driving east from Rowland Heights to Brea, as the 99 Ranch Supermarket and storefronts with only Chinese signs would change into the Trader Joe's and the Cheesecake Factory, outside of which blonde women with freckled shoulders waited beside the fountain for their numbers to be called.

Because I could not drive to the freeway without passing by the entrance to The Country, those gates loomed in my mind like a totem. I imagined a life behind those gates where money was kind. I preferred my imagination, because it transported me from my teenage, middle-class blues: getting stoned on the playground, loitering in the In-N-Out parking lot, or making fun of a classmate from AP Psychology because someone said she pulled out her hair and ate notebook paper.

Most of my brother's friends lived in The Country. Mine did not. He was more popular, whereas I hung around with the scene kids who watched anime. In high school, my best friend was Jonathan Fan, who lived two blocks away, also in the Diamond Bar Hills. As a pair with coordinated tastes, we pretended to like the Blood Brothers because we wanted to be punk. Secretly I couldn't stand them. Jonathan, who is also gay, had a harder edge than me—sharp canines and a trip-wire temper that could send ridicule pouring down on whom-ever he chose at a moment's notice. Leggy Asian girls liked hanging around him, the kind of girls who had highlights in their hair and traded photo booth pictures and had fake IDs. Jonathan was immune from ridicule because he was a boy and was sufficiently bitchy because he was gay. I never learned how to harness this energy.

I was sensitive, easily shocked, and diplomatic. I read too much. I was not someone who usually had a best friend, so when Jonathan entered my life around the seventh grade, I spent as much time with him as I could. At his house, he kept a turtle in a tall vase too narrow for it, until it died one summer of dehydration. He also had this small, hellish dog whose deep, tender hatred for me was beyond reason. This dog would hurt itself if it meant barking at me louder. I believed that, in this dog, I'd seen something true. Whenever I approached, it would holler from the outside, bash its ugly face into the thick glass door, hungry, screaming until its voice ripped, eyes squeezed shut like it was about to come.

Militant aesthetics attracted Jonathan and I because we were both five foot seven, closeted, and genetically predetermined to be ignored. As adults, we would leave the people we came from. We'd go to New York. By then, we were in our twenties, entertaining different versions of metropolitan, gay life—his around Hell's Kitchen, mine around DIY spaces in Bushwick. Some of those fake-ID girls from high school also moved to the city, and whenever we'd get group dinners together, reserving long tables in the backs of restaurants, we'd scroll through Instagram profiles and, one by one, talk shit about the people we used to know, people who stayed behind.

I remember one of the times we returned to Diamond Bar for Christmas, Jonathan and I were sitting in his car, and I thought of how the town seemed even smaller than I last recalled, with its vacant skies over low buildings. I asked him about New York, what he'd come to the city looking for, and his one-word answer stunned me in its frankness.

"Glamour," he said.

Succinct, transparent—as helplessly suburban as incorrigibly gay.

Having also spent my youth closeted, my attractions and aspirations were stoked by a steady flame of inner turmoil. The joke I tell people (also true) is that I discovered I was gay by looking at pictures of the crucifix. I might've been five or six, and the only access I had to images of men with idealized bodies were illustrations of Jesus's stripped body on the cross, which I could stare at as long as I wanted without being questioned or reprimanded. And I did stare at them, because I didn't understand them. At that young age, the crucifixion passed down, even revealed, a deep, erotic truth to me: *Pleasure is the result of someone else's pain.*

I intuited this intimate knowledge in the unchanging pool of California light, an aestheticization of the flat moods I occasionally suffered, which muffled me like a giant white mattress I wanted to hack at with a knife. I was melancholy when I had no excuse to be. Mostly, I was bored. A part of me now thinks this memory is confabulated, but I remember my first suicide attempt was when I was in fifth grade. During some terrifying barrage of insomnia, I woke up, went down to the knife drawer with the idea that I'd know what to do, but once I got there, I was stupefied. The scenario did not pan out the way it did in my mind, so I got tired and confused and eventually went to sleep.

This darkness was in the landscape everywhere: a projection that revealed, in California, a soft and rotten core, the way the palms lie flaccidly dead across the sidewalk after a tropical storm. I spent a lot of time on my desktop computer, playing *Final Fantasy* on CD-ROM, discovering gay porn, and watching, after midnight, marathon sessions of what I now know as the anime canon: *Cowboy Bebop*, *Trigun*, *Serial Experiments Lain*, and *Neon Genesis Evangelion*. For a time, I knew Japanese, but then I lost it. I had dreams of going to Tokyo.

Outwardly, I knew I had to strive to be white. My brother was more successful at it. A year older than me, Josh studied pop stars on *TRL* and the daft and fluttery arrogance of the shirtless Hollister models at the mall. Because I looked up to my brother, I followed whatever he did. Between the two camps, he didn't side with our race, so neither did I. We hung out at the Brea Mall and met our friends at Starbucks. Even though the rich Asian families who lived in the city were conventionally "aspirational," there was something about them that always embarrassed me. All money in Diamond Bar was new money, which is to say flashy, but Chinese money was particularly garish. When a rich family at my father's church gave him, the pastor, a gift of the latest iPhone, I found it obliviously tacky. The iPhone is such a loud commodity, and gifts are supposed to be ornamental. While my father showed it off to friends and family, I thought the gift was an insult because it put him in his place. It read as a message, from wealth, that they knew he didn't have one already. He couldn't afford it.

I was embarrassed to be middle class, and I was embarrassed to be Chinese. While my brother claimed the Asian kids rejected him, it had clearly been the other way around. He's also gay, perhaps less legibly so than me, which is perhaps how he stayed closeted much longer than I did—though it must've come with its own measure of self-loathing. He mercilessly made fun of Asian immigrants he called "FOBs," with, it seemed, the hatred that Jonathan's dog reserved for me. He expressed his disgust whenever we saw them passing by. He made fun of their clothes. It was so frequent, and had gotten so out of hand, that one day in the car, my mother said, delicately, "You know, I'm also a FOB."

While my parents tolerated it when we habitually ditched Chinese class, speaking English well was nonnegotiable. My mother looked down on kids in Rowland Heights who were U.S.-born but still had Chinese accents because they only hung out with their Chinese peers, speaking Mandarin. Instead, my parents wanted my brother and me to be integrated into white society, so they took us to the Norton Simon Museum and the Huntington to be educated in the landscapes and drapery of European painting, and we listened to Handel and Mozart in the car and drove out to L.A. to see the philharmonic.

So it made sense that Josh mixed fluently with whites. He served in student government, was voted onto homecoming court. I remember the morbid glee I felt, sitting in the high school gym during a pep rally, watching him shake his ass onstage at screaming cheerleaders and wrestlers to Missy Elliott's "Lose Control." Josh began picking up the affectations of white teenagers, white silliness that signaled maturity, that they were adult in their frivolity. Whenever I met up with him after school to drive home, it always struck me as queer that he and his friends would tell each other, before leaving, "I love you," and then blow each other kisses. Gay, gay, gay.

I didn't understand this kind of casual flirtiness. It went against all the weight and austerity that I learned at our conservative Chinese church. In contrast to Chinese frugality, both financial and moral, I associated white people with revelry, debauchery, excess, or hedonism (which I spelled "heathenism" for years because I'd heard the word pronounced in church before reading it in a book). This was confirmed by Josh's friends in The Country, who had hot tubs and pool tables and tennis courts and endless parquet floors. It was not merely their wealth that distinguished them but their lifestyle. When their parents were gone for the weekend, they hosted parties with alcohol and slept with one another in vacated bedrooms. The boys had perfect bodies, ran six-minute miles, spent their after-school hours at the gym preparing for wrestling matches. I wanted to be one of the boys. On weekday nights, my brother would tell me about this world, which he held from me at a distance, letting me in only in the telling. He did this, I suppose, because he knew how much I wanted to be like him.

When I did eventually get chosen for student government, he said the only reason I got in was because I was his brother. I wasn't popular, but I was uncontroversial—spent most of my time in AP Studio Art and Journalism, and read about Kierkegaard and Christian existentialism—and I wasn't beautiful.

Eventually I outgrew my teenage awkwardness and learned that pairing discernment and eccentricity could be an advantage. By the time I saw the Breivik Lacoste photos in 2011, I had already outgrown Lacoste, though I did not need to be convinced of the power of fashion to determine the imagination. In the photos, Breivik isn't handsome, but he's attractive enough to pass as a catalog model for Target markdowns.

In other words, he's white, preppy. He knows to make eye contact with the viewer, lips parted in a casual smile. The background is white. The lighting sophisticated. He's wearing a black Lacoste jumper, but underneath is a salmon-colored polo. The collar is popped.

## 2.

A line from a Lutz Bacher print depicting a woman in the passive position of a threesome reads, "Psychological studies reveal there is a strong relationship between cruelty and the sexual impulse." I come across this as a thirty-year-old living in Berlin, around the same time I discover a video file, buried somewhere on my hard drive, that I downloaded so long ago I'd forgotten when. Once I rewatch it, I can't stop watching. I replay it for weeks on end. It's vanilla porno, nothing outlandish or exotic. Early in the video, two men are about to fuck. The bottom looks Turkish, has a short black beard and shaggy black hair. The top is white, typical trade, with tattoos that signify both Williamsburg hipster and conspiracy theorist. When the top starts pressing his dick into the bottom's sphincter, the bottom sucks his teeth as if he's just gotten a paper cut. He starts to moan as the top moves in slowly. The bottom makes a sound like he's just tasted something delicious, and the top smiles and says, "Feel good?" The bottom whimpers in pleasure until, it seems, his partner's dick hits something inside, somewhere complicated that he doesn't understand, and he winces like someone's touched an open sore. "It's a big dick," the top says in a tone of "I told you so"—as if the bottom doesn't really know what he's gotten himself into. The bottom tries to be gallant, tries to keep it cute, and says "Yes, sir" as he rotates his hips, massaging onto the dick in his ass. "There you go," the top says, gaining energy. "Get it nice and deep," the bottom says, which the top takes as a green light to fold over, his arms caged over the bottom's back, and push himself all the way in. The bottom gets nervous, quivers, and props up his ass to ease the thrusts. But the top doubles down, as if to say, "You said this is what you wanted." When he thrusts all the way in, the bottom moans in agony. Clearly in pain, he says, "Fuck, that's a huge cock," and I can't tell if that's his way of asking for him to go easier, or if he's committing himself fully to servicing his partner's ego. The top doesn't slow down. At one point, when the bottom screams his loudest, the top bends over to kiss his cheek, even as he keeps thrusting in and out. The bottom's lost his erection by this point, and keeps squirming, writhing beneath the heat of his partner's stomach, at which point the top grabs the bottom's hair and shakes his moaning head as he presses it deeper into the pillow. The longer they go at it, the top, who keeps fucking at a steady pace, changes his expression from detached to one not exactly benevolent, but amused. Eventually, when the bottom loosens up, the top rewards him with more kisses, as if the kisses were all he was ever after, and says, "That's my boy. This dick's all yours." In the video, the part that gets me off is when the tone shifts, when the bottom loses control of the dynamic and gets humiliated. The reason I keep watching this video is because watching the bottom in pain does something for me. I take pleasure in imagining his pain, and I don't understand why.

3.

Here's an image of the artist Anne Imhof, at the 2017 Venice Biennale, wearing a Balenciaga cap. She is accepting the Golden Lion, the exhibition's top prize, for her performance at the German Pavilion. From Berlin, I flew into Venice for the opening, but I didn't make it to the award ceremony. That morning, I was waiting in line for the Fondazione Prada museum when my friend, who had attended Imhof's performance with me, looked up a news update on his phone and said, "Holy shit, guess who just won the Golden Lion."

Later I bought Imhof's same hat in white, even though I couldn't really afford it. Like Proust's madeleine, her hat served as a capsule that could evoke, for me, an entire era that vanished after the pandemic. These years dated somewhere after the Occupy movement, after the Arab Spring, throughout

Black Lives Matter, and right up to the height of #MeToo, when Harvey Weinstein, Knight Landesman, and Lorin Stein were deposed in one mighty swoop.

Imhof's Venice performance was titled *Faust*. The German Pavilion was palatial, with eggshell columns at the entrance, where chained black Dobermans stalked back and forth. The line was crowded, bodies pushing in from all sides. Loud, industrial beats throbbed from inside the pavilion. Upon entering, we discovered that the pavilion was bisected vertically. Imhof had erected a thick, transparent floor, made from bulletproof glass that split the space into an upper level, where viewers milled, and a basement, where dancers unfurled or lay outstretched on a bare mattress, vaping. There was a taste at the time for fashion models with a certain appearance: androgynous, lanky, intelligent. This was the look of the dozen or so performers, some of them models, in fact, dressed in oversize graphic tees or Adidas track pants. They writhed on the floor and wrestled with each other, within a circle of viewers looking on like witnesses to a cult ritual. The room was thick with the tension between attractive dancers clocking each other in sidelong glances. One was on all fours, head hung low. A man lay facedown on the floor as a woman stood erect upon his back. The vacancy in the performers' eyes registered as soulless boredom, or a sleep deprivation approaching clinical emergency. This was their bargain: What they have is status but what they want is love.

I might've taken this as a warning for the years to come, except the Faustian bargain wasn't on my mind when I moved to Berlin in 2016, in search of new beginnings. I came with dreams of becoming an art critic, but I did not know how to become one. I felt brimming with what is called aesthetic experience, but had not yet developed the articulation to distinguish one kind of intensity from another. I had a romantic picture of what an art critic in Berlin looked like: an eccentric dressed in all-black Issey Miyake, arguing about theory with artists and intellectuals over oysters and cocaine into early mornings, when one could see the sunrise over the TV tower from the balcony doors. To be a critic meant to surround oneself with the iconic, the serious, and the controversial; to wrestle with the ideas of the day; and, as if in reward for this spiritual labor, to remain untouched by boredom. It was a stock image, though it served as a recurring fantasy I entertained during my life in New York at a midlevel job in corporate advertising, the stuff of windowless cubicles and Tupperware salads and closed-lip smiles. I needed to change my life. I thought if I resigned myself to this office-bound career, I would be someone who could turn thirty, and then turn forty, and barely notice the difference. Instead, I quit my job and flew to Germany. I kept telling friends who asked me why that I didn't want to miss out on "the Paris of our time." I was going to Berlin to become an art critic.

In Berlin, I started with nothing. Nobody knew who I was, a bit player in the background who showed up to openings alone, talked to no one, and rode the U-Bahn home by myself with a pretzel I bought at one of the train platform bakeries. At the time, Anne Imhof and her dancers epitomized the heights of the art world. I sometimes recognized the dancers at parties in Berlin: either too early, because they had somewhere else to be, or very late, because they were coming back from something else. I'd often see her music producer and dancer, Billy, at monthly gay parties that went on for three days at a time. Sometimes, he'd be with the two designers of the Berlin-based fashion label GmbH, who were Turkish and Pakistani. They'd bring along their dark-skinned models from Paris, who appeared older than they were, dignified, carrying themselves like diplomats.

At one of these parties, I was sitting inside a shack where club kids passed lines on their phones like oysters on a platter, and I happened to be sitting next to Billy, who introduced himself. At first, I didn't let on that I knew who he was. He spoke like someone who didn't have to work for attention: arrogant, blasé. He portrayed himself as another glitzy club kid whose life, as chronicled through Instagram, was expressed through photo ops at gay monuments around the world, such as Cher's home in Malibu. After a while, we were passing an iPhone around the group with our astrology charts, and when I scrolled through mine uninterestedly, he grinned at me, knowingly, and said, "So you're not a believer."

There it was: the casual, gay flirtiness I recognized in my brother's white high school cohort. In the gardens of these clubs, I glimpsed this levity in the glint of someone's rose-tinted glasses, angled flatteringly beneath the shadow of leaves. I referred to club kids like Billy as "the boys," even though some of the boys were girls. Some of the boys liked me, but I was not one of the boys. I was an outsider. I was both too serious and nervy, too reverent, and the boys were nothing if not irreverent. I was Asian. And none of the boys were Asian. None of Imhof's dancers were Asian. The Asians I knew hung in packs, always on the outskirts looking in, never the center of attention, and seemed only to complain about how they couldn't get laid or command the attention of the boys they desired. It all so depressed me. I tried to distance myself from them, convinced I was the exception. I thought I could be "the only one."

But race wasn't the sole reason. I was always leaving the club alone, coming down from the weekend's cocktail of drugs on the U-Bahn or in a cab, only to collapse on my bed (which was sometimes a pull-out couch) and masturbate myself to sleep. I wasn't fucking anyone during this period of my life. I told people it was because I had been sexually assaulted, which conveniently silenced people's follow-up questions, though that didn't feel like the whole story to me. It's not that I didn't want sex. I craved it, intensely—when I was coming down from ecstasy, I spent hours watching porn, which I paid for online—although when I first moved to Berlin, no man I was attracted to would return my gaze. I was horny. I was a gawker. Under the dim, blue lights at clubs walled in concrete, I stared at men's bodies in harnesses as they pretended not to notice me. I was so certain I was invisible. I never was. They didn't mind my attention, possibly pitied me. Although, to anyone who did look at me, I sneered and diverted my gaze. I was simultaneously picky and desperate, which made me a hopeless case. I told myself that my loneliness, which both tormented and repulsed me, was temporary, although my fear was that it reflected something deeper, perhaps permanent: some characterological defect condemning me to live out my years alone as a misfit.

When I fantasized about the kinds of lives that are immune to loneliness and neediness, I thought of the boys in the garden. The boys were so obviously *fucking*—they were languid and certain, while I was stiff and frigid and alert. But I tried to copy the boys' showy displays of bravura and charisma. In the same way that people who study English as a second language sometimes have better grammar than native speakers, I thought I could pick up social manners that did not come naturally to me but that I could master, just by observing people and observing the scene, which was my favorite thing to do.

It reminded me of when Proust first enters society in *In Search of Lost Time*, and becomes transfixed by these microscopic social mannerisms, his mastery over which will determine how quickly he ascends the social world. Without thinking, I began comparing actual people to characters I'd read about in Proust. Privately, I had this game where I could always locate, in any social setting, who was the Duchesse de Guermantes, the preeminent aristocrat whose elite salon was the pinnacle of the Parisian milieu.

Sometimes, the Duchesse was Wolfgang Tillmans. Sometimes it was Bill Kouligas.

Tillmans, whenever I saw him out, was always surrounded by a phalanx of fashion boys who were fey and alien-looking and vicious. Tillmans had done for Berlin's post-reunification club scene what Proust had done for belle epoque Paris: He photographed an entire era of the liberal demimonde that would have disappeared in time had he not volunteered himself as the culture's documentarian. Rare for artists from the rave scene, often derided as excessive or unintellectual,

Tillmans attained the highest that the art world could offer: prizes, retrospectives, that *New Yorker* profile. For years, I envied my friends who'd been photographed by him, at his apartment or at warehouse parties, or who reported partying with him on Fire Island. I had never actually met him. But news of what he was up to tended to filter back to me. The day Frank Ocean's *Blonde* dropped, I remember, I went to Panorama Bar on the top floor of Berghain and saw one of Tillmans's former lovers. When I sat next to him at the bar, he leaned in and said, "Did you see the new Frank Ocean cover? Guess who photographed the picture."

Through mutual friends, I knew Eugen, who managed Between Bridges, Tillmans's exhibition space in Berlin. Eugen had a goofy Russian accent, wispy brown hair, and a year-round pornstache, whose marked absence was the defining feature I noticed when I saw the editorial shoot he modeled for in *Arena HOMME+*. For the space, he organized symposia about the refugee crisis in Europe, the rise of right-wing extremism, and the resurgence of nationalism. Eugen was the first person I met who lived out my fantasy idea of the intellectual, the kind of man for whom I felt I had to think up a witty opener when I came up to him on the dance floor. Which was rare, because he seldom went out. When a friend had asked Eugen if he would be at a party we were all going to later, he joked, "I can't. I have to be careful about where I show this face." He really only showed up when Roi Perez, his partner at the time, DJ'ed his monthly sets for his prestigious Berghain residency. For the club's yearly garden opening party, I'd gone alone to see Roi play. The DJ booth was set up in a shed that opened out onto a paved dance floor, where sprinklers sprayed water from above. I had been dancing near the front when, out of nowhere, Eugen appeared, locked eyes with me on the floor, and blurted, "Do you have any drugs?" We both giggled, and I shouted, "Yes!" and he immediately brought me into the group loitering behind the DJ booth, where we licked our fingers and dipped them into my bag of MDMA. By the time I got back to the dance floor, I knew the whole interaction had been clocked by this crop of bitchy club kids who knew me but never said hi, yet suddenly approached me now to say, "Oh hey, when did you get here?" If these social theatrics sound exhausting, they were.

I preferred seeing Eugen at Between Bridges, which was always empty when I visited, so we would sit outside and share a cigarette. At the club, he habitually invited everyone to visit him in the space, which was something of a test to see who actually would. I was someone who actually would. This was before I started writing for art magazines, so I was still trying to prove myself, leaving Eugen with erudite one-liners about bricolage that I knew he understood (because he was a translator of Russian avant-garde poetry), but he'd never react, just smile, as if to say, "Babe, this isn't necessary." That was his affect: gossipy, irreverent, a little tired. His lexicon always hovered around fashion, art, and the club, because that was his milieu. When talking about artists, he'd flip through images on his phone of those he revered—usually female—describing them like drag queens. (Of Trisha Donnelly, he'd say, "She's my goddess.")

Whenever Between Bridges had openings, I could never get a hold of Eugen, who was busy and unavailable, so I just showed up and earnestly looked at photographs. It was at one of these events where I met Wolfgang himself. He was as he always appeared: tall, meek, with a crooked, wolfish smile—graceful, but cryptic. He smiled a lot and tilted his head to a slight bow when greeting people. I was looking at the art when he approached me, introduced himself in his low, German accent, and invited me to the afterparty at Ma-Lu 15. I don't know why. I was a nobody. No one caught me chatting it up with Eugen, because I never found him. I was alone, and I didn't look anywhere near as fab as all the androgynous male models who fluttered around Wolfgang at these functions. Maybe he invited every stranger who walked into the gallery—its own kind of principled hospitality. But at the time, it felt like I'd been chosen. Either way, it doesn't matter. I didn't go to the afterparty. I chickened out. Yet I kept turning the episode over in my mind on the U-Bahn ride home. I thought that I had uncovered a secret about power—that those who have the most of it can be the most magnanimous, because they have nothing to gain, and by this time, they're a little bored and hard to impress, so the only pleasures left for them are from the looks on others' faces when witnessing their generosity, to remind themselves that they still are, in fact, virtuosos in spirit.

I met Bill Kouligas at Tresor, the historic music venue that brought techno to Berlin (as all the books say). We were at a show for Amnesia Scanner, one of Bill's artists on the record label he founded, PAN. Amnesia Scanner wasn't techno, but to Bill, I dubbed them "the Britney Spears of deconstructed club," and he laughed and said, "I love that." He took a liking to me. That night, Bill had been hanging out with Billy, whose musical compositions for Anne Imhof's Golden Lion performance in Venice would later be released on PAN.

Meeting Bill did feel like I was getting one step closer to Imhof, whose presence always hovered nearby these years. I wasn't even sure I'd know what she looked like if I saw her. She didn't appear in her own performances, although I saw both Bill and Billy as avatars, or extensions, of her presence, her aura.

After Bill and I were introduced, I noticed immediately that he was strange: inarticulate, reserved, impeccably good-looking. I classified him as that type of artist who themselves might've been awkward when they were younger, disengaged from the infinitesimal manners of social life, and were therefore isolated and private enough to make a lasting work of art that, later in life, they'd be celebrated for, and be suddenly surrounded by fashionable hangers-on who were more socially fluent. At that point in their career, such an artist no longer needs their childhood strangeness but holds on to it anyway as a distancing mechanism that forces people to work harder for their attention. To others, this aloofness might come off as arrogance. But with me, his attention seemed located not outward but inward.

I wanted more face time with Bill, so I asked if he'd like to do coke with my friend Tianna and me. We had enough mutual friends, but I was determined not to name-drop a single one—something I learned from people like Eugen, who name-dropped no one. I knew the only way I could make an impression on Bill was with affect and intelligence. While we crouched in a circle, somewhere in the garden, I tried to cycle through the quickest hot takes I could come up with on the spot (his hometown, Athens? Documenta 14?!) and looking for the split second in his eyes when I had his attention. It was like striking a lighter several times before the flame appears. And once the flame appeared, I was careful not to blow it out. We made plans to go back to the dance floor, but Bill was engulfed almost immediately by others he knew (including a celebrity comedian, Tianna said) who became suddenly interested in Tianna and me after seeing us emerge with Bill. And before we lost him for the rest of the night, he pressed both his hands on my left shoulder, an eccentric gesture that seemed to signal "Thank you."

I knew Tianna from the rave scene in New York because we both came up as club kids—I liked introducing her as a "Black techno icon"—and we had this running joke that we were determined to become "more than the world's greatest party girl." At the time, I was trying to distinguish myself from the club kids I was associated with, aged anywhere from eighteen to twenty-six, often holding uninteresting lives outside nightlife, working at the airport or call centers or at hostel booking agencies, but who dressed up for the rave with an impatience to be noticed: lavish outfits cut from flowing satin; chains, directly sourced from Bauhaus; or vintage looks bought head to toe from the Humana thrift store in Friedrichshain.

As club kids, our highest destiny was to serve as decoration to somebody who had attained a level of status that was evidently not in the cards for us. My cosmopolitan superpower was being a fashionable plus-one who could be conveniently ditched at any moment and still hang. This sometimes took me to strange places at odd hours. Once, Tianna invited me to a hotel party in Mitte, hosted by a Zimbabwean millionaire from Silicon Valley with other various hangers-on he'd picked up at the club: editorial models Tianna knew or DJs from the fetish party circuit. People were sprawled on the bed and smoking on the balcony. The furniture was gold and tacky. The millionaire supplied us with endless coke and ketamine, but only at select moments, when he chose us by name to join him in the bathroom or by the side tables topped with black glass, seemingly designed for this exact purpose. The drugs were mini rewards for doing our jobs: look hot, sway around high, and, if he'd gotten into storytelling mode, listen with fascination.

That was our agreement: smile in service of the main action. Some people loved and hated but nevertheless perfected this role. I'm thinking of one person I knew, a runway model signed to a major agency, whose face reminded people of a young Leo DiCaprio. He had the giggly personality of someone accustomed to being adored. I thought of him as a millennial Duncan Hannah, in that people drew energy from his aura and passed him around like a fertility idol. Social climbers tended to use him as a conduit to get to other people. He usually hung out with people who populated this mythical, borderless state between New York and Berlin: contrarian painters, failing actresses, or Dimes Square denizens of the art-world Twitterati—people who generally brought him around with them to "appear" as a witty ornamentation in the gilded, mirrored rooms they circled in.

The fact that he produced music (which I thought was good) was almost an obligatory social assignment, secondary to his socialite energy, which is a charisma that exhibits star power despite doing nothing. Obviously, he was aware of this, so he didn't have the confidence to own himself as a music producer. He knew Bill Kouligas, and I told my friend he should send Bill some music, but my friend never took this suggestion seriously. Sometimes, he confided to me how disgusted he was by his own self-promotion, and I told him that once he created a work of art he truly believed in, he wouldn't be ashamed to promote it. Look, if Duncan Hannah never got serious about painting, we wouldn't know who the fuck he was. Maybe we won't ever know who this friend I'm talking about is. He needed to get serious, and I wasn't sure he would. This was the source of his self-hatred, which was the chink in his persona that drew you in. He both enjoyed and detested his role as a stylish accessory at the Boom Boom Room or at Louis Vuitton afterparties, but he guarded his status because he knew he was replaceable. I genuinely enjoyed hanging out with him, but he was preoccupied with certain theatrics he had to use to defend his status, like slinking away whenever I tried to introduce him to other friends or knowing when exactly to leave me on read on our Instagram DMs. I could never get him to hang out with me unless I put him on list, and eventually I made myself purposely unavailable to him because I knew that was the only way I could retain his respect.

I liked most people, revered many, but didn't always respect them. These years, there was one person who gained my unwavering respect, purely because he was the single Asian man I knew—"the only one"—whom everyone in the art world loved and name-dropped and invited: Preston. He was a decade older than me and had the air of an old queen or a mafia don: past his prime, but benevolent, judicious, hungry for praise. Years later, somebody told me I was like "a younger Preston," which alerted me that I was morphing into him. For better or worse, I picked up a lot of his social tactics.

Preston had worked for a fashion boutique in New York that produced the cult YouTube series *Model Files*, in which he stars as an out-of-touch casting director. He adhered to the Spice Girls logic of assigning everyone types as if marketing categories: athleisure babe with the metal tee, Lolita in lace, hippie Coachella girl. The tags that got stuck to Preston were "Jungle Asian," "Fashion," or "Southern boy from Arkansas"—word lists for a mood board that evoked his global brand. As a fashion-industry casting director, including his work for the post-internet impresarios DIS, Preston knew how to spot people's talent for inhabiting prescribed archetypes native to a high school cafeteria, ones that an audience might find legible. He described Beyoncé as "class president." His own persona, "Cameron Diaz": a relatable, all-American personality that was messy, but endearing, like a clumsy dog. On celebrity, he said you could either be an "Elvis" or a "Bob Dylan"—define a single, iconic aesthetic repeated over the course of an oeuvre, or become impossible to pin down, changing one's style the moment before it becomes intelligible and thus commodified by the culture.

Preston understood that status was inherently theatrical. Always knowing how to make an entrance, he would arrive to a party during its second or third leg, always "after dinner," ideally with some ingénue, maybe an emerging noise DJ or a trans model from Manila, people who were early in their careers, still unproven, but knew how to command the attention around them, even if they didn't know why. Because that's what Preston did. He spotted talent before anyone else. Preston's assigned type for me was the "Writer," a witty intellectual who could also hang. He teased me by calling me "Joffrey," because that's how Germans mispronounced my name.

It was incredibly flattering when he took you under his wing, how he introduced you to his more recognizable friends in a way that made them feel embarrassed for not already knowing who you were. When my turn came around, I didn't realize he had been training me to see how I'd do, until one night, after leaving a party, he said, "You're good at this."

At the time, in leftist circles, edgelord postures were gaining traction among a certain type of white class-essentialists who told racist and homophobic jokes "ironically" to aggravate more centrist liberals. Preston would sometimes open a remark with "This is gonna sound really racist," which established him as an edgelord, and simultaneously put white people who orbited the art world at ease, because around him they wouldn't have to perform Good Liberal theatrics. Preston flattered people by letting them feel morally superior to him, which should have been beneath him, because it did a disservice to his genius.

I wouldn't copy this exactly, but I did inherit Preston's intuitive understanding of how to placate white fear. For the longest time, I would never call anyone out as racist. It meant losing your cool. Once, in a discussion about white privilege, a white friend had remarked to me that I "always come up with the most un-PC response in conversation." I didn't know how to take this. To suggest that I was un-PC would mean that I wasn't like all the queer and nonwhite people who were always foaming at the mouth—I was *chill*. Was there an internalized shame to all my armchair critiques of identity politics and PC culture? I had no perspective, though what I loathed more than white privilege were the looks of reverent approval whites would grant me for all my nonwhite nobility, my dazzling intersectionality, and I would pour acid on the whole thing with asides like how the best short stories in the *New Yorker* are by Old White Men (even though it's actually Old White Women), and I'd revel for a beat as the temperature in the room changed.

It was perhaps this ingratiating insecurity, a wanting to be liked, that bonded me to Preston. At heart, I found in him a childlike desire to please. When strangers came up to him and asked, "Are you Preston?" he'd blossom like a cactus flower and recycle the same rehearsed bits that guaranteed laughter. He was sufficiently hilarious, and a consummate narcissist. It was always "Preston," on a first-name basis, perhaps christened in the music video he appeared in with Kylie Minogue, where she flirtatiously calls on him like a pet, "Preston, Preston."

On Instagram, he posted pictures of his travels throughout Asia, flying around for reasons that were never quite clear, and because you could never tell which of his stories were true, you didn't ask. I had a nickname for him, "Poverty Jet Set," because he was always running out of cash and seemed to operate solely on mysterious debit cards that were secretly sent to him in the mail. No one ever dared ask about it, because Preston didn't exactly live in the same world as the rest of us. His was a life of velour, layovers, and cheekbones that shattered glass.

Which could be alienating. When people talked shit, I made sure to defend him, always. Though once, an art critic I knew called Preston an "incel," which was aimed at Preston but inadvertently wounded me. I was mortified in his place.

It meant that if I ever reached the status that Preston had, this is what people would say about me. Maybe that's why I never felt alienated from Preston. He seemed harmless, allergic to solitude, and surrounded himself with flattery and chatter almost as a compulsion. Was he lonely? During the entirety of the time I knew him, I'd never seen him in a relationship. After a few drinks, he would lament to me how no one was ever attracted to him, how the gays rejected him. He had difficulty picking up guys because, he said, "Most people assume I'm a bottom because I'm Asian."

He was dependent on praise and attention that was just never enough, which is why, I imagined, he craved dominance in bed. Perhaps he was sexually frigid, and I was someone who understood that. I thought I could understand his body, offer him a level of intimacy only I could provide. At a gay party at a DIY venue, I tried to make out with him on the dance floor, and he yelped, "No!" and scurried out of the room. That was the last and only time I ever hit on him. I don't think he was ever interested in the stuff of romantic relationships—the risk of being rejected, the shame of intimacy. The face you make when you're about to come is always a concession, because it is ugly, grotesque, and needy—a side of sexuality that Preston repressed. He never wanted to be vulnerable, even as insecurity (which is different from vulnerability) oozed out of him. He preferred to throw his affections at men who were as untouchable as a Gucci spread in a magazine. And when these men ignored him, he blamed it on racism or gay-body fascism. This was legible to me because I was guilty of the same. We never brought it up. Though I still carried with me, whenever we went out, a damp sense of unspoken protection over him, because of what we secretly shared, which I was learning wasn't so uncommon with Asian men, of whatever sexuality.

Maybe he felt similarly for me. In a way that no one else ever bothered, he prodded me along in my career as a writer. It was through Preston that I first heard of Caroline Busta, to whom he suggested I should send my writing. Everybody in the Berlin art world knew *of* Carly since she had been the editor of the historic German art journal *Texte zur Kunst*. She traveled often, but when she was in Berlin, she surrounded herself with a ring of luminaries and personalities you had to fight your way through and almost be ushered in by to get her attention.

It took me an entire year after Preston's suggestion to send her my writing, but once I did, she very quickly, and decisively, brought me on as an editor for New Models, the online platform she founded with her partner, Julian, who went by Lil Internet. New Models enjoyed an unparalleled level of clout at the intersection of art, fashion, and nightlife in New York and Berlin. When I first met Carly, she kept bringing up names, asking if I knew them. I'd say I did, even if it was only someone who followed me on Twitter. But if I didn't know them, it felt like a tiny shortcoming, a wound communicated at the level of a micro-expression, which she probably detected, because she'd follow it with an apology, "Sorry, I'm just trying to figure out . . ." She curated her company, just like how her apartment with Julian had an air of careful selection, up on the fourth floor of a tower in Mitte by the Günter Litfin Memorial, overlooking the water. Their flex sense of humor was exemplified by luxury products they'd place around the apartment, like Aesop, on which they'd cover the labels with white stickers that said NEW MODELS.

They had prints and artist editions on their walls, including one by Anne Imhof—a friend of Carly's—depicting Imhof's partner, Eliza Douglas, with her elbows perched on her knees, mouth open in what Imhof has described as "O-Face." At the time, Douglas opened and closed every Balenciaga show in Paris.

I asked Carly about Imhof, whom I saw as austere, and Carly said, "But she's so much fun," and then showed me the latest Instagram Story of Imhof wearing clown makeup like the Joker, for Halloween, standing next to Douglas, chic and tall. I don't know why the clown makeup surprised me. It charmed me. I wondered if I would ever meet her.

When I spent time at Carly's apartment, she always looked thin in her black jeans or Hermès T-shirt. (She told me the shirt was fake, which worked to her credit, because intellectuals knew that to fetishize an original over a copy was the most unintellectual thing to do.) She looked almost haughtily chic, which contrasted the darkness that typified some of her furtive obsessions. Though she spoke with the charismatic voice of a flight attendant, she was privately fascinated with cult leaders, mass killers, and alt-right incels who wrote misogynist manifestos distributed on 4chan. Yet when I think of her, I have this image in my mind of sitting at the dining room table, watching her silhouette against the windows as she lifted onto her toes to pull down the blinds. She appeared to float.

One of the first things Carly said to me when we started working together was "I'm interested in the life of the commodity," which, in one short breath, gave me permission to care about glamour the way I did. She was deft at cunning one-liners about any given artist. She said of a prominent German video artist and writer, "She has to intellectually dominate everything she can't be a part of." A novelist we both knew was "very Hillary Clinton 'hot sauce in my bag.'" Another novelist, much more well known, Carly said, was always "hanging out with certain people, solely so she can write about them." She went on, "But I'm saying this probably because I have a chip on my shoulder, because once, at a party, I heard her refer to me as 'That blonde over there.'"

With Carly, I knew I wanted to pivot into the friend zone, right from the beginning, so she wouldn't compare me to some of the writers she'd worked with at *Texte zur Kunst*, against whom I feared I could not measure up. When I texted Carly, I found myself affecting a casually manic tone seemingly lifted from a gay-adjacent Brooklyn warehouse party email—exclamation points, trailinggggg textttt, ALL CAPS. I mostly thought it was funny, but also nonthreatening. And I also liked that my queerness was coded in my texting as vernacular. In Berlin, she might have associated queerness (affectionately) with nightlife, but she only ever brought up race to ridicule virtue signaling: exhibitions with diverse curation that felt on the nose, Black Lives Matter hashtags on Instagram, that sort of thing.

Her partner, Julian, who had a lot of Black clients in the music industry—he'd shot a music video for Beyoncé and produced music for Azealia Banks—was more likely to try to earnestly think through problems of race, with me or on the New Models podcast, even if his thoughts were half-baked, which he said was part of the process: You had to risk being wrong to find your way to right. While I mostly worked with

Carly, Julian was off on the side of the room, editing videos or putting together the podcast. Tall and almost brutish, he sometimes had the affect of a friendly giant, next to Carly. His face was often screwed up, eyes squinting with brows furrowed, as if he were intensely trying to work out a problem in his head. He didn't make eye contact unless you were directly talking to him, and he usually held himself aloof. I'd heard him joke before about how he has Asperger's, or is "on the spectrum," which can still be true, even if it doubles as a useful performance to keep people at bay.

So, this is stupid and lazy, but if you ever want to put a conversation with someone you've just met on the fast track, you talk about drugs or sex. When I tried this on Carly, she said, about drugs, "We need our vices," in a way that I could tell meant she didn't struggle with any of her own.

In the same conversation, she said that when she used to live in New York, after work she would visit Bjarne Melgaard, the gay Norwegian painter, who was flamboyant and butch, and who lived in an apartment she could see from the northeast corner of the *Artforum* offices, where she worked as an editor. Upon arriving, she'd find his apartment totally smoked out as he sat lighting his meth pipe on one of four massive Knoll couches strewn with wool blankets. He had these two chihuahuas, and whenever she went over, they would be completely crazed, running around, jumping into walls, because of the secondhand smoke.

I said I wasn't surprised, because I thought he had meth face.

"What's meth face? Is it sort of pockmarked?" Carly said, touching her cheeks.

I nodded. "It's Bjarne's face."

I knew this because I was also becoming a junkie. Drugs were cheaper than lunch, and they corroded me from the inside. Most of my binges happened at home, so I could dissociate from my calcifying loneliness. It was easy to lie to yourself, at parties, that you'll always be padded by the laughter and banter of witty acquaintances, but when I went back to my bedroom, I wondered about all the others who paired off after the party while I was finishing off my grams, here and there, with the same SoundCloud mixes from my portable speaker.

I watched porn. I took sleeping pills.

These habits were something I tried to downplay the more I made my name as a respectable writer who ostensibly had his shit together. But behind the curtains were nights of insomnia, the shakes, and powders that always disappeared faster than I'd planned. I didn't tell anybody about the summer mornings I lay sweating and shivering in bed. But at panels at the Grüner Salon or openings at the Julia Stoschek Collection, I put forward the performance of an intellectual, well versed in the theoretical discourses of the age, partly because I had a chip on my shoulder as a sort of ad-man-from-New-York-who-reads-Lacan-once-and-now-fancies-himself-an-art-critic.

Even so, for the first time in Berlin, and to my astonishment, my writing career was starting to take off. Before, I could barely get art reviews printed in magazines unpaid. Now, magazines approached me with paid assignments. I was giddy to finally graduate from the black hole of unanswered pitch emails. Yet this was also the time that I was using drugs sometimes five days a week, just to keep the terrors at bay. Some mornings I sat at my desk, drafting a review, jotting down notes I remembered from last night's opening, but felt rushes of gnawing pain flow up my forearms like a current.

It was withdrawal. Rattling hands, stomach pains.

Once, while visiting me in Berlin, my friend Jean had said, "Almost every one of my best friends are drug addicts," which was also true for me during several years of my life. We suffered equally from romanticizing the transgressive lives of artists, which meant romanticizing drugs. We'd met after he had read some of my theoretical writing published in a techno zine, and we started bonding over art. Both of us wanted to write for *Artforum* one day, swooned over a kind of mythic fantasy from the seventies of the lives of certain of the magazine's early writers. His copy of Rosalind Krauss's *The Originality of the Avant-Garde*, which he gave me, became a book I carried with me to every city I lived in.

Jean had a shaved head and large doggy eyes. He wore a chain necklace, crisp white T-shirts, and a bomber jacket on the back of which he'd had Jenny Holzer's *Truisms* custom screen-printed. He slept with men and women, was by every account handsome. (You can see him in one of Tillmans's photos, dancing shirtless at a Brooklyn warehouse party with his girlfriend at the time, the head of menswear at Helmut Lang.) He'd come from single-mother poverty in Jersey— "white trash" by his words—but had the refinement and acculturation of art and the avant-garde, even if he didn't have the wealth associated with it.

At the time, he was in an open relationship with someone I'll call Kathy, after Acker, one of their heroes. Kathy was a

nonbinary sex worker (whom Proust would've called "a cour-
tesan") who looked like Edie Sedgwick and had a contained
animalistic energy to them (meaning, they had a temper,
which made people obey them).

The first time I spent any real time with Jean and Kathy
together was after an Unter Halloween party in New York,
where I was then spending part of the year. We all split Ubers
to the apartment of a creative director in Williamsburg who
was hosting afters. People from the party, too wired to go to
sleep, were going in and out of the bedroom, engaging in
pansexual group sex on the bed, or were on the living room
floor, sharing a limitless supply of powders. While talking
with Jean at the kitchen island about signaletic communication, I could see over his shoulder into the bedroom, where
my Asian friend was on the bed, splayed on his stomach. He
reached for his poppers on the side table while he was getting
fucked, and said of the man on top of him, "He has the
perfect size dick," and I couldn't tell if that meant big or was
a concession because it wasn't.

When morning turned to evening, someone had dragged
the potted trees in from the balcony, and as people sauntered
around naked, it all seemed natural, Edenic. At some point,
two queer DJs from the scene showed up, and they didn't seem
to react to what was going on inside, so I didn't either. "I can't
believe you two haven't fucked yet," Kathy said to me, sitting
next to Jean, smiling. The way he looked at me showed that
the desire was real. And I desired him. In the blur of the drugs,
Jean and Kathy and I fell into a role-play scenario where the
two of them sat at the dining room table like parents busy
with dinner guests while I crawled between them on the floor,
under the table, trying to get their attention by licking and

sucking their toes as they kicked me away, irritated, like I was a dog.

This was as far as I went. He didn't push. I felt embarrassed. This block—it just made me want him more, coming this close and not being able to touch. It was maddening. In the past, if I had believed that only undesirable men approached me, here was proof to the contrary. My fantasies were being handed to me on a fucking platter. And I still couldn't. This set an ill precedent. I could no longer tout the story that the men I wanted were always rejecting me.

Was I odd? My deepest fear was that I was watching a sexual revolution, a historic liberation enabled by PrEP and marriage equality, simply pass me by. If I didn't figure my shit out in time, it would go, just like that—my youth, the times. I would never forgive myself if I sat this one out. I was wasting the prime of my youth. Increasingly, my sex life appeared like a room with many doors, and each of them opened, at different times, but I couldn't bring myself to walk through a single one. One day, all those doors would close, leaving me standing in this room, alone, hopeless and afraid with only the echo of my own voice.

Because I was so sexually inept, I romanticized the relationship Jean and Kathy had together as a bohemian fantasy: the art historian and the sex worker. Together, they had chemistry, personality. Sometimes, Jean would read to Kathy passages from Georges Bataille's *Story of the Eye* while Kathy gave him a blow job—something of a scene from Acker's 1974 film *The Blue Tapes*, when she gives Alan Sondheim a blow job while he tries to recite to her from a book. I know this because Kathy read me a journal entry while we were railing lines of K, sitting on a floor mattress of an apartment they rented while visiting Berlin.

Because I was fascinated, Kathy would tell me stories about their massage parlor in Brooklyn that they called "the hand job factory," where they often serviced Hasidic Jews who lived in South Williamsburg. They sometimes met higher-paying clients who booked rooms at the Standard and asked them to carry out fetishes on a pay scale that could approach the thousands, depending on the ask. Once, they were paid to gag until they vomited on a client's dick. Another time, there was a guy who tried to pay them less because he was hot and they enjoyed it. (He didn't get away with it.)

When I asked them what their ultimate fantasy was, initially they said they didn't have one, which sounded right for a sex worker. But after I pressed them, they came up with an answer. It was weird. They said it was being in an orgy with a bunch of hot gay men who were uninterested in but amused by their cunt, fascinated by it, and started poking their fingers in it, and then fucking it out of curiosity, just to see if it would start coming.

When Kathy asked me, I said I fantasized about being in a doomed romance with a meth-addicted hustler who was always running out of money, and whenever he came home, bruised from his johns who'd beat him, we'd have desperate chemsex together because we were terrified of climate change.

I said that to be funny. Though the real answer, which I somehow couldn't joke about, was that after I was sexually assaulted, I had fantasies only of gang rape, of men who fucked me sadistically, got turned on by seeing me writhe, which fueled them to go faster. They'd force me to admit I liked the rupturing pain of their dicks ramming my ass, because if I didn't, they'd pound me harder until I did. I tried not to judge my own desires, which did not need to be justified to myself or anyone. Except desire is mutable, even if its mutability is mysterious to me. Eventually, I would outgrow this period, instead fantasizing about this personality who appeared out of nowhere in my mind, a man with a thin but solid jaw and a nasally voice, who was fit and shy and awkward, who apologized before he was about to leak inside my ass, and would look up when he made me moan because he didn't realize how much he was pleasuring me. It seemed that in Berlin, I was this small-town boy surrounded by titans, self-made legends, mean boys who took up space by acting hard and playing hard, and in the privacy of my bedroom in Mitte I fantasized about someone who wasn't noticed when he walked into the room, was gentle and approachable. Someone easy to love. Someone I could trust.

Years later, I did start writing for *Artforum*, and I immediately told Jean. I began by contributing three-hundred-word reviews that ran online. Small, though it was a break for me. Then, when Carly published my essay titled "In Arcadia Ego," written in the vernacular of queer club kids, I was presented to the art world as kind of a discovery in the scene. Not infrequently, strangers would approach me at galleries and clubs and ask, "Are you Geoffrey Mak?" or even, "Are you Gregory?" which meant they'd seen my byline before they heard it spoken. This was totally weird to me. Before, I hadn't written regularly for art audiences.

Now, I felt like I had a critical space I could call my own, which also meant I had a meaningful investment, however small, in the intellectual life of Berlin.

My reach wasn't large, but I liked spending days swimming in research. I found that in a single day, I could move from a theory of Pharmacoporno-Capitalism to a takedown of identity politics through a revisionist history of housing discrimination, effectively getting my paradigm shifted in the two hours it took to finish a spaghetti Bolognese at Schwarzes Café, with the day's press releases folded in the back pocket of my Rafs, my uniform at the time. The more I traversed the art world, I felt like I was discovering a secret city. Compared to New York, the openings here seemed wilder and laxer than anything I had been used to. At Lars Friedrich, they kept their beers in a bathtub full of ice. At the afterparty at Grunenberg, I saw the guest curator walking her dog through the rooms barefoot, while in one of the back galleries, people were sprawled on the floor, lights off, giggling and snorting lines and talking about Tao Lin. To an American, these nights seemed like outtakes from the last city of decadence. Now, I began running into artists I admired more regularly, which I loved. At a studio party, I asked a stranger if he could open my beer with his lighter, and when he turned around, it was Simon Denny. Only twice did I see Hito Steyerl in civilian life: once at Brandenburg Gate during an anti-AfD protest, and the other waiting in the guest list line at Berghain. I still kept an eye out for Anne Imhof, who I was certain would appear, if she ever did, unexpectedly. Somehow, imagining her in pedestrian situations, locking up her bike, or walking out the doors of the Schinkel Pavillon looking for cell phone reception, seemed undignified and exciting.

Regularly, at openings and dinners, I began seeing Billy—the gay, flirty dancer who'd composed the score to Imhof's performance in Venice. At this point, I had no idea what he now knew about me, or my writing, but it seemed he recognized me, if not purely because he saw me at the right places at the right time. After a group of us had gone to get food after an opening, we decided to pair up on rented scooters to get to a party nearby. I got paired with Billy, who directed the scooter behind me while I tried to keep my balance in front of him. Weaving through cars and streetlights, he told me about a friend we both knew, a drag performer from the gay club scene, who was trying to break into the art world. I had never seen her art, wondered if I ever would. I knew the type: club kid trying to get recognized by the art world and getting totally ignored. This happened to a lot of people I knew. And the more I concentrated on my writing, the more I tried to distance myself from the twenty-six-year-old raver I used to be in New York, who practiced dance moves from YouTube in front of the mirror.

If I had been an anonymous raver when I first met Billy in the garden, I was now a persona he recognized: a critic. I had gotten what I had desired in the Berlin art world, which I so wanted to call home even though it wasn't. I learned its rules, parroted the codes. I played the game. Though if my gains arrived bittersweet, it was due to the discovery, the kind that comes only when it's already too late, that the person having the most fun at the party is the one with the most status or the one with the least. When I was still a nobody, I wish I had known how to enjoy it at the time. Where I was now was complicated and insecure, and I knew I could not return to that state of powerless abandon. The game had already begun. This was my social education.

Occasionally, I still did think about that twenty-six-year-old kid I was in New York, when I met my friend Ellis. This was two years before my first trip to Berlin. Like me, he had one foot in the techno scene and the other in the art world. At the time, he worked as a data analyst for a hedge fund and was the only person I knew my age who collected art. We went down to Art Basel Miami together, where he ended up buying art. His tastes were literary, but also digital— epitomized, at their apex, by the painter Albert Oehlen, whose monograph was one of the few books he owned. As a staunch environmentalist, Ellis read only ebooks or books from the library, but he easily read upward of eighty books a year, mostly novels ranging from Jean Genet to the Fifth Season sci-fi trilogy. In the bedroom of his SoHo apartment, he hung a massive painting by his friend the artist Petra Cortright (which he literally bought by DM'ing her on Twitter).

But more than anyone I know, Ellis was an artist of the self. The angles of his jaw and his heavy brow gave him the harsh beauty of a soft-spoken cybergoth. I swear, he sounds and maybe even looks like the art historian Hal Foster, except with bleached-blonde hair cropped to a perennial buzz. Ellis worked out at Equinox seven times a week, so his body looked military-fit, clad mostly in an all-black uniform: mesh tops ordered from Amazon with sleeves he cut off, Balmain jeans, and Rick Owens Adidas. This was, of course, style, though he cited this uniformism as environmental—fewer clothes but also fewer decisions. Always citing the wasted energy of "decision fatigue," he stuck to the same routine always: Soylent for meals at home or macrobiotic dinners at Souen. Everything was timed. Dinner rarely went on longer than ninety minutes, and if you'd arrived late, he'd usually be waiting outside a restaurant reading a book: a soft rebuke. His sleek roboticism found its ideal complement in the modular aesthetic of industrial techno. When I watched the way he danced at raves, it almost looked like an exercise routine—repetitive, with slight variations over time, which visualized the music, and the endorphin rush people often associate with weightlifting would be enough to carry him through to sunrise.

One of his partners, a Chinese performance artist in the downtown scene, described him offhandedly to me as "my slave-master." I knew exactly what that meant. In Ellis, I detected a libidinal drive to service—such as his determination, during dinners, to fill other people's glasses before his own—which made him a master, because he had the power to, at any moment, withdraw that service, regardless if you'd grown dependent on it. His abrupt withdrawals made me wary of him, even many years into our friendship. Because he accepted you in full, it was implicit that you would grant him the same for his rigid boundaries, opened up only on his terms, and then once he decided to close himself off, it was impossible to access him.

His self-effacement could frustrate me. Sometimes, in conversation, he'd deflect questions away from himself, leaving dinner after you talked the entire time, and you having learned nothing new about the man whom you'd just spent an hour with, yourself feeling narcissistic and exposed, possibly used. Even his all-black uniform was like a priest's, and his affected humility both deflects and commands attention. This monastic demeanor also came with his being devoutly straight edge, as if he commanded full mastery over his body. Ellis wanted to train and submit his body to the extremes of discipline to perfection, and he wanted to be (and was) quietly celebrated for it. Yet his being straight edge also meant he denied antidepressants, even as he struggled with severe but high-functioning depression. He decided he wanted to feel it, raw. Such qualities made him patient, gentle, resigned. (Sitting or standing, he had a persistent slouch that almost coded as couture.)

I was also a high-functioning depressive, so we got along. After I was assaulted, he set me up with his therapist on the Upper West Side, whom I wouldn't have seen if Ellis didn't persist in reminding me to schedule a meeting. We'd joked about our therapist's mannerisms. For instance, I wondered, for years, why he would sometimes open his mouth during conversation, and pick at his molars. It was eccentric but forgettable, until one day I figured out that it was our therapist's way of disguising his yawning.

I don't know what Ellis talked about in therapy. Whenever I asked, he'd say, "Nothing really." Although once, our therapist suggested to him that he liked going to raves to feel close to other people's bodies, an intimacy he wasn't getting from sex, except Ellis thought this was laughable. He identified, simultaneously but in different degrees, as bisexual, asexual, and demisexual—"the sexuality spectrum" he'd say. During certain years he had more sex than I ever did (because fair enough: Ellis was hot). Other years, he chose to have no sex at all. Sometimes he tweeted about it, which showed he could joke about it. Most of his friends knew. He stopped short of pride (which would have read to me like an over-compensation anyway) but I detected no shame or angst. He regarded his asexuality, or these wintry panes of celibacy, with warm neutrality.

Unlike anyone I knew, Ellis chose celibacy with quiet elegance. He was free from the torment and self-castigation that characterized my feelings about my own celibacy, which could be voluntary even if it was experienced as involuntary. But Ellis was a strange and gentle man transfixed by solitude. He was tirelessly moved by the Hudson River. He adored cinema verité and slow cinema, often spending overcast afternoons alone at MoMA in those dark, hagiographic theaters that ban popcorn or drinks. These are solitary curiosities. He was not ashamed of them, nor did he care to share them. He imagined himself in the future as single. Or not. It was up to him. Ellis occasionally had partners, and then returned to celibacy. He was in control of his own solitude, as I was not. But one must accept solitude before one can depart from it.

Yet for Ellis, this solitude came with costs. I always detected in him an inner, possibly integral, darkness. I considered it to be not despite but complementary to his inner peace. Occasionally during group dinners, I would look over and catch his face, expressionless, with his hazel-green eyes opened wide, as if staring at something deep inside his mind, somewhere I couldn't reach. It terrified me. Without a beat, I'd zoom back into the group conversation, and then glance back at Ellis a second later. By then, he would have changed his expression to pleasantly neutral, which is how I knew he'd caught me noticing.

I loved him as one of my closest friends for many years, so I didn't need to ask how he felt, I just read his face. I smiled when he laughed, especially at things no one else in the group found funny, since his sense of humor was as unpredictable as his attention. I knew he tired easily of small talk, and would sometimes abruptly leave a conversation, which always stung, no matter how many times it happened. Midconversation, I would be talking, and then suddenly see the spark in his eye snuff out, and I'd think, I've lost you.

One summer, he invited me to spend a week with his friend Brian—an editor and critic, whom Ellis had met on Twitter—at Brian's seasonal rental in the Fire Island Pines. It was a modernist house at the end of the street overlooking the bay. Inside, it had wood-paneled walls and vintage seventies gay-porn mags stashed deep in the coffee table. When Ellis arrived, he said, "I feel like the entire week was a journey to get here." I knew he was talking about his depression, which seemed to ramp up at the same time every year. It weighed on me. Because we shared a bedroom I took it (inappropriately) as my own doomed responsibility to cheer him up, which is why I often stayed with him upstairs, reading, instead of joining the group downstairs that was raucous and rowdy around the pool.

It also served as an excuse to skirt my social anxiety, because Brian made me nervous. He had long hair, was quite tall, had a Hemingway build. (Taxonomically: a "muscle bear.") As a host, his moods would swing from giddy laughter to an irate disappointment with the hint of a sneer on his upper lip. While a group of us would be drinking champagne in the hot tub, he'd fiddle a bit with his phone, and then leave without saying anything. Later, someone would glimpse through his open bedroom door and see him undressed and collapsed on top of the covers.

Brian's summer house was something of a salon—each weekend, he invited a group of queer artists and critics he knew, who were always called "the boys," gay boys who went to underground sex parties at the Cock and also read Eve Sedgwick. I didn't always know who they were. Though I knew they were *somebody*, the way they chatted about artists whose work I had literally learned about in school, except, in this case, they were concern-gossiping about so-and-so's debilitating alcoholism, or about which artists slept with which dealers, something that confounded me, sheltered as I was, because I could never imagine fucking a literary agent.

After a certain hour in the night, I was sure the boys all slept with each other or fooled around—easy, casual—moving between bedrooms downstairs and the hot tub, while I was upstairs, reading. It was learned helplessness at this point. The boys probably looked at me with benevolent suspicion. I wondered what they thought of me. A prude? I wish it were that simple. Why was I even at Fire Island if I wasn't going to fuck? I never told any of this to Ellis, even though he stayed upstairs with me, also reading. Like me, he wasn't one of the boys. With him upstairs with me, I felt secure. The summer rain pelleted the windows, and there was a gentle smell of wet wood. Propped up on his pillow, Ellis flipped through a paperback that he found on one of the shelves, while the boys downstairs were laughing and shouting, ice clinking. Once he got tired, we shut the light and went to bed.

The next morning, the whole house went to the store to pitch in for food. While most people picked up chips and hummus, I bought a hilariously overpriced tray of smoked salmon. I wanted to impress Brian because I wanted to write for him. At that point, everybody in the art world read Brian. He had been one of the early writers to articulate the strengths and pitfalls of the post-internet aesthetic. Now, he edited for *Art in America*, sharing offices with *Interview*, though he had never opened one of *Interview*'s issues in his life until someone happened to bring the latest one with him to the house. After perusing an interview with the artist Zoe Leonard ahead of her show at MoMA, Brian said, laconically, "This is actually good."

I wanted to talk to Brian about art, but suspected I shouldn't, because it would come across, somehow, as gauche. Like business at the dinner table. I noticed, around the house, he'd play a Spotify-generated playlist of Tori Amos and Talking Heads—the sort of anti-curatorial (and automated) "bad taste" that only critics of "high taste" can effortlessly flaunt. At dinner, I asked him who was his midnineties female singer-songwriter of choice, and he said, "Kate Bush." When he asked me mine, I said, "Sarah McLachlan," which triggered a deep and hearty laugh to come barreling from his gut.

"Bold choice," he said.

Around Brian, I knew I had to use bad taste as a way of signaling good taste. When he saw my copy of *Bluets* on the coffee table, he asked who was reading it. When I said it was mine, he sneered as if to say "teacher's pet." Too on the nose, I guess. Should I have gone genre with Patricia Highsmith? Or just camp: Nora Ephron.

Brian was considerably more jovial and open when I ran into him at queer parties in Brooklyn, after the week in Fire

Island. "Off duty," as it were. Outside one of these parties, he asked me, smiling, "Do you like writing reviews?"

I said yes.

"Send me an email."

One of the first artists I wrote about under Brian was the Filipino artist L., who was an old friend of Ellis's. Aligned with socialist politics, L.'s artistic research, sometimes in the documentary format, was focused on working-class entrepreneurs on Taobao, the Chinese shopping platform, or sugar plantation laborers in the Philippines. Harvard-educated, he was a rigorous writer with convictions. He had contributed to *Texte zur Kunst* when Carly still edited it. An artist's artist, he had a cult devotion among critics. David Joselit, the esteemed art historian, bought a piece of his. The writer Michael Sanchez, whose 2011 essay "Art and Transmission" was an era-defining text, had been an early collaborator. While my self-education was somewhere stuck in the post-structural seventies, and its offshoots in the gender studies of the nineties, L.'s work felt strikingly contemporary. He was always talking about nodes and networks or redistributed class alignments in a globalized, post-internet condition.

L.'s features were handsomely refined, and he had a low voice I found sexy, which erupted often into a throaty laugh, like he was gasping for air. Whenever I met up with him, he would greet me with a white smile and clutch my shoulder with a hard, masculine grip. It was part of his princely demeanor: strong but delicate hands that gave away his upbringing. As Preston remarked once about his table manners: No matter how hungry L. was, he always ate slow.

L. was part of this illustrious Asian crew that Preston also circled in. In one episode of *Model Files*, Preston creates the "Asiancy," a satirical all-Asian modeling agency. Except in real life, he actually did surround himself with a coterie of Asians: DJs who played in castles in Spain, fashion designers whose models looked like post-human aliens, and virtual reality artists who rendered futuristic feminist utopias exhibited at the Tate Modern. Once we started hanging out, Preston brought me into the fold. When we went out together in Berlin, we would occupy a corner of the dance floor and command attention in a way I never had in my life. It was jolting. People watched us. This was the first time I hung out with groups of Asians who might be considered aspirational. They came from everywhere: Singapore, Denmark, Sweden, Vietnam. L. was from the Philippines, though his English accent was perfect from a life in international schools.

The word "privilege" dominates digital parlance, but there's an older word that the thinkpiece generation has little idea how to deal with: "aristocracy." L. came from aristocracy. His father had been the finance minister of the Philippines, and his family owned property all around the world, such as their apartment in Prenzlauer Berg, which combined two separate apartments and was furnished with sconces, tasseled curtains, marble side tables, and Asian cabinets with pearl inlay. L.'s parents were collectors, and their paintings hung like monuments in every room in the apartment, including the bedrooms, where he occasionally hosted artists and curators who might be in town for a few days around an opening or fair.

Somehow, L. was able to command, from everyone around him, a relaxed security. I detected in him what is often attributed to Engels, who in *The Condition of the Working Class in England* was free to empathize with the underclasses precisely because, as the son of a textiles mogul, Engels had no fear of ever becoming a worker himself. I remember when I first met L., I thought he had terrible taste in some of the people he surrounded himself with, who were not at the level of his class or intelligence, until I understood that was what made him L. He was unconditionally welcoming, as an ethic. If Preston showed me that Asians could be aspirational, L. showed me that they didn't need to be. He was friends with some of the other Asians I rejected as uninteresting and insecure and sad—common, I suppose. But L. dignified them by considering them preferable company. This was perhaps sprung from a benevolent curiosity, not having come from where the rest of us had. His compassion was enabled by his distance from the paycheck-to-paycheck lives of the people around him: freelancers, writers, struggling artists, or even successful artists, who might've been "reviewed everywhere" and lived lives considered glamorous but sold only a few paintings a year, each at twelve thousand dollars with a 50 percent cut from the gallerist, which meant they made the equivalent of a junior graphic designer's salary straight out of a BA.

Once, in a conversation about the ethics of canceling problematic friends, he said he'd "canceled" only one in his life: a childhood friend whose wedding invitation L. rejected upon discovering that his friend's name had gotten dredged up in the Panama Papers. That was the thing: L.'s proximity to Actual Real Power gave him a sharp, critical seriousness combined with a kind but muscular generosity that posed itself as unassuming and unconditional.

As I looked up to him, L. became a compass for me to use to navigate the social. I rarely detected any anxiety from him. I suppose it was because he kept himself at a remove from art world gymnastics. He didn't fuck with it, or maybe he just didn't care. L. technically lived in Berlin, but he often flew to Milan for months at a time because he was in a yearslong relationship with an Italian man named Fabrizio who worked as a secretarial assistant at an insurance company. Often, they went on road trips through Italy, where L., in the passenger seat, would read passages, audiobook-style, from Gramsci or from the gay philosopher Didier Eribon's autobiography, *Returning to Reims*, an account of leaving a working-class background that was not dissimilar to Fabrizio's. Once, over Campari sodas, I heard a British dealer say, "I'm so fascinated by this relationship, it's so non-art-world," as if L.'s boyfriend were an exotic specimen. She asked, "Do you look at art together?" to which L. coolly replied, "He likes the Caravaggios." I'm certain he detected the condescension. L. must have been used to it everywhere he went—even I had been guilty of it—but he chose not to react, or even sting back, which was evidence of his deeper grace.

For the first time in my life, I had found a group of artists who sourced power in shared solidarity, and who were dedicated to articulating a distinct, Asian aesthetic. Through Preston and his group of friends, I came to know a gallery called 47 Canal. The dealer made a point to create a stable of Asian artists in New York, something that impressed and moved me, because there was no equivalent in the literary world. This was an incredible discovery, something I did not realize I needed until I found it. These were people I'd meet at openings or parties in New York or Berlin, in rooms with long tables and long windows, somewhere on the second floor, and sometimes I would try to picture what I might look like to someone—perhaps myself, as a teenager—watching from the throbbing blueness of street level: lights, glass, teeth. While my teenage ambitions were largely derived from tennis court lawns and popped collars, I suddenly found, in the middle of my youth, what I never realized I had always been looking for: direct contact with a collective, global genius that offered, yes, the corroboration of friendship, but even more—Asian archetypes, who thrived in environments as harsh as the art market. But these were models who emerged in style, models whom I could look up to, and fashion myself after. Their poses were invigorated by the political stakes against which they'd strut. Poses against the commodity. Poses against Western hegemony. Strength came from how you stood your ground.

Circulating in the 47 Canal scene, which extended from New York to Berlin, I met Frank, a white art critic. Frank, I immediately liked. It was the first time I'd gotten close with a white art critic who was my direct contemporary. The week he taught me the word "facture," it became my favorite word for months. He was British, though thoroughly remodeled as an expat when he had worked as a curator for the historic Artists Space in New York, but occasionally he would say "taking the piss" and a frisson of glee would pass over me. Over the course of the summer, we developed our lingo: "PoCo" was for "Postcolonial," and "toxie" referred to "toxic masculinity energy, *but in a good way*," which encompassed anything from muscle queens at Berghain to Gerhard Richter. He was bisexual, finding himself attracted to the submissive qualities in men and the assertive ones in women. He was Vegan Frank, Benzo Frank, Frankie with the baby face and tattoos, the racial anxiety, and the one-hour Skype appointments with his therapist in New York for which he would clear out the entire day. "I'm sorry I can't hang out on Tuesday," he'd say, "I have therapy."

Most people who knew Frank saw him as a white critic who specialized in nonwhite art. He wrote for museum catalogues for Black artists, spoke on panels, covered major, international exhibitions, on assignment, for outlets like *Artforum*, which looked to him as an authority on nonwhite aesthetics. But I was especially moved by how he put Asian art (the subject of the dissertation he would go on to write) on a pedestal for its formations of collectivity and non-Hegelian conceptions of history. I would not have been able to accept that as legitimate had I not come into my own Asian identity through L. and Preston. Frank believed in *nongkrong*, which means "hanging out," something he learned from Indonesian collectives he spent time with during research trips to Jakarta. In Frank's formation, art was the residue of nongkrong, a relational practice that informed aesthetics. The Indonesians tipped Frank, who then tipped me, that nongkrong is the central node from which art, including this very essay, extends. Frank practiced nongkrong everywhere he went, which meant hanging out with him was intentional—challenging, generative, kinky, and fun—it could be life-changing, even if that change was like a slight pivot of the waist.

Though Frank's whiteness never exactly disappeared. The week a white painter's portrait of Whitney Houston landed the cover of *Artforum*, he mentioned he was surprised there wasn't any backlash for a white painter representing a Black woman, and though I wanted to say, "It's because nobody gives a fuck," I detected, in Frank, an instinctual self–negation in favor of received Black critique. I found this type of dynamic hard to work around: white people handling nonwhite complaint with kid gloves, and me, in return, putting on *my* kid gloves for white people. I wasn't used to this, the tables turned. Once, when deciding not to meet up with a group of artists at a nearby bar, he described them as "uninteresting white people with no awareness and nothing to say."

I know it's what he tried not to be. He once quoted to me the white philosopher Shannon Sullivan: "White people often unconsciously and tenaciously hold on to their white privi-lege because of the psychological and economic benefits it affords them." I don't know if or how much he felt implicated in this, but redistribution of privilege was a priority for him, and I sensed it took a psychic toll.

Later, I sent him a quote from the Black historian Achille Mbembe:

> It is simply not true that unless I have undergone the exact same experience as the other, I know nothing about his or her pain and should simply shut up. Insofar as to be human is to open oneself up to the possibility always already there of becoming (an)other, such a conception of self and identity is by definition antihuman.

I don't know why I made these gestures, which I wouldn't have with others. But honestly, this friendship surprised me.

In the past, I'd shied away from having close relationships with other white, male writers, always holding in my mind the tightrope relationship Baldwin had with Norman Mailer, recounted in "The Black Boy Looks at the White Boy" in 1961,

> We liked each other at once, but each was frightened that the other would pull rank. . . . And I think, alas, that I envied him: his success, and his youth, and his love. And this meant that though Norman really wanted to know me, and though I really wanted to know him, I hung back, held fire, danced, and lied.

I didn't want any of that with Frank. Though some of this competition was inevitable, which made me sad. Frank was indiscreet about his own arrogance, and was stingy with affirmation. He almost never complimented me on my writing, and it solicited me to helplessly compliment him *more*, to the point where I was just being sycophantic. I hated this dynamic. It seemed important that he maintained a persona around me that was as flawless as a cover girl: perfect ethics, perfect politics. Because he identified his voice as a critic who foretold unhappy truths about "settler colonialism" and "racial capitalism" and "environmental catastrophe," his contempt for the things that gave him pleasure was the most tellingly human thing about him.

I felt closest to Frank when I felt his pleasure. I remember all the times in the club when we would turn to each other on the dance floor, lock eyes, and suppress our raver grins because we knew the G was hitting and the next hour would be buoyed with a lilac chattiness. The rhythm of our night would be punctuated in sessions where we'd cram into a bathroom stall, and he'd fill his mouth half full of water, and I'd take out my G bottle and squeeze a dose into his mouth like a bird feeding its young. These slapdash, toilet stall drug sessions were aggressively maternal. I was always timing everybody's high, reading faces on the dance floor to see who was feeling what, and when, and *why*. Frank called me the "vibe doctor," because I always carried with me, in my fanny pack, a panoply of uppers and downers that I used, at will, as if painting reds and violets on a canvas. Often I'd ask, "How are you feeling now, and how do you *want* to feel in thirty minutes?" I liked being the source of Frank's pleasure, even if manufactured, which during these moments presented itself to me, blunt and unnuanced, like a primary color. I felt like I was protecting a child who had put his trust in me, eyes wide open and dilated.

But no, we couldn't stay in the rave forever. Back in the art world, everything got weird again. On several occasions, people came up and asked if he remembered them, which is how I know he intimidated other people. He had a prom king persona, marked by a feigned obliviousness to the fact. He maintained a poker face everywhere he went, and so I could never tell if he approved or disapproved of any one person, artwork, or social situation. And because he had a baby face that weirdly didn't emote, people were always throwing their affections at him without quite being reciprocated, which was the essence of his sweet-and-sour charisma: it made you try harder to win his approval.

So because he was difficult to read, I worked harder to read him in ways I would never bother doing with other friends.

When we were in groups, I stopped introducing him to people I was talking to, because I wanted to see whom he would introduce himself to and whom he didn't, so I'd know whom he was impressed by.

Do I sound insufferable yet? I'm telling you, it almost killed me.

But there was a metaphor I often told myself those days: A good swimmer can swim in a pool or an ocean, it makes no difference. And so when I found myself drowning in the undertow of social minutiae, I would tell myself, don't over-think it, *just keep swimming*. In the social barbarism of all these art world rituals—jealousy, sadism, narcissism, sycophancy, betrayal—I would catch glimmers of this slivering thing called tact, nothing short of a supreme virtue, inscribed on the smallest gestures, as if I were kneeling in mud, panning for flecks of gold. This might have been an imaginary projec-tion, but I chose to believe in its presence in plain situations. I chose to read kindness into the surface of things.

I projected this courtesy when I finally ended up meeting Anne Imhof.

Her show *Imagine* at Buchholz was the first of her work I had seen since the Venice Biennale years ago. Frank and I went, because he was writing a social diary for *Artforum* about the show. We arrived right when it opened, but a small crowd had already gathered in front of the doors, on the street, with wineglasses, silk dresses, and leather trench coats. Upstairs, we were greeted by a model/dancer/performer standing on his/her knees on top of a platform erected on an eight-foot-high I-beam. Around the gallery were paintings of orange spray paint on glass, and readymades that seemed sourced according to a butch Gen Xer's idea of youth and excess: bare mattresses, motor helmets spray-painted gold, dartboards, beer, and S&M sex toys like cuffs and whips.

Frank was immediately engulfed by people who knew him, so I went on upstairs. There, I ran into Shui, who made work under their avatar WangShui, and was one of the queer Asian artists I had come to know in Berlin. I'd gotten into a conversation with Shui and their curator from the Julia Stoschek Collection, where Shui was currently showing, when suddenly on my right, Julia Stoschek herself came clattering over in heels with Anne Imhof at her side. Imhof moved with her chin tipped down, eyes focused gently forward. She wasn't tall. She looked hardcore. Deep grooves on either side of her nostrils made her nude face seem unhurried in her leather coat, workmanlike. But by the time I could even register her proximity, Julia Stoschek had succinctly squeezed me out of the circle in her enthusiasm to make introductions. It is a universal party skill to know when it's time to conveniently disappear, and I stood there awkwardly, wondering if it was time for me to conveniently disappear. Then Anne Imhof noticed me. She glanced in my direction, put one foot into the circle, reached her arm between Shui and Julia to separate them, to extend her hand to me, and said, "I'm Anne."

This glinting gesture is the one that endures in my mind as I write this, years later.

In fact, I found this gesture of tact magnificent, because in the time since Anne Imhof had won the Golden Lion in Venice for the performance I saw in the German Pavilion, she had fallen out of favor. She had been stripped of her status. A certain critical establishment, who otherwise might've kept their criticisms silent, now volunteered themselves to call in Imhof for a public reckoning. The great Benjamin H. D. Buchloh described Imhof's depiction of fashionable youth cults as "utterly prosperous," a "fail at any specific critical analysis of class," or otherwise "a narcissistic delusion of social redemption." Rumors had gone around that Imhof's work was sponsored by Adidas or Absolut Vodka, relegating her work to the level of a branded activation.

At the Buchholz show, the mood had the sadistic air of an ancient ritual, as if the tribal leaders had appeared, one by one, to make their verdict known. Billy was there with Serhat Işık, who was wearing a pair of his own trousers from his label GmbH. I saw Bill Kouligas with Amnesia Scanner. By the double doors, I saw the artist Jan Vorisek enter with Carly, who was smiling with white teeth and red lips. There were some models I recognized, who'd walked Balenciaga, but now looked stiff and nervous. At the club, they were at the top of the social hierarchy, but at the opening, they were near the bottom. At the top now were the artists themselves, some of whose work might've succeeded on the theoretical grounds against which Imhof's work was now castigated: Katja Novitskova, Karl Holmqvist, Simon Denny, Christopher Kulendran Thomas, Yngve Holen, Frieda Toranzo Jaeger. I observed one artist stalking around the exhibition with his chin dipped down into a predatorial grin. Another artist ridiculed the press release for lines like "Imhof's art does not want to be critical. It does not stage metaphorical repetitions of societal violence as a means of maintaining an aesthetic distance," though the opening itself appeared to me as its own genre of societal violence. One curator told me she found it "problematic" for a German artist to talk about the capitalistic objectification of the body without acknowledging the entire discourse of American slavery, a below-the-belt but nevertheless damning assessment, impossible to recover from.

Wafting through the gallery rooms was the unmistakable smell of burning.

I left the show feeling what you're supposed to feel after a tragedy—fear, and pity. I pitied how much Imhof had fallen from having been hailed when she won the Golden Lion. But the fear I felt now came from someplace else, somewhere outside of the white walls of the gallery, as my mind's eye had zoomed outward and glimpsed one of the great social truths about status that everyone knows, but needs to witness for themselves to truly understand: that the mighty rise and fall, and vultures will come for the picking. I'm describing a compulsory ritual, whose existence it seems paramount that people in the game not remark upon, by which I mean *the game itself*, and all the punishing intricacies with which it regulates its elusive but brute decrees of status.

All of it was real. None of it lasted.

In less than a year, the pandemic would wipe out this entire world I'm writing about. When I got shut up in a psych ward during lockdown, all the glittery people I used to know ostracized me from polite society. A lot of these people I wrote about now wouldn't notice or greet me if they saw me on the street.

Yes, this is a morality tale.

If by mentioning all this, and bringing it under the floodlights, I reveal cracks in the very illusions and delusions of this ultimately small, arcane, and overly ambitious art world set, it is to suggest a limit to the gallery banter, market gossip, declined invitations—all those status games that will one day evaporate into mist, because it is the art itself that will, in the end, either last or fade after Anne Imhof or Wolfgang Tillmans or Preston or Carly or L. or Frank or me or you are dead. The art that burns most brightly into the future, I believe, crystallizes an integrity of spirit, whose trace could once be glimpsed from an artist's passing, social tact glimpsed by people who were there, people who remember. If it is true that all of art begins in the social, then it is the social wherein our names will be judged. One can only survive the pull of the social tides by guarding and maintaining an inner grace—a *swimmer's* grace, which is a matter of form and endurance, perfected over a lifetime, because otherwise, if your rhythm slips, or you pause and stop swimming, you'll drown.

## 4.

Elsewhere, there was chaos. During the height of the Trump years, I thought of myself as having fled to Berlin, the new capital of the free world, while Merkel was still in power. Yet even in the back tables at bars, I began hearing more and more educated people in casual conversation refer to what they called "the race war," just as Anders Behring Breivik predicted in his manifesto. We were living in a divided world. Over the last three decades, a bifurcation had opened between a group of slighted white men and the ascendancy of the globalized caste among which I moved in those years.

White supremacy was gaining ground. In Berlin, I felt as if I were standing on the top of one of two hills, and when I looked to the right, I could see another world at a distance, different but forming in parallel to mine. Yet over that hill, the sun seemed only to be rising. This crop of new right-wing extremists—typically white, male, young—ostensibly had all the privileges of identity but lacked the status designations that the liberal caste was seen as having the exclusive ability to confer. The extremists were looked down on as freaks with a barbaric sense of humor, insomniacs who spent their lives chatting online, or a "basket of deplorables." These alienated white nationalists were hostile to "globalism" and its world-liness, hostile to the poststructuralism and critical race theory of the universities, and they defined themselves against the mores of equality, high-cultural pretensions, and moral posturing that, in their view, defined the left-wing elites they despised. They stayed in the same cities as their parents, self-identified as "townies," played *World of Warcraft* and called their friends "cucked" and "gay" and "retarded" and ordered testosterone-boosting nootropics on Amazon. Devoid of any discernible moral compass, their single, cardinal rule was to never be "triggered."

Organized online, some of these new white supremacists boasted on message boards with cell phone pictures of guns. They were jokes until they weren't—once all the trolling and the Nazi memes switched suddenly into the real. Across the world, lone right-wing vigilantes launched killing sprees on churches, synagogues, theaters, and universities. In Halle, Germany, a neo-Nazi armed with a 3D printed gun livestreamed his rampage outside a synagogue with a GoPro camera. In the United States, a white supremacist in Char-lottesville, Virginia, drove a car through a march and killed an antifascist protester. Some of these murderers released manifestos online: extended blog posts attributing the decline of Western civilization to multiculturalism.

A striking number of them explicitly pointed back to a single, predictable source from 2011: Anders Breivik. It was easy to see our times as a fulfillment of Breivik's prediction outlined in his manifesto about alienated whites rising against the multicultural left. In forums and chat rooms, these disaffected white men spoke about sabotaging power lines and bombing synagogues with homemade HMTD. They talked about building a new Fourth Reich, or inciting a "RaHoWa"— racial holy war. This surge of mass shootings prompted the Department of Homeland Security, in 2019, to release an official report denouncing "white supremacist terrorism" as one of the most dangerous security threats to the United States. The forty-page report focused on young, white men who were conditioned by hate speech on social media, and their viral ability to incite violence across the country. It was the first time the department, in its history, acknowledged white nationalist domestic terrorism as a threat on par with that of terrorists operating abroad.

During these years, there was a single American personality who caught my attention as emblematic of the times, its anxieties, its treacly aspirations, and its psychopathologies: Elliot Rodger. He was the proto "involuntary celibate," the white male supremacist and Isla Vista mass murderer.

On May 23, 2014, Rodger was twenty-two when he shot and killed six before shooting himself in the head. He demonized all women for his failure to lose his virginity, and plotted murder against them. Two people he killed were white women, Katherine Cooper and Veronika Weiss, members of the Tri Delta sorority at the University of California, Santa Barbara. Christopher Ross Michaels-Martinez, a sophomore at UC Santa Barbara, was also shot and killed at an Isla Vista deli. Half of the six people Rodger killed were Asian men. Rodger himself was Asian. His father is white, but his mother is Malaysian Chinese. Before he hopped into a black BMW, a gift from his mother, to shoot up a sorority, he stabbed his two housemates and a friend of theirs to death: Weihan Wang, Cheng Yuan Hong, and George Chen. "These were the biggest nerds I had ever seen, and they were both very ugly with annoying voices," Rodger writes in the manifesto he self-published the day of the massacre. "In fact, I'd even enjoy stabbing them both to death." After the stabbing and the sorority shooting, he drove down nearby streets, gunning from his car window, but once he caught sight of Jin Fu, another Asian man, crossing the road, Rodger swerved out of his way to hit him.

He hated Asians as much as he hated women, saw the former as a source of shame and the latter as an object of domination—a result of the instability he felt in his own skin. He both hated and revered his father—white, affluent, attractive to women—who worked as a commercial director in Hollywood, and whose second wife was a French reality TV star. They lived in a gated, three-story house and dined at the Four Seasons. He was the kind of man Elliot Rodger could never be. But in his manifesto, a book-length personal essay uninterrupted by chapter breaks, he creates for himself the persona of a glittery citizen of the world. He relishes describing details like vacations in Spanish castles, birthday parties in

Morocco, red carpet movie premieres, and first-class flights. "I always loved luxury and opulence," Rodger writes.

Flaunting luxury overcompensated for the reality that he was a profound misfit. Even with his affluent background, he was bullied so aggressively in high school that his parents put him in continuation school, where he attended class for only three hours and completed the rest of his work at home. He spent most of his free time on the internet, either playing *World of Warcraft* or watching pornography. Rodger writes that his friends "would always joke that there was never a time that they saw me offline." Before committing mass murder, he was an anonymous troll on online message boards, such as PUAhate.com, a site for stymied incels to "hate" on "pickup artists," whom they saw as "chads" who hoarded women. On the forum Bodybuilding.com, he described himself as "the most stylish person in the world. Just look at my profile pic. That's just one of my fabulous outfits. The sweater I'm wearing in the picture is $500 from Neiman Marcus."

This description stunned me—just as much as when I had seen Breivik wearing Lacoste with the collar popped. Rodger was born into the privileges of both economic class and identity, yet somehow, he saw himself as deprived—but of what? Having all that he did, what did Elliot Rodger want?

*I found the answer in the clothes.* The alligator logo, the Neiman Marcus sweater. Just as Breivik wore Lacoste, Rodger turned to fashion because he wanted to buy something that in fact cannot be bought: status. While identity and economic class are thought to be the two, ineradicable divides along which a society stratifies itself, there is that slippery but persistent third, equal to and sometimes implicated in the other two, but still operating with a mind of its own.

Unlike class and identity—which can be associated with material substance—status, one's social rank, is entirely relational. It can be based on lifestyle, education, social capital, and even sexual capital. Status is extroverted, ephemeral, speculative, gossipy, competitive, mercurial. It is a way to get what we want, and is also what we want. Status can be signaled by a price tag, but isn't fixed to one. Its affinities can appear to be random, but they are fiercely defended once attained. Its totems, always arbitrarily assigned, are subject to change. Status isn't stable, it's always in flux: You're either accruing or depleting; there's no equilibrium. You can have it one day and lose it the next. You can lack the privileges of class or identity but still have status, as I and many people in the art world did. And one can just as likely have the privilege of white, male identity and inherited wealth, but lack status, like Elliot Rodger.

Status was the unattainable grail of his short life. Rodger saw sex purely as a status symbol, which he craved and could not attain. He associated sex with the popular boys in school, the way I did with the boys in the club garden. But he wasn't like the other boys. His grievance felt so irreducible—he seemed unwilling to part with it—that he convinced himself he needed to shoot women and stab Asians to death.

The details of the story both horrified and fascinated me. The virgin shooter. The YouTube video recorded at golden hour. His antisocial charisma spawned followers who would hail him as "the supreme gentleman" because he was cultured and wore designer clothes—a distinction that was ostensibly illegible to the wider culture, but not to me. Leading up to the 2016 election, the Trump campaign stoked rancid, misogynistic excitement from these new online incels who took permission from the candidate to exhibit themselves with something like pride. After Trump, incels were no longer just a fringe group on the internet. They were a constituency.

On the left, it seemed negligent, politically speaking, for serious thinkers to ignore the incel phenomenon. But pundits and politicians always spoke about incels with the morbid, self-satisfied fascination afforded only by the luxury of distance in their tailored, blue suits. People in the art world treated incels as an edgelord curiosity. I did not. Born only three years apart, Rodger and I belonged to the same generation. We led radically different lives, existed on opposite sides of the Breivik divide, but at an uncanny level, I felt I knew something about what it was like to be him, as he perhaps could have felt something about what it was like to be me. When I read Rodger's manifesto, I read it through the lens of the one thing I am an expert in: my personal experience.

*My Twisted World: The Story of Elliot Rodger* has picturesque beginnings: Rodger, as a child, running through the fields outside his family's redbrick country house in Sussex, England. In the open fields, unruly and unpopulated, he picks berries with his Malaysian grandmother, whom he calls Ah Mah. "She would always warn me not to touch the stinging nettles that sometimes grew in our fields, but my curiosity got the better of me, and I got stung a few times." There's an erotic tinge to nature's sprawl—throughout his manifesto, Rodger would often compare sex to beastliness ("an evil and barbaric act"), except that all comes later. For now, he is a child who simply asks the world to enrapture him. "The wind was so strong that I feared it would lift up my frail little body and carry me into the clouds." Even at this age, Rodger is a child who can be swallowed up by his own imagination. Outside Rodger's all-boys private school, he likes to play in the woods, away from the other boys. He prefers to be alone. One afternoon, he gets lost, having strayed from the pack: an early, telling image. The rustling trees and the setting sun set off in him a panic not just about the shadows in the thickets— "I've always been afraid of the dark"—but the tantalizing possibility that out there in the woods lurks some complicated secret, something moist and louche, which in fact he will never come to know.

For Rodger, the Sussex country house is the expanse of his innocence, which would shed itself once his family moves to Southern California, where I also grew up. In school, Rodger is subjected to the conspicuous social rank unique to playgrounds. The epiphany that shocks him out of his innocence is precisely that "there were hierarchies, that some people were better than others," he says. "I started to see this at school. At school, there were always the 'cool kids' who seemed to be more admirable than everyone else. The way they looked, dressed, and acted made them . . . cooler."

Before they understand class, or even identity, all children instinctively perceive status—social capital that they know as "cool." For the first time, Rodger understands that he, relative to other boys, is weak and short, effeminate. He is unlike those boys who hang in packs, boys with insouciant, chiseled faces. Lazy boys, sinewy boys in baseball caps under the crisp California sun, swift and easy across the basketball courts, whose echoes of bouncing balls and sneakers skidding on pavement jangle across Rodger's memory. "They always seemed like they were having a good time."

Upon entering school, all are spontaneously and mercilessly assigned, according to the accidents of their lot, a rung along the social hierarchy. This very assignment, so seemingly fixed as to feel natural, is *the* central wound of Rodger's life. For instance, he writes about his lack of social status almost as much as his lack of sex. It's telling that the word "popular" appears seventy-three times throughout his manifesto; "sex," one hundred.

Rodger is rigorously and explicitly misogynistic, yet curiously, this hatred of women doesn't begin with them, but with the boys. The boys bullied him more relentlessly than the girls. The casual and haughty boys, beautiful boys.

> When I became aware of this common social structure at my school, I also started to examine myself and compare myself to these "cool kids." I realized, with some horror, that I wasn't "cool" at all . . . On top of this was the feeling that I was different because I am of mixed race. I am half White, half Asian, and this made me different from the normal fully white kids that I was trying to fit in with.

Rodger's apprehension of status comes first, identity second. He treats status as if its magic were localized in certain totems, like blond hair or skateboards. He gets his mother to take him to a studio on Mulholland Drive to bleach his hair. He buys a skateboard, learns tricks. His mother takes him to

Val Surf to fetch shirts with skateboard logos on them. Rodger writes, "I felt great anticipation for what the cool kids would think of me once they saw my transformation. To my disappointment, no one really cared."

To the popular boys, Rodger's bleached hair and the skateboards and the shirts with the logos don't really read. What do these boys have that he doesn't have? The boys with the hair and the skateboards are all having a good time, but there's something else that distinguishes them: an ease with malice. "I always had the subconscious preconception that the coolest kids were mean and aggressive by nature," Rodger explains.

It's a casual cruelness that has something to do with sex, even if these boys know nothing about sex.

Soon, the adult world would draw near. At a dinner thrown by one of his father's friends, guests mill about the tables dressed in island prints and satin. Rodger's father teases him by giving him a sip of wine, but only a sip. Then in an episode that appears so vivid as to be possibly fabricated, a "boisterous middle-aged man" approaches Rodger while the other adults are distracted. The man asks Rodger how old he is. Rodger says ten years old. Drunk, the man leers. "In the next ten years, you'll have a great time," he slurs, and then repeats the phrase "a great time." He grins. Its knowing luridness terrifies Rodger as if it revealed teeth rotted black. "I had no idea what he meant by that," he writes, "but when a boy reaches puberty a whole new world opens up to him." I imagine young Rodger shutting his eyes, plugging his ears, and running away to hide beneath the white tablecloths while the adults are still laughing among themselves.

When AOL becomes available, Rodger enters AIM chat rooms with anonymous users, some older. An online friend emails him pictures of "beautiful naked girls" unsolicited. When Rodger sees them, an "ominous fear" sweeps over him, and he promptly stops talking to this person, as if slamming the door upon a demonic revelation.

Later, when Rodger begins hanging out at cyber cafés to play video games, he sees an older teenage boy watching online pornography, with the cold blue light of the screen reflecting on his cheekbones and brow. Peering over the teenager's shoulder, Rodger finds himself tantalized by something that should disgust him but doesn't. "The sight was shocking, traumatizing, and arousing," he writes. "I walked home and cried by myself for a bit."

On his first day of high school, he sees the "huge high school boys" and is so terrified that he bursts out crying in the car, begging his father not to force him to get out. "They all seemed so confident and aggressive," he writes of the boys. "Only after the advent of puberty does the true brutality of human nature show its face."

During his first week of high school, upperclassmen hurl food at him during lunch. Girls bully him. Certainly, Rodger is socially awkward, a "shy kid" who was "viewed as the weirdest kid in school." His very appearance seems to signal a feral neediness that triggers instinctual sadism, even in strangers. For instance, it is remarkable to read Rodger walking home one day when a pickup truck drives by, and four boys start launching eggs at him in the street, laughing as they drive off. It's so absurd, so taken out of a high school comedy, that I wonder, Is he making this up?

His hatred for these boys is inextricable from his longing to become them: the cool boys, the popular boys. With his childhood friend James, Rodger is sitting at a Panda Express in a town center in the Palisades. Upon seeing the popular boys arrive, James blurts, "We're fucked." Because they might get bullied? They watch the boys arrive with "a flock of pretty girls"; a boy sits down with two girls and puts his leg up on a chair with "a cocky smirk on his face." These boys probably wouldn't even have noticed Rodger's presence—people who are having fun don't notice people who aren't—yet Rodger imagines they are gloating. "I wanted to pour my drink all over his head," he confesses. Rodger is so livid that they pack up their meals and finish them at James's house.

"An ominous aura clouded over our friendship that day," Rodger describes. In the privacy of James's house, Rodger starts spewing out all his violent thoughts. "I told him my desire to flay them alive, to strip the skins off their flesh and make them scream in agony as punishment for living a better life than me." James is speechless. He looks on with a face that understands, for the first time, that there is a difference between him and his dear friend. Rodger, upon seeing this look, "deeply disturbed by my anger," understands that there are losers and then there are losers who daydream of bloodshed. He goes on. "I wished he could be a friend that felt the same way about the world that I did. But he wasn't that kind of person. He was a weakling."

It is perhaps Rodger's fatal flaw that he, at such a young age, saw cruelty as inextricable from power. It is why he became cruel later in life. "The most meanest and depraved of men come out on top, and women flock to these men," he observes. After high school, Rodger moves to an apartment in Isla Vista, a Santa Barbara neighborhood known for parties: the kind of white, heteronormative fantasia that characterizes the city's famous Greek life. I knew of its reputation, and its legendary houseboat parties, because my brother had gone to UC Santa Barbara, where all the popular white kids at my high school wanted to be.

Because of Santa Barbara's dense display of popularity in the raw, it is perhaps where Rodger's racist hatred becomes most flagrant. During his first weeks in Isla Vista, one of his randomly assigned roommates brings over a friend named Chance, who was Black. Rodger is in the kitchen when he hears Chance bragging to his housemates about his success with girls. Indignant, Rodger marches over to them and asks each of them, apropos of nothing, if they are virgins. They look at him "weirdly" and say they each lost their virginity long ago. He zeroes in on Chance, who says he lost his virginity when he was thirteen to a blonde white girl. Rodger almost throws his orange juice in Chance's face. He writes, "How could an inferior, ugly black boy be able to get a white girl and not me? I am beautiful, and I am half white myself. I am descended from British aristocracy,"—a desperate claim to both race and class—"*he* is descended from slaves. I deserve it more."

Another time, when he visits his mother's house during the holidays, he meets his sister's boyfriend, who is staying over. Furious that his sister, four years younger, has lost her virginity before he has, he is also disgusted that she is dating a half Mexican. "He seemed like the typical obnoxious slob that most young girls are sexually attracted to." One day, while their mother is at work, he arrives to the house unannounced and hears soft moans from deep within his sister's bedroom. Slowly and silently, he approaches, lurks just outside, listening to the sound of her boyfriend "plunging his penis into my sister's vagina through her closed room door, along with my sister's moans. I stood there and listened to it all." Is Rodger aroused in this moment? Exactly this point, where enticement meets revulsion, pushes him over the edge. He refuses to speak to his sister's boyfriend afterward, even begging his mother to kick him out of the house.

His mounting racist vitriol reaches an alarming pitch one night when Rodger drunkenly wanders into a random house party off Del Playa. Nobody notices him. While college students are playing beer pong with red Solo cups to hip-hop music on the speakers, Rodger helps himself to the free beer. On the way to the kitchen, he passes by an Asian man talking with a white girl. The sight fills him with rage. "I see this white girl at the party talking to a full-blooded Asian," he says. "I never had that kind of attraction from a white girl! *How could an ugly Asian attract the attention of a white girl, while a beautiful Eurasian like myself never had any attention from them?*" He glowers at the couple like a creep. Nothing happens.

Then he steps forward to shove into the man, hard, so much that Rodger nearly doubles over. He's drunk. The couple say so, thinking it was an accident, and try to get him water, but Rodger flees into the front yard. Dizzy, temples throbbing, he climbs onto a ledge raised ten feet over the street. The cool air sweeps the stripe of sweat on his hairline. "Isla Vista was at its wildest state at that time, and I saw lots of guys walking around with hot blonde girls on their arm." Below him, the strong and the beautiful that he will never be a part of loiter lazily in between streetlamps, the pavement glittering beneath cones of light. The bass from inside pulses the deck beneath his feet. Somewhere, not too far away, is the ocean. Then in a gesture as cinematic as it is breathless, he extends his arm out, cocked like a machine gun, and pretends to shoot people down, one after another, spewing bullets all over the street and "laughing giddily as I did it."

I take this to be the same "creepy laugh" that, just a few months later, Bailey Maples described hearing from Rodger on the day of the Isla Vista shooting, when she was so close to him she could look in his eyes. She was walking with her boyfriend and, as she described to CBS News, "felt the bullet graze me" when her boyfriend's hand was yanked out of hers. She would not see her boyfriend again until later when she found him wounded, clothes seeped in red.

What could have prevented this? After the massacre, the media were quick to describe the obvious: that Rodger was murderously misogynistic. Those who used the word "toxic" seemed to stop short of another word, "evil." The verdict against Rodger needed to be made and remade, unambiguously, to uphold justice. But if it was intended to prevent future catastrophes, it was powerless.

After the Isla Vista shooting in 2014, copycat killings spawned. In 2015, one killer who opened fire on Oregon's Umpqua Community College wrote a manifesto praising Rodger, while describing himself as a virgin with "no friends, no job, no girlfriend." In 2018, another drove a van over pedestrians in Toronto; he had posted on Facebook, before the attack, "The Incel Rebellion has begun!"

That year, a report from the Anti-Defamation League drew key links between misogyny and white supremacy in the rise of incels, framing the problem as a war over identity.

Although it's Rodger's misogyny, not racism, that commentators tend (or find easier) to emphasize. Jia Tolentino writes, "Incels aren't really looking for sex; they're looking for absolute male supremacy."

Is it that simple, though? In this case, at least, Rodger thought that sex was due to him as a man, which he could not enforce, but that being half white should make him attractive, even if he was held back by his visibly half-Asian face. The former has to do with entitlement (which the press largely attacked) and the latter has to do with grievance (which the press largely ignored). By his own account, Rodger saw his sexual deprivation as a rejection primarily of his racial identity. He writes in his memoir, "I always felt as if white girls thought less of me because I was half-Asian." Then on PUAhate, Rodger wrote to another Asian user, "White girls are disgusted by you, silly little Asian," adding, "Full Asian men are disgustingly ugly and white girls would never go for you. You're just butthurt that you were born as an asian piece of shit."

Very few wanted to acknowledge Rodger's sense of racial inferiority, which was so key to his murderous hatred. Though it had precedent. In 2008, Wesley Yang examined the deadly stakes of Asian male inferiority in his essay "The Face of Seung Hui-Cho," about the full-Asian Virginia Tech shooter, who might be seen as having anticipated Rodger's killing rampage by six years. It's unclear if Cho was a virgin by the time of the 2007 Virginia Tech shooting, though he wasn't getting laid. As a university student, he sometimes took pictures of girls on his cell phone underneath the table during class and sent creepy emails and instant messages to girls, who were made so uncomfortable that they reported him to campus police. He wrote poetry and fiction that was openly violent, to the concern of his writing professors. Yang argues that perhaps "identity politics" might have given Cho a language to articulate his violent sense of Asian inferiority, but he rejected it. "Cho did not think of himself as Asian," writes Yang. "He was a pimply friendless suburban teenager whom no woman would want to have sex with."

Likewise, Rodger could have claimed his identity as Asian within a community, but he rejected this solidarity. There is a long history of literature, from Frank Chin up to Yang, that wrestles with the sexual emasculation of the Asian American male; Rodger could have found this writing invigorating. But instead of advocating for the half-Asian part of his identity, he doubled down on his half-whiteness as an inalienable superiority, and that his involuntary virginity was a "cruel injustice."

Rodger believed that his identity gave him a "right to sex" and that women rejecting him violated that right—as the philosopher Amia Srinivasan points out in the title essay of her 2021 collection, *The Right to Sex*. Of course, she argues, there can be no right to sex: "No one is under an obligation to have sex with anyone else." Identity politics stops here, which is why Rodger found no use for it. Coalitions can organize for, say, the voting rights of citizens of Puerto Rico, but not the right to sex. This applies to Rodger's Asian identity, too. Even if a world in which Asian men are guaranteed a lower rung on the sexual hierarchy might be considered unfair, it does not and cannot mean that Asian men have a right to sex. The fact that this disparity cannot somehow be regulated presents at least one impasse for Rodger, who found no solutions at the policy level for what he perceived as racial discrimination.

In lieu of racial privilege, Rodger turned to class. Just like when he flexed his whiteness on forums, he flaunted his parents' wealth, which he had easy access to. He wore designer clothes and drove a BMW—even as an unemployed college dropout playing *World of Warcraft*. Except flashing his family's wealth didn't work, not in childhood, and not as an adult. In their forums, incels decry "hypergamy," which the website Incels Wiki defines as "marrying up in socioeconomic status." The term can apply to both men and women, but is used pejoratively among these groups to describe women. In a pyramid-shaped infographic listing the qualities a man needs to attract women, at the top are "Famous" and "Someone with lots of power and influence," along with "Very wealthy." Two out of three convey status, not wealth. While the very phrase "socioeconomic status" implies that wealth and status are often conjoined, we know, from Rodger, that the former doesn't guarantee the latter.

His family wealth did not attract women, and this enraged him. Something else was the matter. In her essay on incels, Tolentino writes that "a rich straight white man, no matter how unpleasant, will always receive enthusiastic handshakes and good treatment at banking institutions; he will find ways to get laid"—if we suppose this to be true, why did it not happen for Rodger? He was straight, at least half white, and had inherited wealth, but he wasn't getting enthusiastic hand-shakes and he wasn't getting laid. Why? Because—by his own diagnostic, one he repeated over and over again—he lacked popularity, clout, cool, fame, prestige, or any of the other terms by which status is known. He believed that his low status prevented him from attracting white women, but the only way to get status was by having sex with white women.

The idea that sex is a status-granting thing is a key discovery Srinivasan makes, if only in passing, in her reading of Rodger's manifesto. In her essay on him, she adds, "facts about 'fuckability'—not whose bodies are seen as sexually available (in that sense black women, trans women, and disabled women are all *too* fuckable), but whose bodies confer status on those who have sex with them—are political facts." To say that sex with certain bodies will "confer status" suggests that this, ultimately, was what Rodger craved. In an essay almost entirely preoccupied by racial and gender identity, this line opens the unexplored suggestion that Rodger's grievance wasn't just about identity, but status. Which, Srinivasan notes, is a political fact.

But if status has political stakes, can policy and organizing answer to it? In the conclusion of his essay about the Virginia Tech shooter, Yang writes that "Cho sees a system of social competition that renders some people absolutely immiserated while others grow obscenely sick." Replace "social competition" with its synonym, "status," and the same applies to Rodger.

If we are to understand these murders—and, possibly, prevent future ones—we need to recognize that the life of status is real, and its political stakes can turn deadly. Even if it would be inconceivable to organize liberatory politics around status, which is too slippery a thing to grasp or pin down, and by definition cannot be equitably distributed. There can be no right to status. There can be no redistribution of status. "Cho imagines the one thing that can never exist—the coming to consciousness and the joining in solidarity of the modern class of losers," Yang points out. For both Cho and Rodger, politics were insufficient. Even if ephemeral, status cannot be imagined away, just by closing one's eyes to it. And it cannot be contractually regulated. Even if status deficiencies are felt as real and insurmountable, driving Rodger to mass murder, our politics are not equipped to address his grievances.

Which makes Rodger's crime a political problem without political answers.

But Rodger's problem is also a human problem.

At first, I resisted seeing him *as* human with human needs. He was vermin that needed to be exterminated before it spawned. Like an immunologist's, my motivation was to locate an infecting agent, isolate it, study it by looking as closely as one can manage with the goal of promptly extinguishing it. To be sure, I am still after this purifying goal. But once I started reading the manifesto, something surprised me. While I condemned Rodger, unambiguously, I also related to him. I experienced his pain as if it belonged to me.

What I found in Elliot Rodger was an intimacy I could not refuse: empathy.

The act of empathy is a person's imaginative projection into another's subjectivity, to the point where subject and object appear to be fused. I associate this most closely with the act of reading. When I read about Rodger entering his high school for the first time, terrified by jocks, I imagined myself in *his* body walking down *my* own high school hallways. I find this strange infusion, this confusion—of my own life and another's, strictly in the imaginary place—to be one of literature's greatest pleasures.

Empathy is a complicated pleasure. Only in literature, not politics, can empathy truly be this reckless, this promiscuous. Anyone's experience is up for grabs; no subjectivity is off-limits. In literature, one opens oneself up to this absolute unconditionality, widespread arms welcoming the range and totality of experience, the good and the evil, with an ambivalence so extreme as to appear like moral anarchy. All suffering is opportunity for use in literature's disinterested quest to capture the range of life in its fullness; to survey the sacred and the profane, and declare, with impiety, that all is human. All is human: in awareness of love.

In fact, one can open oneself up to the fullness of one's own humanity only by empathizing with the humanity in others, up to the extremes where it appears antihuman. To imagine the very limits of the human personality—insanity, violence, enmity—is to face the incommensurable abyss of the self, and of the other. One does not need to know to experience, and empathy, which isn't real knowledge as such, falls on the side of experience. Even if unknowable, evil is essential to being human, and one must empathize with it, so that one can love.

I do this, not for Rodger's sake, but for mine and mine alone. My empathy does nothing for Rodger's victims, nor for Rodger—they are all dead. It's unclear if more empathy for Rodger would have made any difference while he was alive. His therapist, who was paid for by his parents and to whom he had emailed a copy of his manifesto just before the shootings, was professionally obligated to at least perform empathy through his face and voice, yet none of it worked. Rodger proved resistant to friendship, such as with James. His Malaysian Chinese mother, a particularly pitiable character who was unwaveringly devoted to him, listened to his deranged rants, showered him with gifts despite her constant disappointment with his report cards and character. People did try to empathize with him, yet he resisted these efforts. To fault these people for not trying harder is misguided.

But to not empathize will always be, in some sense, inhumane. Breivik, the Norwegian shooter, was diagnosed with alexithymia: an inability to recognize one's own feelings and emotions, which precludes one's emotional perception of others. Here, a limit to self-recognition is a limit to the recognition of others, an inability to empathize. The autopsy report of a girl whom Breivik murdered on Utøya island revealed that he had shot her at close range in the mouth, presumably while she screamed for help or mercy. Her lips were unscathed. The crime here is not that no one had empathy for Breivik, but that Breivik did not have empathy for an innocent girl. In the case of murderers like Breivik or Rodger, what good, what point, would our empathy serve?

Though here is where I can't help myself.

I didn't expect to see myself in Rodger's memoir, yet once I read it, I empathized because of my own failures at sex. Before I left the church at twenty-three, I had not had any sex at all, which is to say that for the entire length of time Rodger was alive before he killed himself, I was also a virgin. When I went to New York, I was eager to find men with whom I could cast off my childhood conservatism, finding men in bars and in back-room banquettes. It was clunky, and, in the case of closeted straight-acting men I found on Craigslist, experimental, but it felt appropriately urban, and sometimes it was fun.

After I was sexually assaulted on a Sunday afternoon in 2013, my sexual imagination was colonized by violence in an instant. From then on, the knot of my desire was that I could not distinguish between what I wanted and what I was afraid would annihilate me. Sometimes at sex clubs, I'd find men to pair off with, but after a certain point, I would freeze up, suck my teeth, and tell them to stop. It was the same every time. I felt like a tease. A disappointment. A prude. Potentially unliberated. And this ultimately left men confused and unresponsive to my texts after.

Sometimes during the dusk of New York streets, I would walk by brownstones and look up at bedroom windows and imagine people living lives, sexual lives, categorically different from my own. I wouldn't even make jokes about sex: I did not think of it casually and could not understand how others did. I saw those friends of mine who had sex with ease like upperclassmen; they had broken in the leather of their sex lives and were in a league entirely of their own, above mine. Inconsolable, I sometimes met friends at Metropolitan, the gay bar in Williamsburg where I used to pick up guys but no longer did. I could hardly talk about my issues, and most of my friends knew not to ask. Occasionally, I'd meet someone who'd ask me casually, "So, how's your love life?" and I'd go white in the face.

Like Rodger, I preferred watching others get fucked, on screen or at clubs. Alone in my bedroom, I watched tons of gay porn. I found it absorptive, total in its command over my attention. Powerful enough to obliterate my thoughts. There were times when I'd wake up at three or four in the morning and feel a longing in my chest so urgent that I'd go to my laptop, load several videos at once, and play them at the same time, just so I could get off while listening to all those beastly sounds: the slobbering, whimpering, the snivels and the screams, the screeching, the teeth grinding, the growling, groaning, and howls. It was a collective crescendo of human hideousness, the actors' faces contorting as if they'd dipped their hands in hot oil. The agonized face: human ugliness as the height of intimacy. Sometimes, I was convinced I was in love with these men getting brutally fucked on film, men I knew nothing about but felt close to, simply because I could feel close to their pain, and get off on it by imagining as if it were mine.

Here is where my experience of porn comes close to my most intense experiences of empathy: finding masochistic pleasure in imagining someone else's pain as if it were my own. Pain is the surest route to empathy because pain is the only universal. One reason we return to literature is because it allows us to experience pain, necessarily vicarious, which is irreducible to being human. We empathize most readily and instinctively when we know someone else's pain, and literature can help us do this. It allows us to escape the impenetrable containment of our insufficient individuality. But the self is a transparent vase; though its edges are hard, you *can* see through them. It is possible to look beyond one's self into another's, even if it is only a projection. Empathy is both an extension of solipsism and a way out of solipsism. Pain makes this happen.

Empathizing with pain is one of the greatest human pleasures I know. Through my imagination, I had overcome that seemingly impenetrable but, in fact, profoundly porous membrane between subject and object, myself and the murderer. I had been cast so far into the ocean I could no longer see the shore, by which I mean the contours of my own stupid self. Having plunged into the alterity of someone else's consciousness, I became a punctured, leaky thing. My soul spewed out in all directions, beyond my volition. And when I returned to myself, the remnants of my journey would leave its marks on everything in the known world, which will never look the same.

This is what the human is capable of, and I would not miss it for worlds.

By empathizing with Rodger, I sensed his human problem revealing itself to me, as if it were a private epiphany. In a grotesque fantasia near the end of *My Twisted World*, Rodger imagines himself as a sexual dictator who hoards all the women in the world in concentration camps, which he watches from a high tower, built so he can leer as they starve to death. *"If I can't have them, no one will."* Except when I read this, I was surprised. Why a death camp and not a harem? If he could command anything in his fantasy—torture, captivity—where's the sex? Only here does he tip off that he does not actually want sex. He is afraid of sex. He hated women because they reminded him of this fear, which triggered his fantasy to exterminate them. He apparently prefers for them to vanish from his life, to leave him alone in his solitary fantasies of roaming unpopulated pastures as a child. Women are not rejecting him, but the other way around. He prefers to keep women at a distance, as the gawker in the imagined tower, or alone, eyes closed, and stroking away at all his life's regrets.

"Sex is by far the most evil concept in existence," he writes.

When I started having sex again, after my yearslong dry spell, it was sex for the sake of it. I knew what I wanted and where to get it and had finally decided to get high enough to make it happen. At a chemsex party on May Day in Berlin, I found myself in the middle of a threesome when the guy whose dick I was sucking said to the guy pounding me in the ass, "Fuck him harder," a comically pornified trope that aroused me. I remember I couldn't really fit this guy's dick in my mouth. But when the guy fucking me moved on to someone else, the one whose dick I was sucking said, "Still want to get fucked?" I did, and when he turned me around and fucked me, the blood from my ass dribbled all over my white underwear, which was hooked, in the dark, around my ankles.

Was this not what I wanted? Sex was the thing I had craved most all these years, thinking it would fix all my problems, rescue me. Of course, this solved nothing. The only difference was that now I was an incel who happened to be having sex. All the old troubles were there: my loneliness, my obsession with status, my superiority complex, which was a disguise for my aggrandizing shame. Nothing changed. I can't remember if this surprised me. It should have been obvious from the start.

The pivotal difference between Rodger and me is that he was afraid of intimacy and wanted status, while I had status and wanted intimacy. Maybe I was living a fashionable life, a life of status, but what did I have to look forward to, but more invitations into more exclusive circles, and finding ever-cleverer ways of name-dropping without coming off like I was name-dropping. I gamed for status because I was good at the game, and because I liked the game, even as it drained the life out of me. I became insufferable. My own pettiness repulsed me. There was no longer any point to it. At first, status was a way of attracting people to me. But once they started showing interest in me, I rejected them, ignored them, pushed them away, for made-up reasons that were never the real reason.

Status was a dead end for me, as it was for Rodger. He watched the boys on the football fields or along the back tables of the cafeteria, fetishizing these false idols with mystery and might. One of the opening lines in his memoir is "All I ever wanted was to fit in." The cost he bore was to live a life intoxicated by fears: of sex, of women, of intimacy, of ridicule, of humiliation, of his father, of loneliness, of change, of friendship, of his own ugliness, of aging, and of all the mean boys who had convinced him that to go without power would be to go without love.

I, too, lived in fear. Not once but several times did my greatest fears come true. As an adult, I would come to know sexual violence, psychosis, separation from family. Yet I often returned to a line written by the painter Agnes Martin, who suffered from schizophrenia, "Defeated you will stand at the door of your house to welcome the unknown." Only after I had been defeated in life did I open myself up to receive the unknown, the foreign, the alien, and even the reviled. My defeats might have robbed me of a capacity for surprise, had they convinced me that trauma was only destined to be repeated. But in the single greatest surprise of my life, these defeats did not make me more bitter. I had nothing left to protect, at which point the only thing I *could* do was love. And I would not exclude Rodger from this love.

When I look at Elliot Rodger's face, I don't see a boy who is at all ugly, or unlovable. Nor do I see the incels' idolized "supreme gentleman." I see someone plain: a younger version of myself. Like me, he has a delineated, square jaw. His full lips make him appear feminine or lurid, like mine do, particularly when I'm clean-shaven. With sunglasses, he bears an uncanny resemblance to pictures of me with shades on by the ocean. He doesn't have the snarl of his father's pug-like face, but the low bridge and discreet eyes of his mother, which remind me of my own eyes. When he says that women did not find him attractive, I don't buy it. Only after I stopped committing myself to the myth of my own ugliness did I notice other people noticing me, as if for the first time. But they had been there all along.

When I was young, I was convinced I was ugly. Once I outgrew my youth, I discovered I could hide my ugliness by designing my own allure, yet I felt the need to hold on to my adolescent irritants and tics that, in each new relationship, would sting the people I cared most about: a test to see if people, hurt, would still return to me. I was deft at performing an amenable and charismatic persona, popular and easily liked. But to spite me for being easy to please and hard to impress, the world seemed to decide that I would be easy to like and difficult to love. Because my charms were overcompensations, I respected anyone who was immune to them. All this time, I was incredulous toward anyone who found me beautiful. As someone unhealthily attached to solitude, I was suspicious of human relationships, convinced that all sociality gravitated toward failure. I did not like my paranoias being proven wrong, even as they were, time and again. I was always ready to terminate relationships with people at the first sign things were getting too real, preferring the confirmation that I was, after all, unlovable, so I could simply be left alone. So it would irritate me when this hadn't worked, when friends persisted, recommitted themselves, restated their love. I didn't want to be told that I could be loved. Love is something you really have to struggle for, and I didn't want to work. But I would be nothing if not the sum of this work.

During these years, I was closest with my friend Ellis, the bisexual data analyst who struggled with depression. Because he was so depressed, he seemed attuned to the suffering of others, a sensibility I shared. I knew Ellis's pain, and Ellis knew mine. Empathy contains intelligence, and when two people empathize in mutual synchronicity, it becomes a mind. It breathes and defines and morphs those who make it. We belonged to different strata of class, identity, and status, but our friendship cut through all that and right to the real thing. In no simple way do I say that this friendship saved me.

The foundation of my empathy with Ellis was the shared understanding that we both felt suicidal, often. He had told me about his suicidal thoughts the first time we had dinner. We didn't know each other well, at all, really, so his pain alarmed me.

"I've had them ever since I was young," he added.

I saw that we were the only ones in the restaurant. It was new, with neon sculptures on the walls and average food. I went quiet. My vision condensed into a tunnel around this person, this stranger sitting in front of me. It was cold, even indoors, so Ellis had kept his thick black jacket on. When the food arrived, I detected a chance to break eye contact. I didn't.

"Me, too," I said.

Had he already sensed this?

There is an undeniable closeness when one shares intimate details with strangers, the kind I associated with airports at night and hotel bars. He looked back at me, head slightly bowed, showing me the crown of his bleached blond hair. What I saw was an intimacy I couldn't refuse.

Over the next few years, we met regularly at Souen in SoHo or Green Bo in Chinatown, and we would sometimes talk about our suicidal ideations as if commenting on the wallpaper. It's not so uncommon for young, sensitive boys to fantasize often of suicide, and in this respect, we were not remarkable. Throughout our friendship, we had an unspoken agreement that when we confessed to each other we were feeling suicidal, we would not need to convince each other out of it, or say the other's feelings were wrong or invalid. We'd hear the other person out, acknowledge it, offer one of the basic services of friendship: witness.

Between the two of us, we distinguished the varieties of the suicidal impulse: fatigue, boredom, the death drive, attention, panicked helplessness, deluded martyrdom, a relief from pain (which could be acute, nagging, or numb), or out of revenge. Most of these weren't serious impulses. Some were intellectualized. For instance, Ellis sometimes told me that his ideal model of suicide would be the truest form of altruism, where, like a plant, he could offer himself entirely to other people's sustenance until he was stripped for parts and used to death. (Category: deluded martyrdom.)

He really was in a lot of pain. We had a robust email correspondence, even when we both lived in New York and saw each other regularly. In one email thread, over the course of a year and several thousand words, he wrote me that the sixth grade was the first time he conceived that killing himself might be "a good idea." Years later, during undergrad, he would be diagnosed by a university psychologist at Columbia with major depression. He described his depression to me as like the arrival of monsoons, whose floods he knew came with the seasons, and he would drop everything to make room once they arrived. He told me that during the worst months, he could ideate on suicide more than fifty times an hour, reaching up to five hundred times a day.

Twice in his life, he made a contract with himself. He'd promised he would give himself five years, and by the end of them, if he still wanted to kill himself, he'd do it. Both times he'd made this contract, he still wanted to die at year five. But since, for a few months during the five-year span, he'd had a break from his compulsive ideations, he told himself it meant that the clock had reset and the contract was void. That, and he didn't want to kill himself, not really.

I should say that Ellis felt suicidal in full knowledge that he had no reason to be. He openly understood that he had close friends, a supportive family, a successful career. Depression was wired into his brain. He seemed born to suffer. In times when he could not push forward for his own sake, he did so for others. I thank him for the times when I needed him more than he needed himself, and he chose to stick around to convince *me* to stick around. We had this thing where each time we parted, all he said was "Hang in there."

To love someone who is depressed, even if you are depressed yourself, is to take on the delusion of embodying, in your very presence, the reason that compels someone to stay alive. These were the implicit stakes of our friendship. After the early stages of a relationship, which are typified by novelty and discovery, it eventually slips into routine, and I relished these routine moments with Ellis. At raves, he would always hover around the speaker stacks with earplugs in, so he could get the best possible sound, and whenever I showed up to the party, I knew I would be able to find him there. In the morning, after the party was over, the sun would show brilliantly over the subway gratings in Bushwick's warehouse district, and we'd walk back home saying barely anything to each other. What infused these otherwise unremarkable walks with meaning was my idea that one morning he might not be there. So even boredom was steeped with radiance.

I tried to be entertaining and funny around him. I knew he liked the way I danced, so at parties, I would at least try to dance well, even if I was tired or bored or wanted to sit down. He never asked me, or expected me, to play this role, though I performed it dutifully, out of gratitude, out of faith, out of foolishness, out of frivolity. Now, my mind fixates on the times when he seemed gripped by physical mirth. Like when a techno track he'd recognize would come on in the speakers, and his body would collapse into urgent, childlike glee. Or the carnal look on his face when he dipped his body into the water of a hot tub—he appeared so fully human, reacting to this fleshly sensation.

I mostly just wanted him to feel better. For years, I kept a clipping of "Poem of Regret for an Old Friend" by Meghan

O'Rourke, which I'd cut out of a magazine the week that I'd read it, and taped onto the inside of a floor-level cabinet where I kept my laundry detergent, which meant that every time I wanted to read it, I had to crouch. I imagined its opening lines to be about forgiving, or at least trying to make peace with, a friend's suicide:

> What you did wasn't so bad.
> You stood in a small room, waiting for the sun.
> At least you told yourself that.

In my apartment in Bushwick, I thought of someone waiting for sunrise, which can come on like a glittering lethargy before sudden darkness: the relief of final rest. Sometimes I wondered if loving Ellis meant allowing him to choose that final rest if it's what he ultimately wanted. I did not want to keep him in this life, just for me, if it only made him suffer. It would not be my decision to make, but I could at least allow him, if he chose, to close in on himself fully, finally. I could release him from my dependence, maybe assure him that he could be proud of me if he left me alone, that I'd somehow been made better because of the joy and struggle of our trying friendship, and that I could at last be fine on my own.

Years after I moved out of that Bushwick apartment and lived in Berlin, Ellis visited for a month. I would sit in the kitchen of his sublet, beneath the light of the window, going on about my problems and preoccupations as he cooked me lentils, or soliciting gossipy updates from him on the New York scene. The forks, the metal fridge, the glasses, and the backsplash tiles all seemed glaring, dazzling, frenzied with lazy sunlight as we talked and talked. His last week in the city, we had lunch at an organic café. As he approached the entrance, I saw he was wearing a bucket hat and sunglasses, because it was summer, and the summers in Berlin can be so generous. Over lunch, we talked about some people we both knew, the science fiction he was working on. We spent the entire afternoon there, as we reclined against large pillows. Sometimes my mind drifted out of the conversation, just so I could stare at Ellis and think of how strange he still appeared to me after all these years. He was facing the window, so his pupils, peering at me from his peridot eyes, narrowed to a prick. After this, Ellis would go back to New York, and by the time the darkness of winter came, this lunch would be but a memory of one sunny afternoon when the restaurant's open windows were stormed with light that warmed our backs.

Before we got up to leave, I asked him how he was, and he said he was less depressed than usual, since he was in Berlin, a city he loved. And then, because I knew I might not see him again for a very long time, I decided to tell him something I had often thought I would.

"I say this because I love you: If you ever wanted to kill yourself, you have my permission."

He looked at me, reached over and squeezed my knee. "I hope you wouldn't say that, because it would mean you've given up on yourself."

## 5.

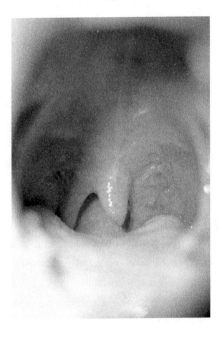

This is a photograph by Wolfgang Tillmans, which I saw, for the better part of my twenties, on a near-weekly basis during the times I spent in Berlin, because until they took it down in 2019, it was hung on the back wall of Panorama Bar. The print itself was larger than my body, so it confronted me physically. The mouth is agape in both ecstasy and emergency: at once a riveting howl of madness, abjection, humiliation, and mirth. The uvula appears like a stalactite hanging over the throat. It always made me think of a cavern opening into a vast, voluptuous distance concealed from the viewer. The negative presence of those hidden leagues is what makes this an encounter with the sublime. During the years when I regularly passed by this photograph—chaos years, all five—it seemed to beckon me with a pulsing question: What do you know about the depths of the human soul? If we are to believe that our understanding of others is but mere projection of our own inner knowledge, then it must be true that what lies in the human depths is no less than the vastness of the cosmos. I passed by this gaping mouth regularly at a time in my life marked by my futile demands for intelligence from a miasma of endlessly renewing confusions. Somehow, I thought of this photograph during these years as a compass that oriented my fears when I really needed it to. The photograph seemed to tell me: Choose to believe. Choose to admit that you do not know. Go deeper still.

Only just now did I ask myself if the view depicted in this photograph is what Breivik might have seen when he shot the young girl in the mouth at close range. Stunned, I look on. My mind can't help but drift toward what isn't in the frame: the unseen upon which thought merely borders. I see the top button of her collar. Her chapped lips on that sunny morning in July. The semitransparency of her hair in motion, strands tending upward. Who is this being—this soul, this human— that I am confronting in this image? Within moments of this view, her body would cross into death. All human knowing stops there. As someone living confronting the moment before death, I am left with this awesome terror—an acknowledgment of my own death, which I can never know. My back turned to the future, I see only what is past. Fingerprints where I touched the dust on my father's record player, the view from the water of Hong Kong Island at moonlight, guns stuffed into a duffel bag with its embroidered sportswear logo in white. I see the green lasers in Jennifer Lopez's video for "Waiting for Tonight" as the club counts down to the new millennium. But as the mind can create images when left alone in the dark, an apparition of light can become an answer to darkness. This might be what is meant by faith. Stupefied or seduced, I turn around and look beyond the threshold of death to see an irreducible vibration breathing with infinite, arrogant life. Is this my body? Take this in remembrance of me. All that is known will be subsumed into the unfamiliar, the novel, the miraculous. Total depravity will at once be conquered by absolute grace. Our entire being will become lifted, loved, and gratified, given over to pleasures of the highest sense in the hope that mortality itself could at last be swallowed up by life.

# ACKNOWLEDGMENTS

No work of art is the product of just an individual, but the result of a collective process. I'd like to thank my agent, Noah Ballard. And my editor, Ben Hyman—my inscrutable analyst, my tireless custodian—who had the insight to tell me what my text was about before I knew. I want to acknowledge your integral role in "Identity Despite Itself," "California Gothic," and "Mean Boys"—you were like a director for these pieces, and I your cinematographer capturing the drivel of my life and turning it into meaning. These three wouldn't have existed without you.

"Identity Despite Itself" is indebted to feedback from Trisha Low, Zoë Beery, and McKenzie Wark, who told me, "Genre and gender—it's the same word in French." For "Mean Boys," I'm grateful for feedback from Amanda DeMarco, Ryan Ruby, Sam Venis, Simon Wu, Pujan Karam-beigi, Amana Fontanella-Khan, Merray Gerges, Nathan Hilgartner, Zoë Beery, Mia Council, Jack Murphy, and Harry Burke, who told me, "None of these are mean boys." Thank you to my professor Katie Roiphe, who edited and work-shopped sections of this book during my MA at New York University's Cultural Reporting and Criticism program, which upgraded my prose and acuity at every level. And thank you to the fastidious support from Bloomsbury editorial—managing editor Barbara Darko, associate editor Morgan Jones, copyeditor Gleni Bartels, and proofreader Jenna

Dutton—for both having my back and saving my ass. Thanks to Drew Zeiba for providing an additional proofread.

Thank you to Wolfgang Tillmans for generously letting me print his photo. And to my brother, Josh, who taught me so much over the years about how to tell stories.

The following names, which are used to identify various individuals who appear in the book, are fictional: Kathy, Jean, Ellis, L., and Frank.

# SOURCES AND WORKS CONSULTED

### EDGELORDS

Goetz, Del. "The Wolf Credo." 1988.

Hebdige, Dick. *Subculture: The Meaning of Style.* Milton Park, Abingdon, Oxfordshire; New York: Routledge, 1979.

Meyers, Lawrence. "Politics Really Is Downstream from Culture." Breitbart News, August 22, 2011. https://www.breitbart.com /entertainment/2011/08/22/politics-really-is-downstream-from -culture.

Nagle, Angela. *Kill All Normies: Online Culture Wars from 4chan and Tumblr to Trump and the Alt-Right.* Winchester, Hampshire, UK: Zero Books, 2017.

Steyerl, Hito. "The Spam of the Earth: Withdrawal from Representation." *e-flux Journal,* no. 32 (February 2012). https://www.e-flux .com/journal/32/68260/the-spam-of-the-earth-withdrawal -from-representation.

Yago, Dena. "Content Industrial Complex." *e-flux Journal,* no. 89 (March 2018). https://www.e-flux.com/journal/89/181611/con tent-industrial-complex.

### IDENTITY DESPITE ITSELF

Butler, Judith. "Performative Acts and Gender Constitution: An Essay in Phenomenology and Feminist Theory." *Theatre Journal* 40, no. 4 (December 1988): 519–31.

Chu, Andrea Long. "The Mixed Metaphor." *New York*, September 27, 2022.

Foster, Hal. "Smart Objects: Hal Foster on the Art of Rachel Harrison." *Artforum*, January 2020.

Joselit, David. *After Art*. POINT: Essays on Architecture 2. Princeton, NJ: Princeton University Press, 2013.

Sedgwick, Eve Kosofsky. "Shame, Theatricality, and Queer Performativity: Henry James's *The Art of the Novel*." In *Touching Feeling: Affect, Pedagogy, Performativity*, 35–66. Series Q. Durham, NC: Duke University Press, 2003.

### THE RULES TO LIVE BY

Bell, Julia. "Really Techno." *White Review*, June 2018.

Crimp, Douglas. "DISSS-CO (A Fragment)." In *Before Pictures*, 183–99. Chicago: University of Chicago Press, 2016.

Reynolds, Simon. "Generation E: British Rave." *Artforum*, February 1994.

### CALIFORNIA GOTHIC

Bersani, Leo. "Is the Rectum a Grave?" *October* 43 (Winter 1987): 197–222.

Dick, Philip K. *VALIS*. New York: Bantam, 1981.

von Kleist, Heinrich. "On the Theater of Marionettes." *Berliner Abendblätter*, December 15, 1810.

Weil, Simone. "The Love of God and Affliction." In *Waiting for God*, 117–36. Translated by Emma Craufurd. New York: G. P. Putnam's Sons, 1951.

## ANTI-FASHION

Bettridge, Thom. "Dark Arts: Notes on Fashion, Content, and Magic." *Spike*, Spring 2019.

Bishop, Claire. "Digital Divide: Contemporary Art and New Media." *Artforum*, September 2012.

Busta, Caroline. "The Internet Didn't Kill Counterculture—You Just Won't Find it on Instagram." *Document Journal*, January 14, 2021.

Dean, Aria. "Poor Meme, Rich Meme." *Real Life*, July 25, 2016.

de Duve, Thierry. "Don't Shoot the Messenger: Thierry de Duve on the Duchamp Syllogism." *Artforum*, November 2013.

Highsnobiety. *The New Luxury: Defining the Aspirational in the Age of Hype*. Berlin: Gestalten, 2019.

Horning, Rob. "Fear of Content." *DIS Magazine*, October 21, 2015.

Kelsey, John. "The Sext Life of Painting." In *Painting 2.0: Expression in the Information Age*. Edited by Achim Hochdörfer, David Joselit, and Manuela Ammer. Munich: Prestel, 2015. Published in conjunction with an exhibition of the same title, organized by and presented at the Brandhorst Museum, November 14, 2015–April 30, 2016.

Krauss, Rosalind E. "The Originality of the Avant-Garde." In *The Originality of the Avant-Garde and Other Modernist Myths*, 151–70. Cambridge, MA: MIT Press, 1985.

Price, Seth. *Dispersion*. Self-published, 2002. PDF. http://www.sethpricestudio.com/writingarchive/DIspersion.pdf.

Sanchez, Michael. "2011: Art and Transmission." *Artforum*, Summer 2013.

———. "Contemporary Art, Daily." In *Art and Subjecthood: The Return of the Human Figure in Semiocapitalism*, 52–61. Edited by Daniel Birnbaum, Isabelle Graw, and Nikolaus Hirsch. Berlin: Sternberg, 2011.

Scarabelli, Taylore. "Styling for Social Media." *Viscose*, no. 1 (2021): 70–75.

Stagg, Natasha. *Sleeveless: Fashion, Image, Media, New York 2011–2019*. South Pasadena, CA: Semiotext(e), 2019.

## MEAN BOYS

Berardi, Franco "Bifo." *Heroes: Mass Murder and Suicide*. Futures 4. New York: Verso, 2015.

Latour, Bruno. "On Actor-Network Theory: A Few Clarifications." *Soziale Welt* 47, no. 4 (1996): 369–81.

Sedgwick, Eve Kosofsky. "Paranoid Reading and Reparative Reading, or, You're So Paranoid, You Probably Think This Essay is About You." In *Touching Feeling: Affect, Pedagogy, Performativity*, 123–51. Series Q. Durham, NC: Duke University Press, 2003.

# IMAGE CREDITS

# A NOTE ON THE AUTHOR

GEOFFREY MAK is a queer Chinese American writer whose work has appeared in the *New Yorker*, the *Paris Review*, the *Guardian*, *Artforum*, the *Nation*, *Art in America*, *Interview*, *Spike*, *Guernica*, *Highsnobiety*, and other publications. He is cofounder of the reading and performance series Writing on Raving. Mak holds an MA in cultural reporting and criticism from New York University's Arthur L. Carter Journalism Institute. He lives in Brooklyn.